The Paris Shopping Companion

The Paris Shopping Companion

A PERSONAL GUIDE
TO SHOPPING IN PARIS
FOR EVERY POCKETBOOK

Fourth Edition

SUSAN SWIRE WINKLER

WITH CAROLINE LESIEUR

CUMBERLAND HOUSE PUBLISHING
NASHVILLE, TENNESSEE

THE PARIS SHOPPING COMPANION
Published by Cumberland House Publishing, Inc.
431 Harding Industrial Drive
Nashville, Tennessee 37211-3160

The original edition of this book was published in the United States in 1993 by Cobble & Mickle Books.

Cover design by Tonya Young
Text design by Julie Pitkin

Library of Congress Cataloging-in-Publication Data
Winkler, Susan Swire, 1950–
The Paris shopping companion : a personal guide to shopping in Paris for every pocketbook / Susan Swire Winkler with Caroline Lesieur
    p. cm.
ISBN-13 978-1-58182-512-1
ISBN-10 1-58182-512-9

TX337.F82P37973 2006
Printed in the United States of America
2 3 4 5 6 7 8 — 10 09 08 07

To my husband,

who allows me to live in two worlds.

Preface to the 4th Edition

Paris has been a destination for shoppers from abroad for over three hundred years. In fact, the first tourist guidebooks to include information on distinctively French luxury goods and the boutiques that show them appeared in the seventeeth century and included mapped itineraries for shopping excursions. Even then, during the time of Louis XIV, the shops were put together as nowhere else, positively seducing their customers. Little has changed and the world still flocks to Paris to be seduced by the charm, elegance, and glamour of its offerings.

This fourth edition of *The Paris Shopping Companion* includes over seventy new shops, each holding to the standard established long ago as Parisian style.

Acknowledgments

Margie Adams, Ron Pitkin, Laurie Harper, Lisa
Taylor, Tracy Ford, Goli Ameri, Lorraine Rose,
Martine Purcell, Mary Hinckley, Wendy Holden,
Arlene Schnitzer, Clinton Smullyan, Gloria Swire,
Jim Winkler, Julia Winkler, Jordan Winkler, Jacob
Winkler, and the shopkeepers of Paris . . . without
whom there would be no book.

Contents

Introduction

Ever since I saw the movie *Gigi* as a young girl, I
have been fascinated by the French and the French
way of life. As a student abroad in Paris, as a graduate student in French literature, as a fashion journalist, and as an importer of French linens for my own
shop, I have pursued the enigma that is French
style.

I still see Paris through an overlay of *Gigi*, with
an eye to what is undeniably and irresistibly French
in a city that is being invaded, like the rest of the
sophisticated world, with the so-called international style.

The Paris Shopping Companion is a very personal
account of Paris as I see it, shop by shop.
Concentrating on what is French by origin or
adoption, it is a customized guide that explains
how to look at each establishment from a French
point of view, as much as a primer that suggests
what to buy at each stop along the way.

To arrive in Paris and take in everything at
once can be confusing, if not overwhelming. In this
book I have tried to sort out the best of the best,
choosing my favorite shops and pointing out the
smartest buys in a variety of price ranges. I have
made a special effort to highlight wise purchases in
even the most expensive shops. These often make
the most distinctive gifts because they come so
beautifully wrapped and packaged.

To the French, shopping is a cultivated activity.
Window-shopping is considered a respectable, even
edifying, pastime. It seems that all of Paris is out
and about on weekends and warm evenings, taking
time to enjoy the beauty of the city, to discuss the
latest changes in the windows of their neighborhood shops, or to critique the newest *couture* fashions along the boulevards. In the realm of design,
all Parisians are experts. They became so by study-
ing the streets and shops of the city, and following
the news in a culture where fashion shows make the
front page and the editorials.

Within a few minutes of arriving in the city, you'll recognize the latest styles. Simply park yourself at your hotel window or in a café and study the self-assured *Parisienne* as she passes by. What is she wearing and how is she wearing it? You'll soon realize that the woman on the street has a savvy that fashion magazines envy. To obtain some of that savoir-faire yourself, adopt her air of confidence and set out to find exactly what you've seen and liked. Or find a shop you admire and let the adept sales help put everything together for you.

You can tour Paris, study Paris, or just walk Paris. But it's shopping Paris that may be the most pleasant and enlightened way to get to know the city, and even those who hate shopping love it in Paris. Even those with little money to spend find their shopping hours well spent. In a culture where style of life is a source of national pride and pleasure, shopping as the French do is an invaluable approach to understanding French culture. All the better if you can take some of that culture home with you.

—*Susan Swire Winkler*

Practical Matters

WHEN TO GO

Paris is a pleasure any time of year, but die-hard shoppers may want to avoid the period from the end of July through August, when many shops and restaurants are closed while their owners and staff are *en vacances* (on vacation) with most of their countrymen. It is always a good idea to check with your local French Consulate beforehand for dates of holidays when shops and banks will be closed.

WHAT TO TAKE

Walking shoes, a detailed street map (I recommend the pocket-size Michelin plan #14), calculator (non-solar), credit cards (must include Visa), automatic teller machine cards, traveler's checks in euros and in dollars, and at least one empty suitcase for carrying your purchases home.

  As a matter of course, I always keep my money, credit cards, and passport concealed under my clothing in a small, flat purse that hangs from my neck.

GETTING AROUND

A city this beautiful is best seen on foot. I heartily recommend a good pair of walking shoes and your map on all but the most rushed or inclement day. When you must, take a taxi (expensive) or the highly efficient métro (subway system). It is economical to buy a *carnet* (packet of ten tickets) for first- (only an advantage during rush-hour) or second-class travel. The bus is fine, and accepts métro tickets, but it's slower and more difficult to figure out, and you must indicate to the driver when you want to be let off.

CASH AND CREDIT

You are assured the best rate of exchange, the interbank rate, when you pay by credit card. Paying by credit card also gives you a clear record of your purchases and expedites your *détaxe* (tax reimbursement). Most Parisian establishments accept credit cards. Remember that there may be a rate fluctuation between the time you purchase and the time your transaction is processed in a bank. Be sure to alert your credit card banks of your travel dates so they don't reject your foreign charges.

Handle your currency exchanges in a local bank (you can shop around for the best rate), which traditionally offers better values than change booths and hotels.

Automatic teller machines are strategically placed throughout Paris, beginning with the arrival terminal at the airport, and are an easy way to get euros. You should be able to draw euros at a good rate (though transaction fees may be higher than at home) directly from your checking account, credit card, or debit card by using the ATMs. Check with your bank before you go for locations of automatic teller machines in Paris that will take your cards. Don't forget your PIN numbers for these cards. They must be 4 digits for the ATMs in Paris.

You may want to bring traveler's checks in euros and in dollars so you'll have some local currency when you arrive and still be able to obtain the most current exchange rate in Paris. It is smart to cash your dollar traveler's checks every two to three days, as needed, to avoid bringing home extra euros that you must then pay to reconvert to dollars.

TAX REFUNDS

As a non–European Union resident you are entitled to a tax refund (*détaxe*) for purchases totaling at least 175€ in one store on one day. If you are shopping with a friend, you may combine your purchases to achieve the total, and share the refund back home. Refunds vary from 12 to 33 percent, with most at about 13 percent, depending on the item. You can more or less make up for your import duty on the same items by following the *détaxe* procedure. (Note that *détaxe* does not apply to antiques.)

When you shop, be sure to have your passport and the proper name and address of your hotel or residence in Paris handy. Request the *détaxe* forms, which the store will fill out with your help in a matter of minutes. You will leave the shop with your *détaxe* forms in a stamped envelope addressed to the shop. If you have paid for your purchases by credit card your refund will appear in dollars as a credit to your card's account; otherwise you will be mailed a refund check in euros. Either way takes about three months.

If you pay by credit card the boutique sometimes offers to write up one purchase slip that includes the tax to be refunded and a second purchase slip with the tax already deducted. In this case, when you have processed your *détaxe* forms upon departing France, the shop will tear up the first slip and you won't have to wait for a refund.

When you are leaving the country (at the airport or train station), you must go to the customs official at the *bureau de détaxe* before you check your luggage—he may want to inspect your purchases, so keep them easily accessible. He will stamp your documents, keep one copy, return one copy for you to mail on the spot in the store envelope, and give you one copy to keep. When the store receives your mailed copy, the refund process begins.

Don't let the *détaxe* process worry you. It's well worth the little effort and it always works.

SHIPPING AND CARRYING YOUR PURCHASES HOME

The simplest and cheapest way to get your purchases back home is to carry them with you in the extra suitcase(s) you prudently packed. I always travel to France with my second-largest luggage piece packed and inside my otherwise empty largest luggage, and return home with both pieces filled. I also take an empty nylon athletic bag or two. Be sure to check with your airline on your luggage allowance.

Be aware right off that the cost of shipping large pieces home may change your mind about making the purchase. Shipping is appropriate when you know you'll never find the same thing in the States or don't want to look for it again, and you are comfortable with the associated costs. A reliable seller should help you arrange shipping and give you the exact costs beforehand.

Smaller items can be shipped by some stores. Again, get a firm shipping price. Ocean transport takes about twice the time at half the cost of air shipment. For items shipped directly from the store, the *détaxe* is automatically deducted without paperwork on your part.

Any post office offers reliable shipping at good rates. Bring your parcel in fully packaged and wait your turn.

U.S. CUSTOMS

Your airline will give you customs forms to fill out during your flight regarding the amount of your purchases. Each traveler is allowed to bring in $800 worth of purchases duty-free. Bona fide antiques, original works of art, and books are also duty-free. You will be charged 3 percent duty on the next $1,000 worth of purchases, and set customs tariffs on anything over that amount. These tariffs vary, but a beaded or embroidered gown, for example, may carry a rate of 33 percent. You may want to pick up the brochure "Know Before You Go" from your local customs office, which details customs information for returning residents.

Never try to fool a U.S. Customs officer. If he pulls you aside to inspect your luggage you can be sure that he'll recognize your new Ungaro gown even without the label, and he knows the difference between an art deco knickknack and a bona fide antique. (In case you don't, a true antique must be at least 100 years old, with the papers to prove it.)

CALCULATING YOUR COSTS

Always carry your calculator to determine how much you're paying in dollars. When the exchange rate is an unknown, let the daily rate posted in the banks be your guide. Don't forget to consider any *détaxe* refund, U.S. Customs duty, and shipping costs in your grand total.

Size Chart

WOMEN'S CLOTHING

American	4	6	8	10	12	14
French	36	38	40	42	44	46
British	8	10	11	12	13	16

Women's Shoes

American	5	6	7	8	9	10
French	36	37	38	39	40	41
British	3½	4½	5½	6½	7½	8½

Baby Clothing

French	Sized to the age of the child. 1m to 18m, "m" meaning months.

Children's Clothing

French	Sized to the age of the child. 2a to 16a, "a" meaning *ans*, or years.

Men's Suits

American	34	36	38	40	42	44	46	48
French	44	46	48	50	52	54	56	58
British	34	36	38	40	42	44	46	48

Men's Shirts

American	14	14½	15	15½	16	16½	17	17½	18
French	36	37	38	39	41	42	43	44	45
British	14	14½	15	15½	16	16½	17	17½	18

Men's Shoes

American	7	8	9	10	11	12	13
French	39½	41	42	43	44½	46	47
British	6	7	8	9	10	11	12

Men's Hats

American	6⅞	7⅛	7¼	7⅜	7½
French	55	56	58	59	60
British	6¼	6⅞	7⅛	7¼	7⅜

THE COUTURE

In recent years the cost of haute couture clothing, the kind that is meticulously and painstakingly constructed to mold to the body of a private client, has become so high that only an estimated 2,500 women in the world are able to make the glamorous shows and required fittings a part of their lifestyle, and the "death of the haute couture" is a hot topic in fashion circles. The French government has even appointed a special committee to bring more relevance to the formidable *Chambre Syndicale de la Haute Couture* by redefining its rules for membership. Happily, for the rest of us, the extravagant collections continue, for their best ideas are distilled into the more moderately priced and often more wearable *prêt-à-porter* (ready-to-wear) collections by the same designers.

Designers put on dazzling shows to debut their collections twice a year for store buyers, the fashion press, and their best customers. While these shows are restricted, in the following weeks you should be able to attend a live or video version of the same in the individual designer's boutiques. For this you must call ahead to reserve, or have your concierge do so.

ALTERATIONS

The better clothing shops will try to accommodate the traveler with fast *retouches* (alterations). I let the shop alter whenever possible because of the very high dressmaking standards and often reasonable prices. Many will deliver altered merchandise to your hotel, gratis.

RETURNS

Returns are not generally accepted.

How to Use This Book

MAPS

The numbers on the main shopping district maps (The Left Bank, The Right Bank, The Marais, and The Sixteenth) are a suggested itinerary that can be helpful even if you don't plan to visit every shop. If the shop has more than one location listed, the first address is the most highly recommended and will be numbered on the map.

ADDRESS

A Parisian street address is followed by the *arrondissement* number. Paris is divided into 20 *arrondissements* (districts), arranged numerically in a spiral outward, beginning with the first around the Louvre. In this book, all addresses are followed by the *arrondissement* number. For example, 5th indicates the address is located in the 5th *arrondissement*.

PHONE AND FAX

When you are calling or faxing from the United States, use the country code for France (33), and city code for Paris (1). If you are calling from within Paris, the code (01) must begin every phone number.

MÉTRO

If you're within walking distance of the shop, this is often the fastest way to get there. The closest métro stop is included in the shop description. If several stops are listed, all are nearby.

OPEN

Store hours change seasonally at many establishments, and most will close for part of August. You (or your concierge) can readily verify open hours by phone.

CREDIT CARDS

The following abbreviations are used for credit cards in this book:

V: Visa, known as *Carte Bleue* or *CB* in France

AE: American Express

MC: Master Card, known as *Eurocarte* or *EC* in France

DC: Diner's Club

PRICE RANGE

The range is from inexpensive ($) to very expensive ($$$$).

INTERNET

Many shops now have websites. The sites listed accept Internet orders.

SHOP TALK

Many of the larger shops have some staff that speak English, while at smaller shops this is not necessarily the case. Keep in mind that every shop wants your business and will do its best to understand what you want.

A glossary of French words and phrases not commonly understood by English-speaking foreigners is included on page 239.

CURRENCY

The euro (€) is the official and only accepted currency in France. Don't bother to bring any old French francs.

The Paris Shopping Companion

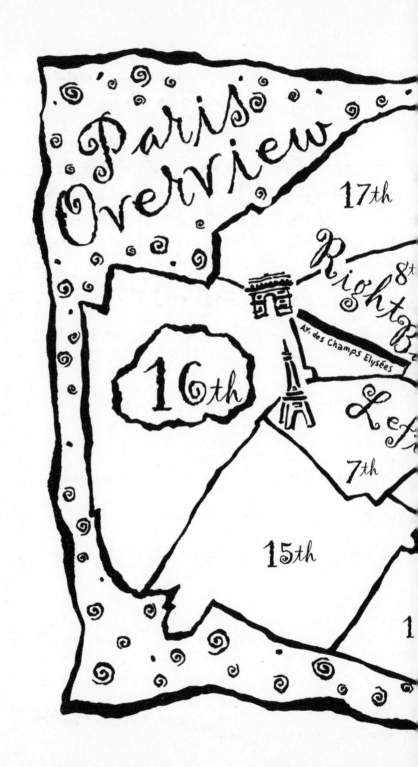

Rive Gauche

The Left Bank, or *Rive Gauche*, is the spiritual home to any student who has ever come to Paris to study at the *Sorbonne* or *École des Beaux-Arts*, and to anyone who has imagined herself in a café sipping wine with Jean-Paul Sartre.

The intellectual tradition that began here in 1215 with the establishment of the University continues in this area known as the *Quartier Latin* (Latin Quarter) since that time when Latin was the tongue of scholars. As you make your way down the Boulevard St-Michel, enjoy the international student milieu, but don't expect to be tempted to do much shopping.

Next door in the Faubourg St-Germain, many venerable French families live in fine old family homes. Here the lifestyle is quiet and understated among those who have nothing to prove, while their centuries' worth of prized but oft-traded possessions stimulate a vibrant antique business throughout the *quartier*.

In these refined surroundings you will find publishing houses, new and old art, meters of fabrics for recovering those inherited pieces of furniture, and the sorts of clothes and accessories that suit a people to whom personal style comes naturally. Somewhere between the conservative and the avant-garde, you'll find some of the most interesting shops in the city.

Map key on following page

Map Key

Where To Stay

RELAIS CHRISTINE

Tucked away at the end of a quiet street is this former private home and garden, now a luxury hotel. The medieval structure houses 51 rooms, including suites and apartments, each done differently, with wooden beams, fabric-covered walls, and antiques. In the fitness room and spa you will see original white stone walls. You won't be disappointed in the quality of this establishment.

ADDRESS
3 Rue Christine, 6th
TELEPHONE
01.40.51.60.80
FAX
01.40.51.60.81
METRO
Odéon
CREDIT CARDS
V, AE, MC, DC
RATES
Double rooms from 345€
Breakfast 20€
INTERNET
www.relais-christine.com

HÔTEL D'AUBUSSON

The massive oak doors at this historic address open to a seventeenth-century townhouse whose beamed ceilings and Aubusson tapestries speak in the present tense, offering every comfort. Thanks to a masterful decor by designer Jacques Granges, the warmth of the beautifully appointed public rooms extends to the guest rooms. Sip an *apéritif* at the Café Laurent, site of the first literary café in Paris, or take your tea in front of the lobby's Burgundian stone fireplace. You'll feel very much at home while staying here. Families can be accommodated in the pavilion wing, and there is a parking garage.

ADDRESS
33 Rue Dauphine, 6th
TELEPHONE
01.43.29.43.43
FAX
01.43.29.12.62
METRO
Pont-Neuf or Odéon
CREDIT CARDS
V, AE, MC
RATES
Double rooms from 270€
Breakfast 23€
INTERNET
www.hoteldaubusson.com

HÔTEL DUC DE SAINT-SIMON

A quiet refuge off St-Germain, this lovely hotel is on one of the most beautiful old streets in Paris. You won't find quarters more gracious than at the Saint-Simon. Every corner exudes sophisticated French charm, and so does the front desk (the very attentive owners happen to be Swedish). Fine antiques, lots of light, an abundance of fresh flowers, and cozy cotton prints make this ambiance unforgettable. The Italian architect Gae Aulenti

ADDRESS
14 Rue Saint-Simon, 7th
TELEPHONE
01.44.39.20.20
FAX
01.45.48.68.25
METRO
Rue du Bac
CREDIT CARDS
V, AE, MC
RATES
Double rooms from 245€
Breakfast 15€
INTERNET
www.hotelducdesaintsimon.com

chose to live here when she was designing the nearby Musée d'Orsay. Make your reservations early because word of this hotel is spreading. Just down the block is the restaurant L'Oeillade, where you can have an outstanding meal before retreating to the hotel bar.

HÔTEL DE L'ABBAYE

ADDRESS
10 Rue Cassette, 6th
TELEPHONE
01.45.44.38.11
FAX
01.45.48.07.86
METRO
Saint-Sulpice
CREDIT CARDS
V, AE, MC
RATES
Double rooms from 200€
Breakfast included
INTERNET
www.hotel-abbaye.com

Built as a convent in the eighteenth century with a vaulted stone entrance, the Hôtel de L'Abbaye is a longtime favorite of many. A classic hotel of charm, its rooms are large enough, quite comfortable, and many overlook the walled courtyard garden and fountain. You'll find modern amenities within the hotel and the Luxembourg Gardens down the street.

HÔTEL LE SAINT-GRÉGOIRE

ADDRESS
43 Rue de l'Abbé-Grégoire, 6th
TELEPHONE
01. 45.48.23.23
FAX
01.45.58.45.48
METRO
St-Placide or Rennes
CREDIT CARDS
V, AE, MC
RATES
Double rooms from 175€;
Breakfast 12€
INTERNET
www.hotelsaintgregoire.com

This stylish hotel is extremely popular with French, American, and English guests who appreciate the elegant decor by David Hicks and great attention to comfort. On a winter's afternoon you'll find them around the roaring lobby fireplace toting shopping bags from the smart boutiques nearby. During summer, the sixth-floor rooms are in demand for their air conditioning, and so is the first-floor double, which has a terrace.

HÔTEL VERNEUIL

ADDRESS
8 Rue de Verneuil, 7th
TELEPHONE
01.42.60.82.14
FAX
01.42.61.40.38
METRO
St-Germain-des-Près or Rue du Bac
CREDIT CARDS
V, AE, MC

Long established in an elegant seventeenth-century building on a quiet street between the Orsay and the Louvre museums, the small and charming Hôtel Verneuil is a favorite of those who appreciate its warm ambiance. Recently, its twenty-six rooms have been redone by decorator Michelle Halard, each a different fashionable mix of classical stripes and toile de jouy, eighteenth-century prints, and modern lighting. While you're on this street don't miss the mural painted by fans of Serge Gainsbourg, in homage to the well-loved singer/composer on the wall outside his home.

RATES
Double rooms from 150€
Breakfast 12€
INTERNET
www.hotelverneuil.com

The Serge Gainsbourg mural, Rue de Verneuil.

HÔTEL DES GRANDES ÉCOLES

A first-choice hotel for Left Bankers on a budget, you will find your fellow guests are here to speak at the Sorbonne, to show Paris to their children, or are simply saving their money for shopping. A short uphill climb from the métro, this refuge is situated off the street in the midst of a small park. You feel the quiet and calm of the countryside as you take your tea on the terrace overlooking trees and flowers. The sunny breakfast room with lace-covered tables is full of guests who return every year. And at these prices, why not? Ask if room #114 is available.

ADDRESS
75 Rue du Cardinal Lemoine, 5th
TELEPHONE
01.43.26.79.23
FAX
01.43.25.28.15
METRO
Cardinal Lemoine or Monge
Double rooms from 105€ (less without bath)
Breakfast 8€
CREDIT CARDS
V, MC
INTERNET
www.hotel-grandes-ecoles.com

Culture Along the Way

ADDRESS
15 Rue Vaugirard, 6th
METRO
Luxembourg
TELEPHONE
01.42.34.23.89
OPEN
Daily, 9 a.m.–sunset

LUXEMBOURG GARDENS

This superb sixty-acre garden created by Marie de Médicis is a place of romantic beauty, whose flowered pathways are designed around fountains, sculptures, and ponds, and whose pony rides and marionette theater provide entertainment for the children.

Luxembourg Gardens

MUSÉE D'ORSAY

The Orsay Museum is a masterful transformation from a train station, and the magnificent architecture by Gae Aulenti is nearly as celebrated as its famous impressionist collection. Works from the late nineteenth and early twentieth centuries are elegantly displayed. At the rooftop café you can sit next to murals by Toulouse-Lautrec and view the white domes of Sacré-Coeur in the distance.

ADDRESS
62 Rue de Lille, 7th
METRO
Solférino
TELEPHONE
01.40.49.48.14
OPEN
Summer: Tue–Wed & Fri–Sun, 9 a.m.–5:30 p.m.; Thur, 9 a.m.–9:15 p.m. *Winter:* Tue–Wed & Fri–Sat, 10 a.m.–5:30 p.m.; Thur, 10 a.m.–9:15 p.m.; Sun, 9 a.m–5:30 p.m. Closed Monday all year

MUSÉE DE CLUNY

Built by the abbots of Cluny in 1330, the collection of medieval art housed here includes the Lady and the Unicorn tapestries in the dazzling mansion adjoining ancient Roman baths.

ADDRESS
6 Place Paul Painlevé, 5th
METRO
Cluny
TELEPHONE
01.53.73.78.00
OPEN
Mon & Wed–Sun, 9:15 a.m.–5:45 p.m. Closed Tuesday

MUSÉE RODIN

Many of Rodin's best-known pieces are set in the large garden surrounding the Hôtel Biron, the exquisite mansion which houses his works. *The Thinker* (the original, of course) sits in the garden above Rodin's tomb.

ADDRESS
77 Rue de Varenne, 7th
METRO
Varenne
TELEPHONE
01.44.18.61.10
OPEN
Tue–Sun, 9:30 a.m.–5:15 p.m. (to 4:15 p.m. in winter); Closed Monday

Left Bank Shops

ADDRESS
Area bordered by the Quai
Anatole France and the Quai
Voltaire, Rue des Sts-Pères, Rue
de l'Université, and Rue du Bac
METRO
St-Germain-des-Prés
OPEN
Hours vary; on Mondays many
open after lunch, if at all
CREDIT CARDS
Accepted by most dealers
$$-$$$$

1. CARRÉ RIVE GAUCHE

Antique shops

A delightful way to get to know a favorite part of
Paris is to explore the old, the beautiful, and the
curious in the antique shops of the CARRÉ RIVE
GAUCHE, an association of neighborhood antique
dealers. You will find anything and everything of
quality in these shops, from the grand to the rustic,
and you will delight in the discovery of dealers
who are both knowledgeable and courteous. And,
it's supposed to be a secret, but you can always dis-
cuss the price.

Explore the ambiance and antiques among the
123 member-dealers found in these eight streets.
Among the most prestigious names are
DRAGESCO-CRAMOISAN, 13 Rue de Beaune,
where you may feast your eyes on a superb selec-
tion of porcelain pieces cho-
sen for their delicacy, subtilty,
and purity of color; GALERIE
DELVAILLE, 15 Rue de
Beaune, where the Delvaille
family has been dealing in
eighteenth- and nineteenth-
century paintings, furniture,
and quality objects since
1860, and is happy to share its
knowledge with you;
GALERIE CHEVALIER, 17

Galerie Delvaille

Altero

Raton Ladriere

Quai Voltaire, with four generations of expertise in fine old rugs and museum-quality tapestries; GUY LADRIERE, proprietor at 11 Quai Voltaire, and authority in all manner of art works, showing small sculptures and objects from the middle ages to nineteenth century; COMOGLIO, 22 Rue Jacob, a traditional source for set designers and antique reproduction fabrics (ask to see the upstairs apartment); and GALERIE CAMOIN DEMACHY, 9 Quai Voltaire, with its magnificently stylish arrangements. Smaller shops filled with fascinating objects for the home are found at every turn. GALERIE DUCHANGE ET FILS, 12 Rue des Saints-Péres, shows coffee tables and cabinets fashioned from eighteenth-century Chinese doors and coromandel panels.

ADDRESS
3 Quai Voltaire, 7th
TELEPHONE
01.42.60.72.15
FAX
01.42.61.00.69
METRO
Rue du Bac or Palais-Royal
OPEN
Mon, 2–6:30 p.m.;
Tue–Sat, 10 a.m.–12:45 p.m. &
2–6:30 p.m.

ADDRESS
4 bis Rue de la Grande
Chaumière, 6th
TELEPHONE
01.46.33.72.39
FAX
01.43.54.90.76
METRO
Notre Dame des Champs or
Vavin
OPEN
Tue–Sat, 9:30 a.m.–12 p.m. &
2–6:15 p.m.
CREDIT CARDS
V, AE
$$
INTERNET
www.magasinsennelier.com

2. SENNELIER
Art supplies

Chemist Gustave Sennelier opened the family firm in 1887 when he invented a revolutionary type of pastel crayon, now available in over 500 colors and sold throughout the world, and the Senneliers continue to create new products and colors. Van Gogh shopped here, as did Picasso. Celebrated and aspiring artists from Paris and around the world know SENNELIER for its history as well as its complete selection of supplies and colors extraordinaire.

The original shop, located next to the ÉCOLE DES BEAUX-ARTS, just a glance across the Seine to the Louvre, looks much the same as it did 100 years ago, its wooden shelves jammed to accommodate the most modern materials alongside the traditional. Upstairs with graphic and technical supplies you'll find wooden easels made by another branch of the family.

Certainly no artist should miss this store, and I can't think of a more inspiring gift for the young painter than a giant pastel crayon in a brilliant Sennelier color.

Sennelier

3. GALERIE ROBERT FOUR
Tapestry arts and restoration

If you have an interest in tapestry, this is a great place to come for a quick education. The rooms here display 400 pieces of old and contemporary works, just possibly the largest collection in the world.

Robert Four owns one of Aubusson's ancient tapestry workshops and continues its tradition of vertical method tapestry, training its own weavers. There are only a handful of such restorers in France, qualified by three years of courses and a long practicum. So if you bring Grand-Aunt Clotilde's hunt hanging here for a touch-up, it will be in the most nimble of hands and well worth the hefty fee, as new tapestries start at 9,500€.

Both new and old are available here as well as small cushions with antique tapestry insets beginning at 300€—about one-third the cost of new and in mint condition. Or, purchase a canvas kit (from 700€), complete with yarns and needles, and whip up your own seat cushions for those tired dining room chairs.

ADDRESS
8 Rue des Saints-Pères, 7th
TELEPHONE
01.40.20.44.96
FAX
01.40.20.44.97
METRO
St-Germain-des-Prés or Rue du Bac
OPEN
Mon–Sat, 10 a.m.–7 p.m.
CREDIT CARDS
V, AE
$$$-$$$$

Galerie Robert Four

ADDRESS
54 Rue Jacob, 6th
TELEPHONE
01.47.03.07.18
METRO
St-Germain-des-Prés
OPEN
Mon–Sat, 10:30 a.m.–1:30 p.m.
& 2:30–7 p.m.
CREDIT CARDS
V, AE, MC
$$$

4. ADELLINE
Jewelry

Adelline Roussel crafts jewelry with character out
of 22-carat gold and semi-precious stones, sold
exclusively in this small shop. The look is modern
and handmade, yet delicate, as she sets often asym-
metrical colored stones in simple settings. If you
love rings, earrings, and bracelets that have color
and elegance, don't miss this stop. Pieces begin at
220€.

ADDRESS
38 Rue Jacob, 6th
TELEPHONE
01.42.60.01.85
METRO
St-Germain-des-Prés
OPEN
Mon–Sat, 10:30 a.m.–7 p.m.
CREDIT CARDS
V, MC
$$

5. LA MAISON IVRE
Pottery and table linens

If you love the South of France and want to bring
its sunshine into your kitchen back home, this is a
convenient and friendly stop for Provençal *faïence*
and the table linens that show them to their best
advantage. Pieces come also from Alsace, Corsica,
Lyon, and the Loire valley. Owner Sylvine
Nobécourt chooses her varnished clay pots, art
ceramics, and stoneware from twenty artisans' studios and pairs them with traditional provincial-
style textiles. There are table sets in typical bright
prints (8€) as well as traditional and elegant white
quilted cloths (61€). For a magical touch take home
a lavender-filled wand (25€). The shop will arrange
shipping for you, and yes, this can be expensive.

6. VICKY TIEL

Women's eveningwear

Here you'll discover a ravishing collection of ball-gowns, cocktail dresses, and wedding gowns tucked into a flower-filled courtyard in one of the oldest buildings in Paris. And you're not the first. The Hollywood crowd has been coming here since American Vicky Tiel established herself in Paris in the 1960s with the help of Elizabeth Taylor.

Glamour has its price, beginning here at 2,500€, but also its standards. The team of seam-stresses on the premises is rarely idle, fashioning voluptuously draped frocks from silk, chiffon, wool, taffeta, and beads for women both French and non-French who have a special understanding of what it is to be "dressed" for an evening. This is also a top-of-the-list stop for brides-to-be and their mothers.

ADDRESS
21 Rue Bonaparte, 6th
TELEPHONE
01.40.51.70.57
METRO
St-Germain-des-Prés
OPEN
Mon–Fri, 10 a.m.–6 p.m.;
Sat, 12–6 p.m.
CREDIT CARDS
V, AE, MC
$$$$

7. MONA

Women's clothing and shoes

This is just the spot for the Left Bank lover of bohemian chic who would never be caught crossing over to the Avenue Montaigne. If you ask, the shop will help you put together their well-chosen pieces from top designers (Chloe, Alai, Lanvin among them) with their fabulous selection of shoes for just the right measure of nonchalance.

ADDRESS
17 Rue Bonaparte, 6th
TELEPHONE
01.44.07.07.27
METRO
St-Germain-des-Prés
OPEN
Mon, 2:30–7 p.m;
Tues–Sat, 11 a.m.–1:30 p.m. &
2:30–7 p.m.
CREDIT CARDS
V, AE, MC
$$$-$$$$

ADDRESS
27 and 36 Rue Bonaparte, 6th
TELEPHONE
01.43.54.89.99
FAX
01.43.29.81.69
METRO
St-Germain-des-Prés
OPEN
Tues–Sat, 10 a.m.–12:30 p.m. &
2–7 p.m.
CREDIT CARDS
V, AE, MC
$$$

8. LIBRAIRIE ABBAYE-PINAULT

Autographs, manuscripts, historic documents, rare books

Even if you don't expect to make a purchase, you will certainly want to take a peek in the window displays at LIBRAIRIE ABBAYE-PINAULT. Monsieur Pinault has possibly Europe's finest collection of these fascinating bits of history. His library of 30,000 autographs, primarily from literary figures of the twentieth century, includes letters from Colette and musical notes from Eric Satie. Sometimes you can pick up something interesting, perhaps signed Gide or Cocteau, for 460€. The most important pieces are in the 3,800€ range, though you can always find a bookmark for 38€. You can count on fair pricing here as M Pinault is an official expert before the Parisian Court of Appeals. Among the 5,000 volumes of rare books are a fine representation of illuminated manuscripts from the fifteenth to twentieth centuries.

ADDRESS
33 and 54 Rue Bonaparte, 6th
TELEPHONE
01.43.26.57.95
METRO
St-Germain-des-Prés
OPEN
Mon–Sat, 11:30 a.m.–7 p.m.
CREDIT CARDS
V, AE
$$$

9. FABRICE

Costume jewelry (N.54)
Home accessories (N.33)

Always fresh and inventive, createur Jackie Riss has been designing and selling her jewelry here since the 1960s, to the raves of the French fashion press, now with the help of her daughter Alexandre. The neighboring boutiques show styles from the avant-garde to retro to ancient Greece, globetrotting through time for inspiration. A necklace of silk, pearls, and stones and a wide rounded bracelet inset with clear and colored crystals may lie next to an African collar of large exotic wood beads and another of verdigris that's built like armor. These windows never fail to delight.

The intriguing juxtaposition of material and design is exciting to the Parisian customer, who is undaunted by the choice and has a knack for putting it together. If you buy, you may assume that confidence too! The collection changes each season, and recently featured a collection of resin butterfly pins in spring colors poised to fly right off your lapel (from 150€).

10. J. PANSU
Home accessories, handbags

Happily, this well-established textile manufacturer has opened a boutique featuring its charming and highly desirable look in ready-made items you can carry home with you. Sturdy and fashionable purses made from Pansu's heavy stripes are all the rage here (from 103€), and they're definitely not your grand-mother's handbag. You'll find as well classic cushions (from 57€) and wall hangings from their tapestry mills, rugs, footstools, and so on, available in a fresh and modern style and in colors *a la française.*

ADDRESS
42 Rue Bonaparte, 6th
TELEPHONE
01.43.54.34.20
METRO
St-Germain-des-Prés
OPEN
Mon, 2–7 p.m.;
Tue–Sat, 10 a.m.–1 p.m. &
1:30–7 p.m.
CREDIT CARDS
V
$$

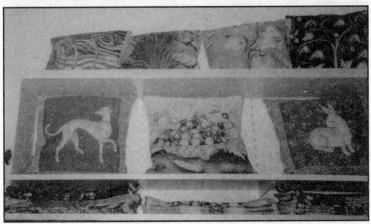

J. Pansu

ADDRESS
38 Rue Bonaparte, 6th
TELEPHONE
01.43.29.12.71
FAX
01.43.29.77.57
METRO
St-Germain-des-Prés
OPEN
Mon–Sat, 10 a.m.–6:30 p.m.;
closed two weeks in August
CREDIT CARDS
V, AE, DC
$$$

11. NOBILIS
Fabrics and wallpaper; period and contemporary furniture

It is only fitting that so many of the city's most beautiful interiors stores make their home in one of Paris's most refined neighborhoods. NOBILIS has brought fine fabrics to the discerning fingertips of the haute bourgeoisie since 1928. Here is where they come to choose coverings for their most noble pieces of furniture and for the walls of their period apartments—and you may too.

If your taste runs to glass and steel, you will be pleased to know that Nobilis has added contemporary choices to its classic damasks and chinoiserie prints. Choose a Napoleonic-style chair and cover it in a brilliant geometric. Plan to carry them home, since Nobilis won't ship. Whether you come to buy or browse, you won't feel lost or unwelcome as you flip through the fabric boards.

Along the Way

The church ST-GERMAIN-DES-PRÉS is the oldest in Paris. The tower and belfry have stood since the 10th century and are now surrounded by Romanesque additions. At its zenith, when its riches and allegiance belonged to the pope, the church rivaled the city of Paris in power.

Today it is known for evening concerts of classical music and a garden statue given by Picasso in tribute to his poet friend Apollinaire. Entering the glass doors to the sanctuary you'll find relief from the noisy bustle of street life on the Boulevard St-Germain. To prolong the calm, explore the more tranquil neighborhood to the north of the boulevard.

For a nearby lunch or dinner, two reliable standbys are conveniently located across from each other, and they're both hopping from noon to the wee hours, indoors and out: the corner entry to LE PETIT ZINC (N.11 Rue Saint-Benoit) feels smallish until you open the carved wooden doors into the belle epoque palace with its intimate dining rooms serving a classic menu; if you want a very good, very quick steak dinner, cross over to LE RELAIS DE L'ENTRECOTE (N.20 Rue Saint-Benoit) where reservations are not taken, but no sooner are you seated than a waitress is at your table. Here is a formula menu where your choices include a delicious *profiterole desert*.

Le Petit Zinc

12. PETIT FAUNE
Children's clothing

Very civilized clothing for your little fawn from infancy to age six. The small collection is entirely in cotton, mostly Liberty of London prints, and wool that is hand-knitted. If a lovely little dress at 50 to 80€ doesn't suit your budget, perhaps you would like to bring back for her an adorable doll rattle wearing a smaller version of the same dress and a boating hat in a matching print for him, each for 20€.

If you're a do-it-yourselfer, head directly to the LES OUVRAGES DU PETIT FAUNE boutique. Here you will find sewing kits for ten different patterns or five knitted outfits. A detailed pattern, including cloth, buttons, and even the PETIT FAUNE label will cost you about one-third of the completed garment on the Rue Jacob.

ADDRESS
33 Rue Jacob, 6th
TELEPHONE
01.42.60.80.72
METRO
St-Germain-des-Prés
OPEN
Mon–Sat, 10 a.m.–7 p.m.
CREDIT CARDS
V, AE
$$$

LES OUVRAGES DU PETIT FAUNE
Sewing Kits Only
ADDRESS
13 Rue de Mézières, 6th
TELEPHONE
01.42.22.63.69
METRO
St-Sulpice
OPEN
Mon, 2–7 p.m.;
Tue–Sat, 10 a.m.–7 p.m.
NO CREDIT CARDS
$

ADDRESS
32 Rue Jacob, 6th
TELEPHONE
01.55.42.00.39
FAX
01.46.34.45.18
METRO
St-Germain-des-Prés
OPEN
Mon–Fri, 10 a.m.–7 p.m.
CREDIT CARDS
V, AE, MC, DC
$$$$

13. HERVÉ L. LEROUX
Custom women's evening and cocktail attire

Mysterious and elegant, this black boutique is back-drop to its sensational designs. Couturier Hervé Leger has changed his name to open a new label based on his famous bandage dress, but reaching a higher level of sophistication. Draped custom gowns are made–to–measure on the premises from a viscose jersey with a heavy lining that hugs and sculpts the body to the Leroux shape, which is very sexy and, yes, expensive. But what is a perfect figure worth? Long dresses start at 4,000€ and tops, skirts, and short dresses of a similar allure are also in the collection. Fabrication takes three to five weeks, with one fitting suggested, though in a pinch, the atelier can work its magic without you. His color palette, all solids, is geor-geous!

Hervé L. Leroux

14. LA MAISON RUSTIQUE
Books

If you are interested in French style but only read pictures in French, this is a bookstore for you. The publisher Flammarion has built an attractive shop in the guise of a rustic refuge for its beautifully photographed titles specializing in interior decoration, gardening, nature, and *l'art de vivre*. While some titles are offered in English, would an English translation of *The Art of Folding Napkins* really help?

You may receive a Flammarion book catalog free of charge from this address.

ADDRESS
26 Rue Jacob, 6th
TELEPHONE
01.42.34.96.60
FAX
01.42.34.96.62
METRO
St-Germain-des-Prés
OPEN
Mon–Sat, 10–7 p.m.
CREDIT CARDS
V, AE
$$

15. PIERRE MADEL
Antique fireplace accessories

If you practice the fine art of lighting and keeping the hearth burning, or if you simply like to decorate your fireplace, you will be drawn to the warmth of Pierre Madel's shop, founded just after World War II. All crafted in iron and bronze, the beautiful old chimney plaques, andirons, screens, log tools, and screens from the seventeenth century onward are cleaned and buffed to look spiffy in any twenty-first-century room. And if your style is specifically Napoleonic or Empire, you'll find that, too. You can count on them to handle the shipping.

ADDRESS
22 Rue Jacob, 6th
TELEPHONE
01.43.26.90.89
FAX
01.40.46.07.09
METRO
St-Germain-des-Prés
OPEN
Tue–Fri, 3–7 p.m.;
Sat, 11 a.m.–12:30 p.m. &
3–7 p.m.
CREDIT CARDS
V, AE, MC, DC
$$$

ADDRESS
6 Rue Jacob, 6th
TELEPHONE
01.46.34.61.55
METRO
St-Germain-des-Prés
OPEN
Tue–Sat, 11 a.m.–7 p.m.;
Mon, 2:30–7 p.m.
CREDIT CARDS
V, AE, MC
$$
INTERNET
www.huile-leblanc.com

16. HUILERIE J. LEBLANC
Cooking oils

The Leblanc family has been hard at work in the coun-
tryside pressing some of France's finest olive and nut
oils since 1878. How fortunate that they have brought
them to this Rue Jacob address, where purchasing and
shipping are so easy. With four generations of exper-
tise behind this cheerful shop, Anne Leblanc will help
you choose a fine pineseed, walnut, or pistachio oil, or
perhaps one scented with truffle. And she will explain
exactly how best to use it. There are convenient sets of
three oils already packaged for your suitcase (30€), and
all the fixings for salad dressings, including stone-
ground mustards and fruit vinegars.

Huilerie J. Leblanc

ADDRESS
1 Rue de Furstenberg. 6th
(furniture)
2 Rue de Furstenburg
(fabrics)
2 bis Rue de Furstenburg
(accessories)
TELEPHONE
01.46.33.73.00 (furniture and
fabrics)

17. PIERRE FREY
Fabrics, furniture, home accessories, rugs

Patrick Frey carries on the tradition of his father, Pierre
Frey, Parisian decorator par excellence. He has a won-
derful way with textile creations fashioned from Frey
signature fabrics into welted pillows, cashmere throws,
handbags and luggage, table covers and bedroom

linens, and smaller well-priced gifty items. The looks run from eighteenth-century style to freshly colored stripes. Across the street you will find the superb BRAQUENIE collection of fabrics and rugs based on eighteenth- and nineteenth-century documents from Braquenié archives, acquired and stylishly updated by Frey.

01.43.26.82.61 (accessories)
METRO
St-Germain-des-Prés or
Mabillon
OPEN
Tue–Sat, 10 a.m.–6:30 p.m.,
(furniture and fabrics);
Mon–Sat, 10 a.m.–7 p.m.
(accessories)

ADDRESS
3 Rue de Furstenberg, 6th
(BRAQUENIE)
TELEPHONE
01.44.07.15.37
FAX
01.44.07.16.39
METRO
St-Germain-des-Prés
OPEN
Tue–Sat, 10 a.m.–6:30 p.m.

ADDRESS
22 Rue Royale, 8th (accessories)
TELEPHONE
01.49.26.04.77
METRO
Madeleine
OPEN
Mon–Sat, 10 a.m.–7 p.m.
CREDIT CARDS
V, AE
$$$

Place de Furstenberg

Along the Way

The PLACE DE FURSTENBERG is one of the most charming in Paris, and a frequent location for movie scenes and publicity spots, yet it remains hidden from the crowds. Fragrant mauve-blossomed trees carry perfume across the way to the tiny DELACROIX MUSEUM, 6 Rue de Furstenberg, where the great Romantic painter lived and produced his passionate works.

ADDRESS
4 Rue de Furstenberg, 6th
TELEPHONE/FAX
01.43.26.56.91
METRO
St-Germain-des-Prés
OPEN
Mon and Sat, 2:30–6:30 p.m.;
Tue–Fri, 11 a.m.–6:30 p.m.
CREDIT CARDS
V, AE, MC
$$$

18. YVELINE
Antiques

Yveline has an eye for the unusual that will delight the
jaded antique hunter. In this lovely shop where alle-
giance is to distinction rather than to a specific period,
you may find that fascinating dining set, a nineteenth-
century still life, or wonderful wooden hands for the
sofa table. The gracefully articulated hands were once
artist's models and are a specialty here, selling in the
range of 300€ per pair. With forty years' involvement
in antiques, everything Yveline chooses is quite special.

ADDRESS
9 Place Furstenberg, 6th
TELEPHONE
01.43.25.23.20
METRO
St-Germain-des-Prés
OPEN
Mon, 1–7 p.m.;
Tue–Sat, 11 a.m.–7 p.m.
CREDIT CARDS
V, MC
$$-$$$

19. NOLITA
Home accessories

Come here for a charmingly sophisticated version of
French shabby chic, particularly if your favorite femi-
nine adolescent is ready to transform her bedroom into
a boudoir. She'll fall for the omnipresent decoration
here, from chandeliers and lampshades to sofas and
cushions to faux crystal knobs that attach to her wall
for hanging up clothes, pretty in pink or green (30€).

Nolita

20. PIXI & CIE
Collectible figurines

To see the French as they see themselves, stop in at
PIXI, a miniature world of hand-painted lead figures
that begins with the toy soldier and extends to
charming representations of Parisian life. Look
closely at the nanny, the red-cheeked policeman,
the baker and his baguettes, the well-turned-out
golfer all teed up, or the jazzman at his horn.

If you have runway taste, this haute couture collection is a must. Wonderfully executed figurines
modeling the finest French couture fashions of the
century are presented, each in her own small box
that stands open for display with a reflection strip
for viewing the handsomely painted garments from
all sides, complete with the designer's logo opposite.

For the young and hip are lots of inexpensive
knickknacks with plenty of gift potential.

ADDRESS
6 Rue de L'Échaudé, 6th
TELEPHONE
01.46.33.88.88
FAX
01.43.29.74.28
METRO
Mabillon or St-Germain-des-
Prés
OPEN
Mon–Sat, 11 a.m.–7 p.m.
CREDIT CARDS
V, AE
$$
INTERNET
www.pixieshop.com

Along the Way

The OPEN AIR FOOD MARKET, beginning at St-Germain and running down the
Rue de Seine and Rue de Buci, is one of the most picturesque in Paris. In the early
hours the merchants begin arriving to arrange their stands with an artist's eye for
color, shape, and texture, so for shame if you touch the merchandise! From 9 a.m. to
1 p.m. and 4 to 7 p.m., Tues–Sat, and on Sunday mornings, the streets are jammed
with Parisians doing their daily marketing. This time-honored tradition has the mak-
ings of a terrific picnic.

☕ LA PALETTE
Café

LA PALETTE was a favorite hang-out of mine dur-
ing my student days, and nothing here has
changed. Forever (since 1903) a neighborhood café
filled with a lively mix of students, artists, dealers,
and their patrons, you'll find the outdoor tables
crowded whenever there's some sun, and the inside
full of chatter. Baguette sandwiches, delectable fruit
tarts, and the flavor of this artsy quarter are avail-
able all day.

ADDRESS
43 Rue de Seine, 6th
TELEPHONE
01.43.26.68.15
METRO
Mabillon or Odéon
OPEN
Mon–Sat, 9 a.m.–2 a.m.; hot
meals served noon–3 p.m.;
snacks from 3 p.m.–2 a.m.
NO CREDIT CARDS
$

ADDRESS
1 Rue Jacob, 6th
TELEPHONE
01.46.34.00.36
METRO
St-Germain-des-Prés

ADDRESS
21 & 36 Galerie Vero-Dodat
TELEPHONE
01.44.76.00.76
METRO
Palais-Royal

ADDRESS
10 Avenue Victor Hugo, 16th
TELEPHONE
01.55.73.00.73
METRO
Victor-Hugo

ADDRESS
30 Rue de la Trémoille, 8th
TELEPHONE
01.44.43.04.04
METRO
Alma-Marçeau
OPEN
Mon–Sat, 10:30 a.m.–7 p.m.
CREDIT CARDS
V, AE, MC
$$$-$$$$
INTERNET
www.byterry.com

21. BY TERRY
Makeup and skin care products

Parisiennes seeking the ultimate in glamour and refinement come to Terry de Gunzburg for their faces. Her exacting background in the sciences and as makeup artist to the stars has brought the highest level of quality to her crèmes and pigments. Just to walk into her boutiques is a treat for the eyes, as the array of colors is dazzling. To make sense of it all, schedule a makeup session: one hour concentrating on day or evening (110€), or take 90 minutes for a private lesson—they do half your face and you do the other (165€). The woman who has everything will surely want to stop in at the Vero-Dodat address where they will mix pigments and creams to suit, truly haute couture makeup.

ADDRESS
51 Rue de Seine, 6th
TELEPHONE/FAX
01.43.54.57.65
METRO
St-Germain-des-Prés
OPEN
Tue–Sat, 11 a.m.–1 p.m. &
2–6:30 p.m.
CREDIT CARDS
V, AE
$$-$$$$

22. JACQUELINE SUBRA
Antique jewelry

Don't hesitate to buzz open this gem of a shop. Jacqueline and her daughter will invite you to admire their collection of the real thing in jewelry from the late 1800s through the 1960s, much of which now inspires fashionable fakes. Their selections over the past quarter-century, from the coffers of families with taste but diminishing means and from dealers who know of their reputation, represent the finest examples from each stylistic period. But don't worry, Madame assures me that there is always a selection at 100€ for little gifts.

23. GALERIE DOCUMENTS
Original posters

I hope that proprietor Mireille Romand is in when you come to call. As great-great-granddaughter of the founder of this institution, she will be able to explain to you (in English) everything about the vast domain of original posters in her remarkable collection. Her ancestor, a print dealer, began collecting posters when they were just being invented, and this shop was the first in the world to sell them. All are from the early days of lithographic posters (about 1870 to 1950), which explains their superb color.

Choose from the 1,000 or so posters announcing air and motor expositions, theatrical events, interesting inventions, and more, each with historic and artistic value and reliable documentation. If you're not set on a Toulouse-Lautrec, which you can also find here, you may pick up something wonderful for much less.

ADDRESS
53 Rue de Seine, 6th
TELEPHONE
01.43.54.50.68
METRO
St-Germain-des-Prés
OPEN
Mon, 2:30–7 p.m.;
Tue–Sat, 10:30 a.m.–7 p.m.
CREDIT CARDS
V, AE
$$-$$$$

24. GALERIE JEANNE-BUCHER
Art gallery

This highly respected art gallery has proven an uncanny ability to recognize important new art since its beginnings in 1925. The cubists and surrealists were shown here early on, and gallery director Jean-François Jaeger can probably still pull a Miro, Picasso, or Dubuffet from his vaults for the serious buyer. His current stable of international artists has its future in good hands.

ADDRESS
53 Rue de Seine, 6th (Inside courtyard)
TELEPHONE
01.44.41.69.65
FAX
01.44.41.69.68
METRO
Odéon or Mabillon
OPEN
Tue–Fri, 9:30 a.m.–6:30 p.m.;
Sat, 10 a.m.–12:30 p.m. & 2:30–6 p.m.
CREDIT CARDS
V
$$$-$$$$

Galerie Jeanne-Bucher

ADDRESS
28 Rue de Buci, 6th
TELEPHONE
01.44.07.15.03
METRO
St-Germain-des-Prés
OPEN
Mon–Sun, 10 a.m.–8 p.m.

ADDRESS
44 Rue Cler, 7th
TELEPHONE
01.45.51.00.83
METRO
Latour-Maubourg
OPEN
Tue–Sat, 10:30 a.m.–7:30 p.m.;
Sun, 10 a.m.–2 p.m.

ADDRESS
81 Rue St Louis en l'Isle, 4th
TELEPHONE
01.40.46.89.37
METRO
Pont Marie
OPEN
Mon, 3–8 p.m.;
Tue–Sun, 10:30 a.m.–8 p.m.
CREDIT CARDS
V, AE, MC, DC
$$

25. OLIVIERS & CO.
Olive oils and condiments

Here is a fast-growing chain and a good spot for picking up inexpensive gifts with the taste of Provence that will be prized back home. A good selection of products (beginning at 6€), all from the Mediterranean, centers on a large selection of quality olive oils, and includes tapenades, patés, herbs, spices, vinegars, and moves on to ceramic table accessories. Plan to pack them in your bags as the store does not ship to the U.S.

ADDRESS
30 Rue de Buci, 6th
TELEPHONE
01.43.54.56.73
METRO
St-Germain-des-Prés
OPEN
Mon, 11 a.m.–7 p.m.;
Tue–Sat, 10 a.m.–7 p.m.

ADDRESS
342 Rue Saint Honoré, 1st
TELEPHONE
01.42.60.10.75
METRO
Tuileries
OPEN
Mon–Sat, 10 a.m.– 7 p.m.

26. COMPTOIR DES COTONIERS
Women's clothing, all ages

The mother-daughter concept has taken off like mad here with COMPTOIR boutiques popping up all over town. Girls from fourteen to fifty-four are flocking to them for stylish, mostly casual, pieces that are well-made and well-priced. If you don't want to dress exactly like your daughter, there are plenty of basics to choose from. You can even find an item or two for baby. Listed are some of the most strategic addresses.

ADDRESS
33 Rue des Francs Bourgeois,
4th
TELEPHONE
01.42.76.95.33
METRO
St-Paul
OPEN
Mon–Sat, 10 a.m.–7 p.m.;
Sun, 1–7 p.m.

ADDRESS
25 Avenue Victor Hugo, 16th
TELEPHONE
01.40.67.15.84
METRO
Victor-Hugo
OPEN
Mon–Sat, 10 a.m.–7 p.m.
CREDIT CARDS
V, AE, MC
$$

27. EDEN PARK
Casual wear for men, women, and children

A team of unconventional French rugby players
launched EDEN PARK the year they won the
French national cup wearing the pink bowties that
became the brand's logo. While the rugby shirt is
their staple, they offer several collections of week-
end wear, from sport to suits, primarily for boys
and men, in their warmly wooded family-oriented
boutiques. Even their most casual attire is elegant,
as you would expect, with a touch of the eccentric.

ADDRESS
10 Rue de Buci, 6th
TELEPHONE
01.43.26.74.91
METRO
Mabillon
OPEN
Mon, 2:30–7 p.m.;
Tue–Sat, 10 a.m.–7 p.m.
CREDIT CARDS
V, AE, MC, DC
$$$

ADDRESS
7-9 Rue de Buci, 6th
TELEPHONE
01.43.26.19.34
METRO
Mabillon
OPEN
Mon–Sat, 9:30 a.m.–8:30 p.m.;
Sun, 9:30 a.m.–7 p.m.
CREDIT CARDS
V, MC
$

28. AQUARELLE
Florist

The genius of this florist is found in his "bouquet of the week," a 20€ arrangement that comes in a pretty fabric vase that you, the perfect guest, can pick up in the shop on the way to dinner and put right onto your hostess' table. Of course, they'll also deliver anywhere in town for 9€.

Aquarelle

☕ LE PROCOPE
Restaurant

ADDRESS
13 Rue de l'Ancienne-Comédie, 6th
TELEPHONE
01.40.46.79.00
METRO
Odéon
OPEN
Mon–Sun, noon–1 a.m.
CREDIT CARDS
V, AE, MC
$$

Stop by at least to take a peek at the first café in Paris. Le Procope opened in 1686, though the décor has been updated to nineteenth-century style. The likes of Voltaire and Diderot, Robespierre and Ben Franklin have sat, sipped, and thought here. This was also the city's first ice cream parlor.

29. BOIS DE ROSE
Children's clothing

It's no secret that all the aristocracy comes to BOIS DE ROSE to outfit their little darlings for special occasions. Yes, the hand smocking found here is outstanding, but so are the prices. For example, a hand-smocked gold silk dress for a four-year-old is a mere 95€ here, while we would expect to see it at several times that anywhere else. This shop is consecrated to refined clothing for children, hand-sewn and hand-embroidered in Madagascar. From layette to nightshirts to cortege attire, there is something special to wear for every happy family occasion from babyhood to age twelve. The collection updates frequently and outfits are coordinated for boys and girls (accessories are from 5€ and ceremonial outfits from 56€). If you don't find exactly what you want, it can be custom made in two months.

ADDRESS
30 Rue Dauphine, 6th
TELEPHONE/FAX
01.40.46.04.24
METRO
Odéon or Pont-Neuf
OPEN
Mon–Sat, 10:30 a.m.–7 p.m.;
Sunday by appointment
CREDIT CARDS
V, AE, MC, DC
$$

Bois de Rose

☕ LA ROTISSERIE D'EN FACE
Restaurant

ADDRESS
2 Rue Christine, 6th
TELEPHONE
01.43.26.40.98
METRO
St-Michel or Odéon
OPEN
Mon–Fri, noon–2:30 p.m. & 7–11 p.m.; Sat, 7–11:30 p.m.
CREDIT CARDS
V, AE, MC, DC
$$

Light and appealing in both ambiance and cuisine, owner and star chef Jacques Cagna's homey bistro draws a smart crowd, and is a favorite among Americans. They come here for its spit-roasted entrées, imaginative daily specials, and luscious desserts. You can have a three-course lunch for 42€, or a main dish and wine for 18€. Reservations are recommended.

ADDRESS
1 Cour du Commerce Saint
André, 6th
TELEPHONE
01.43.54.32.66
METRO
Odéon
OPEN
Tue–Sat, 11 a.m.–7:30 p.m.;
Sun, 2–7 p.m.
CREDIT CARDS
V, AE, MC
$$

30. TERRE DE SIENNE
Toys

Young and old of any tender age will be carried
away by this charming boutique specializing in old-
fashioned toys. The magical atmosphere here can
bring back childhood memories or inspire the
desire to play as a child of yesteryear. Everything
sold here is new, with the look of the past.
Montgolfiers (hot air balloons) are a specialty, and
found in various sizes beginning at 14€.

Terre de Sienne

La Jacobine

☕ LA JACOBINE

Restaurant, tea salon

ADDRESS
59–61 Rue Saint-André des Arts, 6th
TELEPHONE
01.46.34.15.95
METRO
Odéon
OPEN
Tue–Sun, noon–11:30 p.m.
CREDIT CARDS
V, MC
$$

Stop in here for a bit of history and a quick bite. A colorful series of paintings commemorating the French Revolution adorn the walls of this cozy salon located in one of the city's oldest passageways. Salads are gigantic, and even the pastries are made on the premises. While the theme is 1789, both the dining and the décor are ultra-fresh. Serving lunch, weekend brunch, tea, and dinner.

ADDRESS
4 Rue des Quatre Vents, 6th
TELEPHONE
01.44.07.37.64
METRO
Odéon
OPEN
Tue–Sat, 10 a.m.–7:15 p.m.;
Sun, 10 a.m.–1 p.m. &
1:30–7:15 p.m.
CREDIT CARDS
V, AE, MC
$$

31. SABRE
Tableware

What you'll find here is fun for your kitchen table. In the colorful cutlery collections, designed and produced by the Gelb family, everything is well-made, dishwasher safe, and a joy to look at. Many of the plastic handles are in bright prints from polka dots to florals and plaids, others are a variety of shaped solids offered in tons of tones. There are even natural woods, as well as plastics imitating horn and tortoise. They're sold by the piece (from 10€) or place setting. I find it irresistible, and doubt that you'll be able to leave without at least a serving piece. Some co-ordinating dishware is also sold here.

Sabre

Ustencia

ADDRESSS
95 Rue de Seine, 6th
TELEPHONE/FAX
01.56.24.20.20
METRO
Mabillon
OPEN
Mon, 2:30–7 p.m.;
Tue–Sat, 10:30 a.m.–7 p.m.
Closed August
CREDIT CARDS
V, MC
$$

32. USTENCIA
Gadgetry for kitchen and home

Here is a unique concept shop chock full of ingenious utilitarian gadgets that you can't live without. How about a plastic purse holder for your toilet paper? Or black silicon hot-pads and molds? Or a trans-parent tape measure made to hold the picture of a growing child at each increment? There's a good selection of highly designed coffee makers and unusual kitchen aprons. Everything here is fun and ergonomic, and hand-picked by M Chassagny, a design fair enthusiast. Furniture is upstairs.

33. GERARD MULOT
Bakery

This attractive neighborhood bakery is always crowded with locals in the know. They come for the tempting pastries, *pain aux noix* (walnut bread), and fresh chocolates in bright red boxes. If you're a macaroon fan, don't miss them here! Or try "L'Amaryllis," a delectable house creation of dried fruit macaroon filled with pastry cream and decorated in fresh raspberries.

ADDRESS
76 Rue de Seine, 6th
TELEPHONE
01.43.26.85.77
METRO
Odéon
OPEN
Thur–Tue, 6:45 a.m.–8 p.m.;
Closed Wednesday
NO CREDIT CARDS
$$

34. SOULEIADO
Fabrics, wallpapers, home accessories, clothing

You may already know this enchanting store by its American name, Pierre Deux. This is the authentic version of the well-loved French provincial print.

It all began when Charles Démery, a native of Provence, found 40,000 wooden fabric-printing plates from the eighteenth and nineteenth centuries in his uncle's barn. The enterprise he created in 1938, to produce textiles from traditional provincial fabrics by the old methods, has succeeded by the highest standard. M Démery has modernized and popularized this ancient art of his region, and his fabrics are recognized and appreciated well outside of France.

This shop glows with the warmth of the sun, colors, and lifestyle of Provence. The original motifs have been modernized by enlarging or diminishing them, mixing them, and reproducing them in rich tones. Choose to join the ranks of those seduced by SOULEIADO, and you, too, will re-cover your sofas and chairs, wallpaper your bed-

ADDRESS
3 Rue Lobineau, 6th
TELEPHONE
01.44.07.33.81
METRO
Mabillon, Odéon
OPEN
Mon–Sat, 10:30 a.m.–7 p.m.
CREDIT CARDS
V, AE, MC, DC
$$$

room, throw a new quilt on the bed and linens on the table, strew lavender sachets throughout your home, and put everything from Kleenex to hats in print-covered boxes. Then revitalize your wardrobe with shawls and folklorique skirts, blouses, and trousers.

Fabrics cannot be shipped by the shop to the U.S., but they are cheaper here than in the States.

ADDRESS
4 Rue du Tournon, 6th (florist)
TELEPHONE
01.46.34.10.64
METRO
Odéon or Mabillon
OPEN
Mon–Sat, 9 a.m.–9 p.m.;
Sun, 9 a.m.–2 p.m. & 3–6 p.m.

ADDRESS
46 Rue du Bac, 7th (gift boutique)
TELEPHONE
01.42.22.22.12
METRO
Rue du Bac
OPEN
Mon–Sat, 9 a.m.–9 p.m.;
Sun, 9 a.m.–2 p.m.
CREDIT CARDS
V, MC, DC
$$-$$$$

35. AU NOM DE LA ROSE
Roses, gifts

Scented garden roses, with strains dating back to the seventeenth century, are freshly cut every day for this irresistible shop. The sixty varieties of roses here are favored by those in the fashion world seeking the perfect shade of bud or bloom. Bouquets are beautifully wrapped in white paper tied with a rose, and look terribly Parisian. The Rue du Bac location has a boutique selling rose jam, rose soaps, and other gift possibilities made of roses.

ADDRESS
8 Rue de Tournon, 6th
TELEPHONE
01.44.27.07.08
METRO
Odéon
OPEN
Mon–Sat, 11 a.m.–7 p.m.
CREDIT CARDS
V, AE
$$$-$$$$

36. MARIE-HÉLÈNE DE TAILLAC
Jewelry

When you enter you'll wonder what all the fuss is about. The boutique is minimal in design, its sparse grouping of display cases within walls of a pleasant eggshell blue. But ask to see what's hidden in the drawers and you'll find the jewels in dazzling colors that Mme de Taillac is famous for. The *creatrice* spends six months a year in Jaipur, India, to be near the Gem Palace, where she finds inspiration and hand-picks stones. There, her refined and original designs are handcrafted and hand-faceted in the Indian tradition from precious and semi-precious stones set in 22-carat gold. In her Paris shop she offers unique pieces that are modern in style yet ancient in technique, each beautifully balanced in both color and material. Simple pendants begin at 80€, earrings at 175€, rings from 800€, and the well-publicized scarf necklace is around 10,000€. For the most serious shopper, there's a private showing room.

37. MARIE MERCIÉ
Women's and men's hats

Hats off to Marie Mercié, who designs headgear with humor, grace, and history. A walk through her boutique is like a whimsical world tour, taking you from Fontainebleau to Africa. Since her first collection in 1985, she has brought contemporary chic to this important Parisian accessory by creating hats that will be noticed for their daring without losing their elegance, winning the hearts and heads of younger French thoroughbreds. If you want to wow them at Ascot, consider the straw adorned with a perfect giant sunflower, marred by a housefly.

There are no limits to shapes, colors, and decorations of her millinery and its loosely coordinating jewelry and handbags. Custom orders are possible. Men's hats are at the Rue Tiquetonne address.

ADDRESS
23 Rue St-Sulpice, 6th (women's)
TELEPHONE
01.43.26.45.83
METRO
St-Sulpice

ADDRESS
56 Rue Tiquetonne, 2nd (men's)
TELEPHONE
01.40.26.60.68
METRO
Etienne-Marcel
OPEN
Mon–Sat, 11 a.m.–7 p.m.
CREDIT CARDS
V, AE, MC
$$$

Marie Mercié

ADDRESS
18 Rue Mabillon, 6th
TELEPHONE
01.46.33.84.74
METRO
Mabillon
OPEN
Tue–Sat, 10:30 a.m.–6:30 p.m.
CREDIT CARDS
V, A, MC
$$$$

38. MAISON LA CORNUE
Cooking ranges, cooking classes

LA CORNUE is the absolute queen of the cuisine, both in its beauty and its command of your recipes. Built to order by a single artisan, start to finish, it may take several months until at last you'll have in your kitchen a true source of "ooh-la-la!" The Chateau line is offered in twenty-six porcelain enamel colors that can be trimmed in brass, nickel, copper, or stainless, and is priced accordingly.

Cooks may also sign up for lessons given on the premises. Three-hour tasting demonstrations (80€) are offered three Thursdays a month.

ADDRESS
14 Rue Princesse, 6th
TELEPHONE
01.40.51.81.10
METRO
Mabillon
OPEN
Mon–Sat, 11 a.m.–7 p.m.

ADDRESS
5 Rue des Rosiers, 4th
TELEPHONE
01.48.87.04.26
METRO
St-Paul
OPEN
Tue–Sat, 11 a.m.–7 p.m.;
Sun, 2–7 p.m.
CREDIT CARDS
V, AE, MC
$$

39. NADINE DELEPINE
Costume jewelry and accessories

This is just the place to pick up charming yet inexpensive little baubles that can bring any old outfit up-to-the-minute. It could be a lambskin lace flower to pin on your tee (25€), a Swarovski crystal–studded ceramic butterfly on a neck ribbon, or orange crystal pearls tied with a satin rose (45€). An endlessly creative mix of materials comes out of the workshops behind the boutiques, which also allow for a brisk business in custom bridal accessories. Purses, hats, and scarves round out the collection.

40. THE VILLAGE VOICE
American bookshop

Parisian Odile Hellier opened her shop over a
decade ago to carry on the American literary tradition in Paris, and a fine literary hangout it has
become. You will find current bestsellers here, as
well as two floors of English-language books by
English-speaking writers the world over. Specialties
are new American writing and English translations
of contemporary French works.

The *Village Voice* Readers Series brings a major
writer here every month or so for a reading and
book signing. There is also a good selection of
American magazines.

ADDRESS
6 Rue Princesse, 6th
TELEPHONE
01.46.33.36.47
METRO
Mabillon
OPEN
Mon, 2–7:30 p.m.;
Tues–Sat, 10 a.m.–7:30 p.m.;
Sun, 1–6 p.m.
NO CREDIT CARDS
$$

41. AU PLAT D'ÉTAIN
Toy soldiers

Since 1775, before the French Revolution, young
Parisians have been coming to this store to admire
the first lead soldiers and listen to grownups talk
military strategy in the back room. It still draws the
serious enthusiast of military metal, dealing in the
venerated French makers C. B. G., Mignot, and
Lucotte, as well as the English houses Tradition and
Marlborough.

The battle scene dioramas are spectacular. If
you shun combat, look for the beautifully dressed
Cyrano de Bergerac sporting a nose almost as long
as his sword, or the aristocratic carriage and four,
filled with passengers who could be fleeing revolu-
tionary wrath. Soldiers begin at about 25€.

ADDRESS
16 Rue Guisarde, 6th
TELEPHONE
01.43.54.32.06
METRO
Mabillon, Saint-Sulpice, Saint
Germain-des-Près
OPEN
Mon–Sat, 11 a.m.–12:30 p.m.
& 2–7 p.m.
CREDIT CARDS
V
$$$

Along the Way

On the PLACE ST-SULPICE, a magnificent church shares space with the towering
FOUNTAIN OF THE CARDINAL POINTS, its aura of religious serenity intact. On
glorious summer days you may come upon book and antique fairs here, and on July
14, one of the grandest of Bastille Day balls. The boutiques facing the square are
equally elegant.

ADDRESS
6 Place St-Sulpice, 6th
(women's)
TELEPHONE
01.43.29.43.00
METRO
St-Sulpice

ADDRESS
12 Place St-Sulpice, 6th (men's)
TELEPHONE
01.43.26.84.40
METRO
St-Sulpice

ADDRESS
38 Rue du Faubourg St-Honoré
(women's)
TELEPHONE
01.42.65.74.59
METRO
Concorde

ADDRESS
32 Rue du Faubourg St-Honoré
(men's)
TELEPHONE
01.53.05.80.80
METRO
Concorde

ADDRESS
8 Rue de Grenelle, 7th (shoes
and accessories)
9 Rue de Grenelle, 7th (men's
and women's accessories)
TELEPHONE
01.45.44.39.01
METRO
Sèvres-Babylone
OPEN
Mon, 11 a.m.–7 p.m.;
Tue–Sat, 10:30 a.m.–7 p.m.

ADDRESS
5 Avenue Marçeau, 16th (exhi-
bition space)
TELEPHONE
01.44.31.64.00
METRO
Alma-Marçeau
OPEN
Tue–Sun, 11 a.m.–5:30 p.m.
CREDIT CARDS
V, AE, MC
$$$-$$$$

42. YVES ST-LAURENT RIVE GAUCHE
Women's and men's clothing

St-Laurent was the king of Paris fashion since his
first collection for Dior in 1968. He had the
genius to introduce collections that kept the fash-
ion world wildly excited, season after season, and
his innovations have become classics. The YSL
you buy today, now designed by Stefano Pilati,
remains elegantly cut and enormously comfort-
able, and will still be so when you put it on ten
years from now.

St-Laurent was the first designer to open a
prêt-à-porter boutique, taking the formality and
high prices out of fashion found in the rarified
couture milieu. The Left Bank location is his
largest, but located out of the tourist hub it's qui-
eter than the others. Come here for the quickest
and most attentive service and to best view the
extensive collection. In the women's boutique
downstairs look for suits, dresses, skirts, acces-
sories, and leathers, upstairs for shoes and furs.
The Avenue Marçeau location, once the haute
couture headquarters, is now home of the Yves
Saint Laurent Foundation, and is an exhibition
space for shows on YSL and various artists.

43. PIERRE HERMÉ
Pastries, chocolates

Described by connoisseurs as the "Picasso of pastries," Pierre Hermé has established himself in a jewelbox of a shop, offering small cakes, tartes, chocolates, petit fours, macaroons, and other gems that some deem "incomparable." Using the finest ingredients and with every possible attention to detail, he produces new collections twice a year of the great French classics, updated. They must be tasted to be fully appreciated.

ADDRESS
72 Rue Bonaparte, 6th
TELEPHONE
01.43.54.47.77
METRO
St-Sulpice
OPEN
Tue–Sun, 10 a.m.–7 p.m.
CREDIT CARDS
V, AE, MC, DC
$$$-$$$$

44. CACHAREL
Women's, men's, children's clothing, layette

CACHAREL offers much more than the flowered blouses and shirts that once made its name. The revved-up designs by Cléments and Ribeiro, an English/Brazilian couple, are young and contemporary. Cacharel embodies their look of simple sophistication with a punch and is an easy family stop for an immensely wearable, decently made, well-priced wardrobe for everyone. The ambiance feels as fresh as the collection, quite in contrast to the mad crush at the nearby department stores.

If you care less about the newest designs and the perfect ambiance, try CACHAREL STOCK for last year's designs at discounts of 30 to 40 percent.

ADDRESS
64 Rue Bonaparte, 6th
TELEPHONE
01.40.46.00.45
METRO
St-Germain-des-Prés
OPEN
Mon–Fri, 10:30 a.m.–7 p.m.;
Sat, 10:30 a.m.–7:30 p.m.
CREDIT CARDS
V, AE, MC
$$-$$$

CACHAREL STOCK (discount)
ADDRESS
114 Rue d'Alésia, 14th
TELEPHONE
01.45.42.53.04
METRO
Alésia
OPEN
Mon, 2–7 p.m.;
Tue–Sat, 10 a.m.–7 p.m.
CREDIT CARDS
V
$$

ADDRESS
53 Rue Bonaparte, 6th
TELEPHONE
01.43.29.01.90
METRO
St-Germain-des-Prés

ADDRESS
5 Rue Montmartre, 1st
TELEPHONE
01.40.41.99.51
METRO
Les Halles

ADDRESS
23 Rue de Grenelle, 6th
TELEPHONE
01.45.49.28.73
METRO
Rue du Bac

ADDRESS
2 Rue Guichard, 16th
TELEPHONE
01.42.15.18.85
METRO
La Muette

ADDRESS
25 Rue Tronchet, 8th
TELEPHONE
01.40.17.07.41
METRO
Havre-Caumartin

ADDRESS
9 Rue Bréa, 6th
TELEPHONE
01.55.42.14.72
METRO
Vavin
OPEN
Mon–Sat, 10:30 a.m.–7 p.m.
CREDIT CARDS
V, AE, MC
$$

ADDRESS
28 Rue du Four, 6th
TELEPHONE
01.45.48.39.31
METRO
Mabillon or St-Germain-des-Prés
OPEN
Mon–Sat, 10 a.m.–7 p.m.

45. PRINCESSE TAM TAM
Lingerie, swimwear, sleepwear

If you're planning a day in the country, in your underwear, come to PRINCESSE TAM TAM to buy it. Mostly cottons, with little that's very transparent or peekaboo, the cut remains feminine, even without much lace. Denim stitching or floral prints in dark colors is the look here. It's perfect for teens and for women of the world who love to feel cozy in their jams.

46. POM D'API
Children's shoes

The multicolor mosaic storefront has tremendous kid appeal among the artfully austere facades of this grown-up city. Inside it's filled with fanciful POM D'API label footwear for baby to sixteen years.

Whether it's beaded sandals, tennies in bright color combos, or leopard-skin-like booties, these shoes won't fail to please the modern child. After all, this family has been pleasing the generations since 1870.

Pom d'Api

ADDRESS
13 Rue du Jour, 1st
TELEPHONE
01.42.36.08.87
METRO
Les Halles or Etienne-Marcel
OPEN
Mon–Sat, 10 a.m.–7 p.m.

ADDRESS
140 Avenue Victor Hugo, 16th
TELEPHONE
01.47.27.22.00
METRO
Victor-Hugo or Pompe
OPEN
Mon–Tue & Thur–Fri, 10 a.m.–1 p.m. & 2:15–7 p.m.;
Wed & Sat, 10 a.m.–7 p.m.
CREDIT CARDS
V, AE, MC
$$-$$$

47. DINH VAN
Jewelry and watches

The distinctive DINH VAN esthetic relies on simple forms for a pure, minimalist beauty. Trained at Cartier, the French-Vietnamese designer has had his own shops and devoted following since the 70s, producing pieces that have become near cult items. Currently everyone is mad for his Chinese Pi in its many iterations, from a flat silver circle hanging from a black cord, to hammered 22-carat gold, to those with diamonds, all intended to bring happiness.

ADDRESS
58 Rue Bonaparte, 6th
TELEPHONE
01.56.24.10.00
METRO
St-Germain-des-Prés
OPEN
Mon, 1–7 p.m., Tue–Sat, 10:45 a.m.–7 p.m.
CREDIT CARDS
V, AE, MC
$$$

48. GEORGES RECH
Women's clothing; men's clothing

RECH is a smart stop for anyone looking for discreetly cut pants or skirts, jackets or coats. His separates are cited as among the best in Paris by the French fashion press, but you'd never know it with-

ADDRESS
54 Rue Bonaparte, 6th
TELEPHONE
01.43.26.84.11
METRO
St-Germain-des-Prés

ADDRESS
273 Rue St-Honoré, 8th
TELEPHONE
01.42.61.41.14
METRO
Concorde

ADDRESS
23 Avenue Victor Hugo, 16th
(women's)
TELEPHONE
01.45.00.83.19
METRO
Étoile
OPEN
Mon, 11 a.m.–7 p.m.;
Tue–Sat, 10 a.m.–7 p.m.

ADDRESS
27 Avenue Victor Hugo, 16th
(men's)
TELEPHONE
01.45.01.69.53
METRO
Victor-Hugo
OPEN
Mon–Sat, 10:30 a.m.–7:30 p.m.

ADDRESS
100 Rue d'Alésia,14th
(outlet)
TELEPHONE
01.45.40.87.73
METRO
Alésia
OPEN
Mon, 1–7 p.m.;
Tue–Sat, 10 a.m.–7 p.m.
CREDIT CARDS
V, AE, MC, DC
$$-$$$

ADDRESS
5 Rue du Vieux-Colombier, 6th
TELEPHONE
01.42.22.75.83
METRO
St-Sulpice

ADDRESS
20 Rue du Boccador, 8th
TELEPHONE
01.49.52.09.98
METRO
George V

out a close look. Clothes that seem to hang straight on the rack take a shape of their own when you step into them, even if you're not French. There's something to flatter every figure, each in a dozen or so fabrics. While these classics come well priced in his Synonyme line, the George Rech line is trendier and pricier. Menswear, including his ever-popular suits, is found only in the Sixteenth.

49. VILEBREQUIN
Men's and boys' beachwear and shoes

For a woman vacationing on the sands of St-Tropez, trying on swimsuits from a beach vendor is half the fun. But if you are male, you won't want to miss the opportunity to shop at Vilebrequin in town. After thirty years, this St-Tropezien line of swim trunks (which double as shorts), sunglasses, and beach shirts has moved into Paris with three boutiques offering its stylish gear year round. The famous trunks come in a nylon carrying pouch and include a removable waterproof pocket. There are five men's cuts, with most ending up just a few inches above the knee, not so skimpy as you might expect from the town made famous by its nude beaches. All in all, everything here is quite fashionable, even a bit preppy. If you're gift shopping for an American man you'll probably want to buy a size up: a large Frenchman is the size of a medium American. Men's trunks run about 100€, and boys' from 60€. The father-son collection is a big hit, and so is the new addition of beachy shoes in raffia.

ADDRESS
281 Rue St-Honoré, 8th
TELEPHONE
01.40.15.64.06
METRO
Concorde or Madeleine
OPEN
Mon–Sat, 10 a.m.–7 p.m.
CREDIT CARDS
V, AE, MC
$$$

50. JAMIN PUECH
Handbags

If you've been looking for a truly original bag, you'll find it here. Forget the status symbol lookalike. At JAMIN PUECH they take a fine classic material, say leather or silk, in a fashionable shape, and to give it a bit of character may whop it, distress it, add a few beads, trims and embroideries, and maybe some fringe, until it looks like it's been on the road with a rich groupie. They're terribly stylish and definitely for the individualist.

ADDRESS
43 Rue Madame, 6th
TELEPHONE/FAX
01.45.48.14.85
METRO
St-Sulpice
OPEN
Mon–Fri, 11 a.m.–7 p.m.;
Sat, noon–7 p.m.

ADDRESS
68 Rue Vieille du Temple, 3rd
TELEPHONE
01.48.87.84.87
METRO
St-Paul
OPEN
Tue, noon–7 p.m.;
Wed–Fri, 10 a.m.–7 p.m.;
Sat, 11 a.m.–7 p.m.
CREDIT CARDS
V, AE, MC
$$$

Jamin Puech

ADDRESS
60 Rue du Cherche-Midi, 6th
TELEPHONE
01.45.49.45.96
METRO
Sèvres-Babylone
OPEN
Tue–Sat, 10:30 a.m.–7 p.m.
CREDIT CARDS
V, AE, MC
$$–$$$

51. LES CONTES DE THÉ
Teas and teapots

Cultivators of teatime will find a treasure trove here. More than 100 varieties of tea are sold alongside the products and accoutrements that complete a perfect tea service. I come here for the extraordinary selection of teapots that Mme Dattner has chosen from around the world. Whether you prefer Russian motifs, reproduction Meissen, English teapots in all colors, Chinese or Japanese services, or pots in the shape of a house, you'll find them all in this delightful little shop.

ADDRESS
27 Rue du Cherche-Midi, 6th
TELEPHONE
01.45.48.83.79
METRO
Sèvres-Babylone
OPEN
Mon–Sat, 10:15 a.m.–7 p.m.
CREDIT CARDS
V, MC, DC
$$$

52. MISE EN DEMEURE
Home décor

You'll find everything for the home here. For all your homes, in fact. MISE EN DEMEURE is choc-a-bloc with its own well-done reproductions and antiques from the eighteenth and nineteenth centuries as well as its modern line. If you have a lot to furnish in a hurry, you needn't feel overwhelmed, as the experienced staff is happy to help you, in English, to put it all together. They are even quite willing and capable of doing it up for you, from your chairs and sofas to linens and tableware. And, they ship all over the world. Be sure and see the antique mirrors, upstairs. This establishment also deals with the trade.

Along the Way

The MARCHÉ BIOLOGIQUE (organic market), on the Boulevard Raspail between the Rue de Cherche-Midi and the Rue de Rennes, is where *tout* Paris comes to do its weekly organic marketing. On Sunday mornings from 9 a.m. to 1 p.m., vendors are open for business, drawing health, and quality-conscious Parisians to their open-air stands for wonderful jams and honeys, savory buckwheat *galettes* (pancakes) filled with vegetables and cheese to consume on the spot, and creamy unpasteurized goat cheeses that you can take back to your hotel but not back to the U.S. This large and popular market becomes increasingly crowded as the morning wears on, so it's best to go early.

53. À LA REINE ASTRID
Chocolates

The ultra-rich bittersweet chocolate here is not to be missed by lovers of such things. Established in 1935 in memory of Queen Astrid of Belgium, these candies are definitely French in taste, from the top-selling nougatine with 99.8 percent pure cocoa, to the praline specialty. All, however, are fit for a queen.

ADDRESS
24 Rue du Cherche-Midi, 6th
TELEPHONE
01.42.84.07.02
METRO
Sèvres-Babylone

ADDRESS
33 Rue Washington, 8th
TELEPHONE
01.45.63.60.39
METRO
Georges V
OPEN
Mon–Sat, 10 a.m.–7 p.m.
CREDIT CARDS
V, AE, MC
$$

54. LOXWOOD
Women's clothing and accessories

This is one of those wonderful shops where you can coordinate an entire outfit, from cashmere pull to silk scarf to leather skirt. And when you walk out with a matching purple suede bag and moccasins, you'll still look conservative. Despite the English name, LOXWOOD is very French, quite elegant, and not terribly expensive.

ADDRESS
14 Rue du Cherche Midi, 6th
TELEPHONE
01.42.22.11.21
METRO
Sèvres-Babylone
OPEN
Mon, 11 a.m.–7 p.m.;
Tue–Sat, 10 a.m.–7 p.m.
CREDIT CARDS
V, AE, MC
$$

ADDRESS
8 Rue du Cherche-Midi, 6th
TELEPHONE
01.45.48.42.59
METRO
Sèvres-Babylone or Saint-
Sulpice
OPEN
Mon–Sat, 7:15 a.m.–8 p.m.;
Closed Sunday

ADDRESS
49 Boulevard de Grenelle, 15th
TELEPHONE
01.45.79.11.49
METRO
Dupleix
OPEN
Tue–Sat, 7:15 a.m.–8 p.m.;
Closed Monday
NO CREDIT CARDS (except
by Internet)
$
INTERNET
www.poilane.fr

55. POILÂNE
Bakery

Lionel Poilâne is the best-known bread baker in
Paris. The Pain Poilâne sign is in the window of
dozens of eateries throughout the city, and there is
always a line at his own famous bakery on the Rue
du Cherche-Midi. Visitors are sometimes treated to
a walk through his basement kitchen where bare-
chested bakers fire brick ovens filled with a dough
of stone-ground flour, water, and Brittany sea salt.

It is rightly said that each batch has its own
character, and though it varies, POILÂNE is the
standard bearer for the loaf that's crusty on the outside and mildly sour on the inside. While you're
here, pick up some little shortbread cookies to stash
in your purse, and consume an apple tart on the
way out. You may now order from their website for
U.S. delivery, paying by credit card.

ADDRESS
4 bis Rue du Cherche-Midi,
6th
TELEPHONE
01.45.44.95.54
METRO
St-Sulpice or Sèvres-Babylone
OPEN
Mon–Sat, 10:30 a.m.–7 p.m.

ADDRESS
2 Rue Tronchet, 8th
TELEPHONE
01.47.42.28.82
METRO
Madeleine
OPEN
Mon–Sat, 10 a.m.–7 p.m.

ADDRESS
40 Avenue Montaigne, 8th
TELEPHONE
01.47.23.07.26

56. ERÈS
Women's swimwear, lingerie

Early each December ERÈS brings in a new collection of swimsuits that actually stay up under water
while you are swimming. The shop maintains its
reputation as an up-to-the-minute house for beachwear design, thoughtful enough also to sell tops
and bottoms separately. What more could a girl ask
for? Perhaps some coordinating cover-ups: T-shirts,
shawls, skirts, long shirts with long sleeves, knee
pants, or dresses that can double as evening wear?
Erès has it.

During winter they show long body suits as
streetwear under the above. Swimsuits begin at
about 115€, one-piece or two, with or without
cups. This is a sophisticated but simple collection,
designed with many bodies in mind. If you find
that you need more selection, go to GALERIES
LAFAYETTE.

METRO
Franklin D. Roosevelt
OPEN
Mon–Sat, 10:30 a.m.–7 p.m.

ADDRESS
6 Rue Guichard, 16th
TELEPHONE
01.46.47.45.21
METRO
La Muette
OPEN
Mon–Sat, 10:30 a.m.–7 p.m.
CREDIT CARDS
V, AE, DC
$$$

57. COMTESSE DU BARRY
Gastronomy and foie gras

Founded in 1908 and always ahead of its time in gastronomic preparation and conservation, the COMTESSE DU BARRY is purveyor of an extensive line of regional southwestern cuisine sold from its many boutiques throughout France. Its original specialty, foie gras, is available in terrines, tins, blocks, and medallions, with or without truffles, and traditionally prepared with a bit of salt, pepper, and armagnac. All the offerings here, including duck and goose confits, duck breasts, and prepared dishes are free of chemical additives. They are ingeniously hermetically sealed to ship worldwide, and can easily be ordered from the website, www.comtessedubarry.com. The shops are lovely; likewise, putting together a gourmet dinner on the web can be lots of fun.

ADDRESS
1 Rue de Sèvres, 6th
TELEPHONE
01.45.48.32.04
FAX
01.45.49.06.27
METRO
Sèvres-Babylone
OPEN
Mon, 2:30–7 p.m.;
Tue–Sat, 10 a.m.–7 p.m.

ADDRESS
93 Rue St-Antoine, 4th
TELEPHONE
01.40.29.07.14
METRO
St-Paul
OPEN
Mon, 2:30–7:30 p.m.;
Tue–Sat, 10 a.m.–1 p.m. &
2–7:30 p.m.

ADDRESS
111 Avenue Victor Hugo, 16th
TELEPHONE
01.44.05.01.89
METRO
Victor-Hugo
OPEN
Mon–Sat, 11 a.m.–1:30 p.m. &
2:30–7 p.m.

(continued on next page)

ADDRESS
88 bis Avenue Mozart, 16th
TELEPHONE
01.45.27.74.49
METRO
Jasmin
OPEN
Closed Monday;
Tue–Sat, 10:30 a.m.–1 p.m. &
2:30–6:30 p.m.
CREDIT CARDS
V, AE, MC, DC
$$
INTERNET
www.comtessedubarry.com

ADDRESS
13 Rue de Sèvres, 6th
TELEPHONE
01.45.48.87.90
METRO
Sèvres-Babylone
OPEN
Mon, 1–7 p.m.;
Tue–Sat, 10 a.m.–7 p.m.
CREDIT CARDS
V, MC
$$

58. CHANTELIVRE
Children's books

This is probably the largest children's bookstore in Paris, boasting over 10,000 volumes, and just the spot to shop for a budding francophone. Let little Mary and Johnny amuse themselves in the toy and story corner while you pursue their transformation into Marie et Jean.

For the youngest child are brightly colored hard-paged books that can be understood whatever the mother tongue. For the student are Babar and Maurice Sendak—French versions of what they have at home—which are fun and instructive since they already know the stories. The same is true for the French-language videos and CDs of Disney favorites, but make sure they are the proper format for your VHS before you buy!

You will also find audio cassettes of French songs and stories, some English and bilingual books, and a collection of book illustration posters that includes Babar classics and *The Little Prince*.

59. LE BON MARCHÉ

Department store, gourmet grocery

Once the old lady of Paris department stores, LE BON MARCHÉ is now among the most chic, after a full facelift by her owners, the luxury group LVMH. Thankfully she still plays the game the old-fashioned way, with a helpful sales staff and very fair prices.

The enormous food department, *"La Grande Épicérie de Paris,"* whose best-of-everything staples are peppered with specialties from around Paris (including Fauchon products) and regional France, is the favorite neighborhood supermarket. On the floor above is *"Le Delicabar,"* a trendy stop for refueling that specializes in gourmet arrangements of vegetables, fruits, and chocolate. If that doesn't pick you up, the magnificent bar lighting will!

ADDRESS
24 Rue de Sèvres, 7th
38 Rue de Sèvres, 7th (gourmet grocery)
TELEPHONE
01.44.39.80.00
01.44.39.81.00 (grocery)
METRO
Sèvres-Babylone
OPEN
Department Store: Mon–Wed & Fri, 9:30 a.m.–7 p.m.; Thurs, 10 a.m.–9 p.m.; Sat, 9:30 a.m.–8 p.m.;
Grocery: Mon–Fri, 8:30 a.m.–9 p.m.; Sat, 8:30 a.m.–8 p.m.
CREDIT CARDS
V, AE, MC
$$-$$$

AU SAUVIGNON

Wine bar

ADDRESS
80 Rue des Saints-Pères, 7th
TELEPHONE
01.45.48.49.02
METRO
Sèvres-Babylone
OPEN
Mon–Sat, 8 a.m.–9 p.m.; closed August
CREDIT CARDS
V
$$

For a simple lunch, snack, or glass of wine, AU SAUVIGNON is a longtime award winner. The full corner view from this spotless establishment is superb for people watching, and while only cold plates are served here, nothing can beat their tartine made with a slice of Poilâne bread and charcuterie, fois gras, or a cheese platter, accompanied by, perhaps, a sauvignon blanc?

ADDRESS
71–73 Rue des St-Pères, 6th
TELEPHONE
01.45.48.88.37
METRO
Sèvres-Babylone
OPEN
Mon–Sat, 10 a.m.–7 p.m.
CREDIT CARDS
V, AE, DC
$$$-$$$$

60. SABBIA ROSA
Lingerie

This is where French starlets often come for their most glamorous underthings, so when you are planning an evening of stardom you'll want to stop here. The seamstresses downstairs stitch luxurious little nothings from silk satins, handworked Calais lace, and fine-gauge cottons.

With patterned bras that can hold their own under an evening shawl, to Brazilian-style undies, to sultry satin pajamas, you'll have no problem changing even the most modest image at Mme Rosa's. If you don't find what you had in mind, the workshop will be happy to whip it up for you.

Sabbia Rosa

61. SHADÉ
Costume jewelry and accessories

The fresh vision of Marilyn Sfadj brings what's new
and stylish from both the designer studios and the
craftsman's atelier to her elegant little boutique, a
gentlewoman's shop from the marble floor to the
romantic chandelier.

Besides pieces from the likes of Lacroix,
Lagerfeld, Kenzo, and Dior that often come directly from the fashion shows are handcrafted items
she has sought around France, many unique to her.
A hair barrette decorated with hand-dyed and hand-
sewn fabric buds I spotted here took the artist three
hours to make and sold for 60€, with matching earrings for 38€. There are bags, sunglasses, hats,
shawls, and lots of hair and jewelry pieces to catch
your fancy in Mme Sfadj's ever-changing fantasy.

ADDRESS
63 Rue des Saints-Pères, 6th
TELEPHONE
01.45.49.30.37
METRO
Sèvres-Babylone or
St-Germain-des-Prés
OPEN
Mon–Sat, 11 a.m.–7:30 p.m.
CREDIT CARDS
V, AE, MC
$$-$$$

Along the Way

If you're on the search for fabulous footwear, you must scout out the Rue de
Grenelle, 7th. Metro Saint-Sulpice.

Begin with CHARLES KAMMER (N.7), whose very style-oriented shoes are
grabbed up by shoeaholics as well as by everyone else who likes to dress up their
feet. The prices here make it easy to walk out with a closetful of moods, from
straight-laced to embroidered baroque, all of a quality that may even outlast the
style. Telephone: 01.42.22.35.13; open: Mon–Sat, 10 a.m. to 7 p.m. $$-$$$.

March onward to STEPHANE KÉLIAN's (N.13, bis) flagship store carrying both
men's and women's shoes as well as his designs for Gaultier and Martine Sitbon. His
look is his own, highly styled but seemingly handcrafted. Telephone: 01.42.22.93.03;
open: Mon–Sat, 10 a.m. to 7 p.m. His other boutiques are at N.26, Avenue des
Champs Élysées, 8th; N.5, Rue du Faubourg Saint-Honoré, 8th; and N.20, Avenue
Victor Hugo, 16th. $$$

At N.17 is CHARLES JOURDAN, whom we've loved since the sixties, and
whose designs for the sophisticate are kept updated by Patrick Cox. Telephone:
01.45.48.48.98; open: Mon–Sat, 10:30 a.m. to 7 p.m. $$$

Down the street PATRICK COX (N.21) shows his sophisticated footwear designs
for men and women. He has a talent for taking a basic and adding a twist.
Telephone: 01.45.49.24.28; open: Mon–Sat, 10 a.m. to 7 p.m. $$$

IRIS (N.28) shows Chloe, Proenza Schouler, Veronique Branquinho, and other
top createurs who are all manufactured in the Iris factory in Italy. This bright white

boutique is full of stand-out designs. Telephone: 01.42.22.89.81; open: Mon–Sat, 10:30 a.m. to 7 p.m. $$$.

Busy boy designer BRUNO FRISONI (N.34) has found a moment to open his own shop with his styles as always favoring a glamorous retro look. Some are easier to look at than to wear. Telephone: 01.42.84.12.30; open: Mon–Sat, 10:30 a.m. to 7 p.m. $$$.

At the pinnacle is CHRISTIAN LOUBOUTIN (N.38–40), whose red-soled shoes are oh-so sexy yet remain the height of elegance. Hand-finished and ultra-comfortable (unless you end up with a stilletto that's a bit taller than you can manage), you'll never regret the fortune you spend on these.You'll find espadrilles here for a mere 195 to 250€. Telephone: 01.42.22.33.07; open: Mon–Sat, 10:30 a.m. to 12:30 p.m. & 1:30 to 7 p.m. $$$-$$$$.

ADDRESS
22 Rue de Grenelle, 7th
TELEPHONE
01.42.22.82.40
METRO
St-Sulpice
OPEN
Mon–Fri, 10:30 a.m.–7 p.m.
CREDIT CARDS
V, AE, MC, DC
$$-$$$

62. HAGA
Curiosities

You're bound to find a small antique something to slip into your luggage, or at least an object that looks well-traveled. In the hunt you may come across black lacquered elephant bookends (75€), a big-handled magnifying glass, an antique cane, or a carved ivory box (1,000€). Much of what you'll find here is old, and it's all cleaned up and ready for your map-room.

ADDRESS
37 Rue de Grenelle, 7th
TELEPHONE
01.45.48.26.13
METRO
Sèvres-Babylone
OPEN
Mon–Sat, 11 a.m.–7 p.m.
(workshop, call for an appointment)
CREDIT CARDS
V, AE, MC
$$$-$$$$

63. ÉTIENNE BRUNEL
Evening dresses and wedding gowns

If you dream of floating into some midsummer's night, come here for your fairy costume. Mireille Etienne Brunel creates wedding dresses and evening wear from *le fil à lumière*, a synthetic transluscent thread that makes up a fabric that can only be described as, well, dreamy, or maybe as cobwebs glistening with dew. A wedding dress here, which is what she loves most to design, will run 2,000 to 3,500€ and upward. Or if you have the fingers of a real fairy princess you can buy the fabric by the meter and make your own. Either way, a purchase here and you are guaranteed some enchanted evenings.

64. ÉDITIONS DE PARFUMS FRÉDÉRIC MALLE
Perfumes

Frédéric Malle has created a "publishing house of perfumes" whose authors are nine of Europe's top noses, each of whom was called upon to develop a fragrance without regard to budget or market direction. The result is a sophisticated range of perfumes for the woman who defies trend.

Grandson to the founder of Christian Dior Perfumes, Malle evidently has a nose for marketing as well as an educated appreciation of fine scents. In every aspect, his Éditions de Parfums is set in the future. The elegantly minimalist shop, designed by Andre Putman, is decidedly calming and determinedly scent-free, with specially designed smelling columns so as not to cause olfactory confusion. Simple identical bottles contain fragrances with such suggestive names as *Musc Ravageur* and *En Passant*. So if you don't want to smell like your grandmother, or like anyone else back home, come here and let Frédéric or his assistant Catherine help you determine which scent is right for you.

ADDRESS
37 Rue de Grenelle, 7th
TELEPHONE
01.42.22.77.22
METRO
Sèvres-Babylone
OPEN
Mon–Sat, 11 a.m.–7 p.m.

ADDRESS
140 Avenue Victor Hugo, 16th
TELEPHONE/FAX
01.45.05.39.02
METRO
Victor-Hugo
OPEN
Mon–Sat, 1–7 p.m.
CREDIT CARDS
V, AE, MC
$$$

Éditions de Parfums Frédéric Malle

ADDRESS
27 Rue de Varenne, 7th
TELEPHONE
01.42.22.78.33
FAX
01.45.44.87.25
METRO
Rue du Bac
OPEN
Mon, 2–7 p.m.;
Tue–Sat, 10:30 a.m.–7 p.m.
CREDIT CARDS
V
$$$

65. DÎNERS EN VILLE
Table arts

This is one of the best spots in Paris to inspire your table, and you'll come away full of fresh ideas along with the treasures in your shopping bag. When the Comtesse de Mandat Grancey first displayed a table mixing old with new in place settings, a taboo was broken. Parisian hostesses embraced the license to dress their dining table with more room for whimsy.

The Countess has gathered charming examples of reproduction glassware, flatware, dishes, linens, and centerpieces, much of it elegantly arranged on tables set throughout the store. Even if you already have enough in flatware and china settings, you will be tempted to grab up accessory pieces and table linens in a variety of colors and patterns so vast that you may miss dinner trying to narrow your choices.

ADDRESS
79 Rue du Bac
TELEPHONE
01.45.48.80.93
FAX
01.45.44.74.16
METRO
Rue du Bac
OPEN
Mon, 12:30–7:30 p.m.;
Tue–Sat, 10:30 a.m.–7:30 p.m.
CREDIT CARDS
V, AE, MC
$$
INTERNET
www.dupeyron.com

66. RYST DUPEYRON
Wine Shop

The old wood paneling and mosaic floor of this classic wine shop are background to the amber hues of its armagnacs and to the reds of its famed bottles of bordeaux. While the selection here is extraordinary, drawing on reserves Monsieur Ryst began stocking in 1905, it is never daunting as the shop will advise you on your purchases and even allow you to taste its vintages. A perfect stop for that celebratory bottle of champagne, whose label can be personalized while you wait, this fine address offers an experience that can be appreciated equally by the oenophile and the novice. And, you can continue to order from its very comprehensive website, www.dupeyron.com, where you'll not only find access to the cellar, but gift packaging, personalized labeling, and wine paraphernalia.

67. MAÎTRE PARFUMEUR ET GANTIER
Fragrances and gloves

When the infallible "nose" Jean Laporte profitably
sold off his last successful enterprise (L'Artisan
Parfumeur), he claimed it took no more than a walk
in his garden in Bourgogne for him to invent an
entirely new line of fragrances for women, men,
and the home, sold exclusively in these beautifully
restored eighteenth-century shops.

If you want to avoid the commercial scents one
smells everywhere in Paris, and that even your
Parisian taxi driver will recognize, come here for an
hour well spent exploring original and subtle com-
positions with a salesperson who speaks English
and guides your search for a fragrance that projects
the real you. Eau-de-toilette is sold here, not perfume, and yes, it does last until your evening bath.
The thirty-plus scents are of the highest quality and
sell for around 60€ a bottle. If, in true Parisienne
style, you seek a lifelong fragrance that to your
friends and family will become synonymous with
you, the boutiques will continue to fill your orders
by mail within ten days. Be sure to pick up their
mail-order brochures for both personal and household fragrances. Also worth reordering are candles
in glass and home fragrance sprays. Once you've
lived with Laporte scents, you'll keep writing back
for more.

ADDRESS
84 bis Rue de Grenelle, 7th
TELEPHONE
01.45.44.61.57
METRO
Rue du Bac

ADDRESS
5 Rue des Capucines, 1st
TELEPHONE
01.42.96.35.13
METRO
Opéra
OPEN
Mon–Sat, 10:30 a.m.–6:30 p.m.
CREDIT CARDS
V, AE, MC, DC
$$$

68. THE REAL MCCOY
American food items

Can't get through another day abroad without your
Doritos? Ready to trade in your morning croissant
for a box of Aunt Jemima's Pancake Mix? After
gorging yourself in the finest European chocolate
shops do you still crave a Hershey Bar? Rest assured
you'll find the goodies here to satisfy your
American taste, but be prepared to pay through the
nose for them.

THE REAL MCCOY is the junk food junkie's
French fix, and a mainstay for Americans living in
Paris who need their pecan pie for Thanksgiving
and chocolate-chip cookies after school.

ADDRESS
194 Rue de Grenelle, 7th
TELEPHONE
01.45.56.98.82
METRO
École-Militaire
OPEN
Daily, 10 a.m.–8 p.m.
CREDIT CARDS
V, AE, DC
$$$$ (compared to back home)

ADDRESS
9 and 11 Place du Palais
Bourbon, 7th
TELEPHONE
01.47.05.13.30
FAX
01.45.51.50.11
METRO
Assemblée Nationale
HOURS
Mon–Fri, 10:30 a.m.–7 p.m.;
Sat, 10:30 a.m.–6:30 p.m.
CREDIT CARDS
V, AE, MC
$$-$$$$

69. BOUTIQUE MP BOITARD
Table and giftware

At this elegant address you'll be rubbing shoulders
with the privileged Parisienne who knows that a
petit cadeau (gift) from MARIE-PIERRE BOITARD
will be both well received by her discerning friends
and exceptional enough for her own salon or table.
No wonder Mme Boitard is able to hold to this
high standard: formerly a designer for Haviland
china, she creates many of the beautiful objects in
her shop. Perhaps best known are the gilt-edged
baroque crystal goblets in a royal blue or blood red.
The exclusive collections here include table ser-
vices, embroidered linens, glassware, masculine
gifts, distinctive objects for the home, and an imag-
inative line of fashion accessories that includes
purses, belts, and slippers. Among her antique items
are my favorite resilvered vases. You can rely on the
good taste of Mme Boitard for the most extraordi-
nary centerpiece or the small gift of a pretty jewel-
ry bag, everything signed MPB, for expenditures of
15 to 10,000€. Brides able to register here are lucky
indeed.

70. À LA PLAGE
Women's and girl's beachwear

You'll be on the beach year-round in this sunny shop, and find everything a girl would want to take off or put on by the sea (except her sunscreen), along with seaside changing cabins for trying them. It's not just about swimsuits here, but also coordinating shoes, hats, purses, shirts, and playtime jewelry, all from American designer Thomas Maier. Matching orange leopard swimsuits here for *Maman* (117€) and *fille* (42€) represent good clean fun!

ADDRESS
6 Rue de Solférino, 7th
TELEPHONE
01.47.05.18.94
METRO
Solférino
OPEN
Tue–Sat, 10:30–6:30 p.m.
ADDRESS
17 Rue de la Pompe, 16th
TELEPHONE
01.45.03.08.51
METRO
Muette
CREDIT CARDS
V, MC, DC
$$-$$$

À la Plage

ADDRESS
25 Quai Anatole France, 7th
TELEPHONE
01.42.60.86.23
METRO
Musée d'Orsay
OPEN
Mon–Fri, 10 a.m.–1 p.m. &
2:30–6:30 p.m.; Sat by
appointment
CREDIT CARDS
V, MC
$$$-$$$$

71. J. KUGEL
Antiques

This venerable house has moved to a new Left Bank
home, worthy of its centuries of top drawer décor.
A vist to the Kugel collections in the magnificent
Hôtel Collot is a must for both the amateur and the
connoisseur. Cross its Palladian threshold decorated
with statues and columns into one of the largest
and most prestigious antiques galleries in Europe,
where you'll discover furnishings from the sixteenth
century, a Renaissance salon, fine examples of sil-
ver, furniture, sculpture, ivories, jewelry, scientific
instruments, and paintings through the mid nine-
teenth century. The Kugel family has been in
antiques for five generations, with an eye for the
most original objects of quality. A great education
can be had here, just a stone's throw across the
Seine from the Louvre, and you may do further
research in the 20,000-volume library on the
premises. Whether you collect or merely browse,
why not begin at Kugel?

ADDRESS
65 (shoes), 67 (birth through
16), and 86 (Yam Jr., girls
12–16) Rue de l'Université, 7th
TELEPHONE
01.45.55.63.70
METRO
Solférino

ADDRESS
320 Rue Saint-Honoré, 1st
TELEPHONE
01.49.27.94.82
METRO
Tuileries

ADDRESS
50 Rue Etienne-Marcel, 2nd
TELEPHONE
01.40.26.20.90
METRO
Etienne-Marcel

72. BONPOINT
*Children's clothing, shoes, and furniture; women's clothing and
maternity (Rue de l'Université only)*

Founded by sisters not so long ago, BONPOINT
has become an instant classic. The sweetly dressed
darlings in carriages adorned with Alsacian lace and
pique from the layette collection grow up to shop
for their flannels and tweeds, or pleated skirts and
velvet vests to age sixteen. They spend the years
shuttling in and out of the main boutique at N.67
with Nanny, admiring the young ladies and gentle-
men in the displays who are smartly attired in vel-
vet gloves and lace collars. The rough-and-ready
look is here, too, in the refined forms of a soft
leather bomber jacket with sweater and lined cords
or western wear. The Rue de l'Université location is
doubtless the best stop in Paris for a complete
child's wardrobe that is elegant, sophisticated, and
exceedingly well made, with furnishings and toys

for the very young at the same address, and the small discount store selling last year's collection just down the street. At Bonpoint even a window stop is worthwhile.

Bonpoint

ADDRESS
12 Avenue Montaigne, 8th
TELEPHONE
01.47.20.42.10
METRO
Alma-Marçeau

ADDRESS
15 Rue Royale, 8th
TELEPHONE
01.47.42.52.63
METRO
Madeleine

ADDRESS
64 Avenue Raymond Poincarré, 16th
TELEPHONE
01.47.27.60.81
METRO
Victor-Hugo
OPEN
Mon–Sat, 10 a.m.–7 p.m.
CREDIT CARDS
V, AE
$$$-$$$$

ADDRESS
42 Rue de l'Université, 7th
(Outlet store)
TELEPHONE
01.40.20.10.55
METRO
Solférino
OPEN
Mon–Sat, 10:30 a.m.–6:30 p.m.
$$

ADDRESS
16 Rue de Bellechasse, 7th
TELEPHONE
01.45.51.36.13
METRO
Solférino
OPEN
Mon–Sat, 10 a.m.–7 p.m.

ADDRESS
12 Place St-Sulpice, 6th
TELEPHONE
01.46.33.03.15
METRO
St-Sulpice
OPEN
Mon–Sat, 10 a.m.–7 p.m.

ADDRESS
14 Rue Castiglione, 1st
TELEPHONE
01.42.60.52.82
METRO
Tuileries, Concorde
OPEN
Mon–Sat, 10 a.m.–7 p.m.

ADDRESS
3 bis Rue des Rosiers, 4th
TELEPHONE
01.48.87.80.11
METRO
St-Paul
OPEN
Mon–Sun, 11 a.m.–8 p.m.

ADDRESS
74 Avenue des Champs-
Elysées, 8th (Galerie du
Claridge)
TELEPHONE
01.45.63.33.38
METRO
Franklin D. Roosevelt
OPEN
Mon–Sun, 11 a.m.–8 p.m.
CREDIT CARDS
V, AE, MC, DC
$$$

73. ANNICK GOUTAL
Perfumes

The tiny boutique on the Rue de Bellechasse, very near the Musée d'Orsay, is my favorite of the ANNICK GOUTAL parfumeries. It was her first, and the experience to be had here is delightful. While your shopping companion is invited to plop in a comfy chair the charming shop director will assist you in discovering which of the Goutal fragrances is the real you. She is devoted to the ideals of the late Mme Goutal.

This concept of a personalized scent has made Goutal an icon in the fragrance world. In her line of twenty-some perfumes is a scent made to reflect each type of woman, masculine scents, and 'Eau de Bonpoint' for children (Mme Goutal was sister to the founder of BONPOINT). Goutal drew from personal experience to create her perfumes, as in Eau de Camille, which evokes the garden where her younger daughter played. A grown-up Camille Goutal has found her place in the business and continues to create new scents alongside the top classics Eau d'Hadrien, Petite Cherie, and Gardenia Passion. The first Goutal beauty institute has just opened at the Rue Castiglione address, based on a new line of scented creams named Splendide.

Annick Goutal

74. MOISSONNIER
Reproduction furniture

The eighteenth century has not yet come to a close
at MOISSONNIER, a superb maker of reproduction furniture that even Louis XVI would find stylish today. While the forms here are classic, allowing you to choose among 140 traditional designs of
furniture pieces and chairs, each perfectly executed,
it is the highly individualized finishing touches in
patina and upholstery that can bring your pieces
into the twenty-first century. Additional new space
on the Rue de l'Université provides a homey setting
for these sumptuously wowie pieces.

Founded in 1885, the house of Moissonnier is a
long-established name among decorating profes-
sionals and only at this recently opened location do
they work directly with the client. You can rely on
the very original ideas (and perfect English) of in-
house design consultant Patricia Fletcher to help
you decide everything from the coloration of your
wood to the tones used on the inside of a drawer.
She can even come up with outstanding choices in
upholstery fabrics if you let her. From final order to
delivery takes about three months. You can request
quotes from their website: www.moissonnier.com.

ADDRESS
28 Rue du Bac and 52 Rue de
l'Université, 7th
TELEPHONE
01.42.61.84.88
FAX
01.42.61.84.89
METRO
Rue du Bac
OPEN
Mon, 2–7 p.m.; Tue–Sat, 11
a.m.–7 p.m.
CREDIT CARDS
V, AE, MC
$$$
INTERNET
www.moissonnier.com

75. IUNX PARFUMS PARIS
Scents and bath products

"Iunx" is ancient Greek for a fascination with and
seduction by scent. But a modern seduction it is in
this conceptual black boutique where all products
are unisex, and the architecture, display, packaging,
and design are high tech. Eau de toilettes (23€ for
15mL), shampoos (26€), body washes, bath gels
and leaves, and candles that burn for 100 hours
(42€) come in over sixty universal scents that vary
according to the season. Romantic olfactory tonics
like *cendre de bois de hetre* (ashes from beech tree), and
rhum avec datte et miel (rum grog with date honey) can
set you apart in a crowd, or identify you as a cou-
ple. The experience here is exceptional.

ADDRESS
48 & 50 Rue de l'Université,
7th
TELEPHONE
01.45.44.50.14
METRO
Rue du Bac
OPEN
Mon–Sat, 10:30 a.m.–7 p.m.
CREDIT CARDS
V, AE, MC
$$-$$$

ADDRESS
37 Rue de Verneuil, 7th
TELEPHONE
01.42.60.25.40
METRO
Rue du Bac
OPEN
Tue–Sat, 2–7 p.m.
CREDIT CARDS
V, AE, MC
$$-$$$

76. LE CABINET DE PORCELAINE
Ceramic decorations

Ceramicists Samuel Mazy and Didier Gardillon
take much of their inspiration and their standards
from the porcelain tradition at Sèvres. Shuttling
between their workshop in the Dordogne and this
outstanding little boutique, the two idealists are
busy reproducing the old and creating new objects
of refinement. To achieve perfection they don't hesitate to reject those pieces that don't fully succeed.
The crème de la crème are for sale here. You may
find a porcelain bouquet imagined for Marie
Antoinette (2,000€), or a simple ceramique tulip in
a vase (45€). There are varieties of animals, chandeliers, humorous plates of ceramique food, and an all
white collection of formal decorative objects for
the occasional table. Prices are very reasonable for
the fine quality.

Le Cabinet de Porcelaine

☕ L'ATELIER DE JOEL ROBUCHON
Restaurant

ADDRESS
5 Rue de Montalembert, 7th
TELEPHONE
01.42.22.56.56
METRO
Rue de Bac
OPEN
Mon–Sun, 11:30 a.m.–3:30 p.m. & 6:30 p.m.–midnight
CREDIT CARDS
V, AE, MC
$$-$$$

Master chef Joel Robuchon has a restaurant that you can try for a quick and delicious lunch, no reservations accepted. It's a new concept for Paris: open kitchen in the middle, dishes added to your bill as you order (à la Chinese dim sum), and most unusually, no smoking allowed! The menu is modern (I had a vegetable mille-feuille and coffee); service fast at bar-style seating, no tables; it's minimalist in style with black marble, good lighting, and maroon leather chairs. Prices are low and you can stop in for lunch and be out of there in under an hour. Dinner may have a much longer wait.

77. CORINNE SARRUT
Women's clothing

Sarrut style epitomizes what the French call "the classics revisited." Known for her berets in fashionable colors and clothes that ooze Parisian charm, the designer always has a good selection of separates that flow over the body. Be advised that this is a boutique for the figure that requires no alterations.

ADDRESS
4 Rue du Pré-aux-Clercs, 7th
TELEPHONE
01.42.61.71.60
METRO
St-Germain-des-Prés
OPEN
Mon–Sat, 10 a.m.–7 p.m.
CREDIT CARDS
V, AE, MC
$$

Rue du Pré-aux-Clercs

ADDRESS
6 Rue du Pré-aux-Clercs, 7th
TELEPHONE
01.40.20.44.12
METRO
St-Germain-des-Prés or Rue du
Bac
OPEN
Mon–Fri, 10:30 a.m.–1:30 p.m.
& 2:30–7 p.m.; Sat, 10:30 a.m.–
7:30 p.m.
CREDIT CARDS
V, AE, MC, DC
$$

78. LES PRAIRIES DE PARIS
Women's clothing

Here is a shop for the young sophisticate who
prefers the simple cut of the ingenue in her
streetwear. There is very little color to distract from
the line of these quietly feminine dresses and sepa-
rates. The stylist here spent twenty-nine years at
Barney's and has developed a collection of easy-to-
sport basics that are quite romantic.

ADDRESS
7 Rue du Pré-aux-Clercs, 7th
TELEPHONE
01.49.27.03.95
METRO
St-Germain-des-Prés
OPEN
Mon, 2:30–7 p.m.;
Tue–Sat, 11:30–7 p.m.

79. LAURENCE TAVERNIER
Men's and women's loungewear

While you're busy investigating wardrobe possibili-
ties on the rest of the street, send monsieur ahead
to scout out something immensely relaxed for the
two of you to don in your chamber. The Tavernier
collection is sober and civilized, yet modern in its
choice of color and simple detail. He may choose

for himself a well-styled nightshirt or pajamas of shirting cotton in any of twenty-seven colors, with cashmere slippers.

And for you, choose perhaps a ruffled-cuff nightshirt with a shawl for cool nights in front of the fire. If he's not with you this is a good stop for an intimate gift: the men's collection also includes underwear and swim trunks.

Laurence Tavernier

ADDRESS
43 Rue Boissy d'Anglas, 8th
TELEPHONE
01.47.02.14.77
METRO
Madeleine
OPEN
Mon, 2:30–7 p.m.;
Tue–Sat, 11:30 a.m.–7 p.m.

ADDRESS
32 Rue du Bac, 7th
TELEPHONE
01.49.27.01.69
METRO
Rue du Bac
OPEN
Mon–Sat, 10:15 a.m.–7 p.m.

ADDRESS
3 Rue Benjamin-Franklin, 16th
TELEPHONE
01.46.47.89.39
METRO
Passy
OPEN
Mon, 2:30–7 p.m.; Tue–Sat,
11:30 a.m.–7 p.m.

ADDRESS
6 Rue Gustave-Courbet, 16th
TELEPHONE
01.44.05.17.11
METRO
Victor-Hugo
OPEN
Mon–Sat, 10:15 a.m.–7 p.m.
CREDIT CARDS
V, AE, MC
$$$

ADDRESS
8 Rue du Pré-aux-Clercs, 7th
(women's)
(2 entrances)
Irié Wash (men's, across the
street)
TELEPHONE
01.42.61.18.28
01.40.20.10.55 (Irié Wash)
METRO
St-Germain-des-Prés or Rue du
Bac
OPEN
Mon–Sat, 10:15 a.m.–7 p.m.
CREDIT CARDS
V, MC
$$-$$$

80. IRIÉ
Women's clothing; men's clothing

There is a reason why well-dressed women from fifteen to fifty-five stop in here weekly. It's cheap chic, with the emphasis on chic, and it's abundant in these designs by Japanese-born, Kenzo-trained, Parisian-minded Irié. Refreshingly original, charming, and comfortable, his collection is born of contrasts: a refined tea suit cut in a bottom-hugging stretch fabric, quiet wool blazers in loud colors, and chameleon-like tight little skirts that take on the demeanor of whatever they accompany. Perhaps the sharpest contrast of all is the solemn Italian interior, filled with marble and music, under a low white ceiling. Irié is famous for his little black suit, the store classic, which is revised for each season.

At the new IRIÉ WASH across the street, men will find suits and separates from synthetic fabrics that scream "fashion" and are all machine washable, even the suit in silver lame. Come here with a date or your grown sons.

ADDRESS
10 Rue du Pré-aux-Clercs, 7th
TELEPHONE
01.42.22.89.63
METRO
St-Germain-des-Prés
OPEN
Mon, 2–7 p.m.;
Tue–Sat, 11 a.m.–7 p.m.
CREDIT CARDS
V
$$-$$$

81. ISADORA
Costume jewelry

These bright and chunky baubles are full of fun and character. Isadora works exclusively on Bakelite, a hard plastic-like material developed in the 1930s. But the product is nothing retro. What she began fifteen years ago as witty, figurative jewelry now includes many modern geometrics in stark black and white or vivid colors.

In her studio, Isadora cuts her material from sheets, dying and rubbing it to perfection, while her mother handles sales to a loyal clientele that includes the Los Angeles County Museum gift shop. Prices and selection are best at the source, with earrings beginning at 40€, necklaces at 115–200€, and rings and bracelets in between. She also has a nice collection of costume jewelry from 1900 through the 1950s.

82. FOREVER
Fine linens

The trousseau-style linens at FOREVER are hand-sewn and embroidered with contemporary young newlyweds in mind. Traditional percale cottons for the bed and linen for the table are made fanciful with a light smattering of romantically modern handiwork, in colors from white to the most current pistachios and lilacs. For later, there's a line of layette linens and baby clothing in cashmeres and wool. They make it easy to order or register for gifts online. For those who want something a little different, there is a made-to-order label, Vis-à-Vis, with 300 color possibilities. Both collections are *luxe*.

ADDRESS
18 Rue du Pré-aux-Clercs, 7th
TELEPHONE
01.45.44.46.24
METRO
St-Germain-des-Prés
OPEN
Mon–Sat, 11 a.m.–6:30 p.m.
CREDIT CARDS
V
$$$
INTERNET
www.forever.fr

83. NATHALIE DURIEUX
Wedding gowns and cocktail attire

What girl wouldn't want a poetically feminine dream dress created just for her wedding day by Nathalie Durieux? It's a fortunate bride who may choose between "Ava," a white silk satin corset with feathered angel wings over a tulle skirt, and "Anais," a satin princess-cut gown with a pale rose tulle underskirt and hand-painted train, or an equally heavenly confection. Mme Durieux, coming from the couture world, prefers to design for the client's personality. For the betrothed who makes an appointment well in advance, the dress can be completed within a week of taking measurements. To wear one may not be worth a second marriage, but you might consider a second wedding. Hand-painted gowns from 2,500€.

ADDRESS
3 Rue Perronet, 7th (boutique and workshop)
TELEPHONE
01.42.22.04.05
METRO
St-Germain-des-Prés
OPEN
Tue–Sat, 9:30 a.m.–1:30 p.m. & 2:30–7 p.m.; and by appointment
CREDIT CARDS
V, MC
$$$–$$$$
INTERNET
www.nathalie-durieux.com

ADDRESS
30 Rue des Saints-Pères, 7th
TELEPHONE
01.45.48.54.67
METRO
St-Germain-des-Prés

ADDRESS
33 Rue Vivien, 2nd
TELEPHONE
01.40.39.05.50
METRO
Bourse
OPEN
Mon–Sat, 9 a.m.–7 p.m.
CREDIT CARDS
V, AE, MC
$$

ADDRESS
196 Boulevard Saint-Germain,
7th
TELEPHONE
01.42.84.12.12
METRO
St-Germain-des-Prés
OPEN
Mon–Sat, 10 a.m.–7 p.m.
CREDIT CARDS
V, AE, MC
$$
INTERNET
www.fragonard.com

84. DEBAUVE & GALLAIS
Chocolates and teas

Founded as a pharmacy in 1800, DEBAUVE & GALLAIS began dispensing chocolates as a medicine to such eminents as King Charles X, and later to Napoleon. It's certainly worth a stop, even if you're not a chocoholic.

While the chocolates are a bit sweet for my taste (though children adore them), the decor remains that of an eighteenth-century apothecary, with candies enticingly displayed in semicircular wooden pharmaceutical cases, potted ferns, marble columns, and the original scales and tea boxes.

85. FRAGONARD
Scents and gifts

This parfumeur from southern France has brought a bit of Provence to St-Germain with a bang. The newly opened shop is bustling with Parisians and visitors alike who are attracted by its refined scents, beautifully packaged as perfumes, eau de toilette,

Fragonard

creams, soaps, and other natural cosmetics, and its charming gamut of embroidered linens. This is a wonderful stop for gifts that have great appeal at modest prices. There are pouches printed or embroidered specially for travel as well as souvenirs, jewelry, men's shorts, and hobbies from 15€; provencal clothing; and lots for the beach. Chances are you'll find something for everyone here. Some items can be purchased from the website. In FRAGONARD tradition, the company has established perfume museums at #9 Rue Scribe, 9th (Le Musée de Parfum) and #39 Boulevard des Capucines, 2nd (Le Théatre-Musée des Capucines).

86. MADELEINE GÉLY/ALEXANDRA SOJFER
Umbrellas, parasols, and canes

Umbrellas and canes have been walking out of Madeleine Gély's shop since 1834, and this is undoubtedly the most famous address of its kind in Paris. When it was purchased by Alexandra Sojfer, a young family friend who was herself raised in the umbrella trade, the tradition continued. The umbrellas are made exclusively for her, many in the establishment's original styles. Though the umbrella may be new, it could have been appropriate for a gentleman 150 years ago, or for a modern gentlewoman.

For the littlest mademoiselle, don't overlook the pink folding parasol with the green frog handle. There are antique and collector pieces as well as reproductions—umbrellas and canes with handles in carved wood, bamboo, or molded synthetic. You may choose one with fold-out spectacles or a hidden whiskey flask, or an animal head from her zoological garden. These aren't necessarily the cumbersome loads of yesteryear. Many will fold into a purse or satchel and Madame offers a handsome array of her own umbrella fabrics, which she is happy to match to a handle of your choosing.

ADDRESS
218 Boulevard St-Germain, 7th
TELEPHONE
01.42.22.17.02
METRO
St-Germain-des-Prés
OPEN
Mon–Sat, 9:30 a.m.–7 p.m.
CREDIT CARDS
V
$$-$$$

ADDRESS
226 Boulevard Saint-Germain,
7th
TELEPHONE
01.45.44.95.77
METRO
St-Germain-des-Prés
OPEN
Mon–Sat, 10:30 a.m.–7 p.m.

ADDRESS
21 Rue Boissy d'Anglas, 8th
TELEPHONE
01.42.65.24.45
METRO
Concorde
OPEN
Mon–Sat, 10:30 a.m.–6:30 p.m.

ADDRESS
51 Rue François 1re, 8th
TELEPHONE
01.45.61.02.55
METRO
Franklin D. Roosevelt
OPEN
Mon–Sat, 10:30 a.m.–7 p.m.
CREDIT CARDS
V, AE, MC
$$$$

87. JOHN LOBB
Men's shoes

JOHN LOBB is for the gentleman who appreciates a handmade shoe and boot of the finest quality suedes and leathers, particularly if his foot requires a specially made fit. The hundred-year-old luxury label, originally English, has been bought by Hermès, and while most models are still made in England, the custom footwear is made in France. For a custom shoe, go to the Boissy d'Anglas address. This is the top of the line in men's shoes, with prices to match.

ADDRESS
175 Boulevard St-Germain, 6th
(Women's clothing and accessories)
TELEPHONE
01.49.54.60.60
METRO
St-Germain-des-Prés

ADDRESS
70 Faubourg St-Honoré, 8th
(Women's)
TELEPHONE
01.42.65.20.81
METRO
Concorde

ADDRESS
194 Boulevard St-Germain, 7th
(Men's)

88. SONIA RYKIEL
Women's, men's, and children's clothing & home items

The architect of the skinny knit has built a modern château worthy of her elegant collections. Her St-Germain headquarters showcasing women's clothing and accessories and porcelain for the table are large, light, and easy to shop in. Here you will find her trademark knits in cotton and wool, understated in color and shape but dramatic in effect and always comfortable. The look is true Parisian chic, and it's made to travel. Pack her culottes, tight sweater, and jersey jacket in your carry-on, throw on some of her gold jewelry, and you could land anywhere in style. Her collection has expanded to velours and other simple fabrics.

The original small shop is at 4 Rue de Grenelle.

Next door at N.6 are delightful fashions for the modern child to age sixteen. The moderately priced SONIA line designed by her daughter Natalie is for the jeans and T-shirt set.

SONIA RYKIEL HOMME, the comfy men's store, offers a complete wardrobe for the modern monsieur.

TELEPHONE
01.45.44.83.19
METRO
St-Germain-des-Prés

ADDRESS
4 Rue de Grenelle, 7th
(Women's sex toys)
TELEPHONE
01.49.54.66.21
METRO
St-Sulpice

ADDRESS
6 Rue de Grenelle, 6th
(Children's)
TELEPHONE
01.49.54.61.10
METRO
St-Sulpice

ADDRESS
61 Rue des Saints-Pères, 6th
(SONIA)
TELEPHONE
01.49.54.61.00
METRO
Sèvres-Babylone

OPEN
Mon–Sat, 10:30 a.m.–7 p.m.
CREDIT CARDS
V, AE, DC
$$$

SR (outlet)
ADDRESS
64 Rue d'Alésia,14th
TELEPHONE
01.43.95.06.13
METRO
Alésia
OPEN
Tue, 11 a.m.–7 p.m.;
Wed–Sat, 10:30 a.m.–7 p.m.
$$

☕ AUX DEUX MAGOTS
Café-Restaurant

ADDRESS
170 Boulevard St-Germain, 6th
TELEPHONE
01.45.48.55.25
METRO
St-Germain-des-Prés
OPEN
Daily, 7:30 a.m.–1 a.m.
$$$

AUX DEUX MAGOTS has possibly the most inviting sidewalk café in the city. Come here while you're waiting for your hotel room to be readied. No matter how jet-lagged you may feel, you'll know you're in Paris when you arrive here.

Inside, mirrored walls, red banquettes, snappily turned-out waiters, and the ghosts of Sartre and Hemingway, who both had tables here, epitomize café life. Settle in over a frothy café au lait and people watch to catch up on fashion trends before embarking on your Left Bank shopping tour. Just next door is the equally popular CAFE DE FLORE (N.172 Boulevard St-Germain).

ADDRESS
37 Rue de la Bûcherie, 5th
TELEPHONE
01.43.25.40.93
METRO
Saint-Michel
OPEN
Daily, noon–midnight
NO CREDIT CARDS
$-$$

89. SHAKESPEARE AND COMPANY
Books

The inscription stamped on the inside cover of every book purchased here reads, "Shakespeare and Company Kilometer Zero Paris." And this is indeed the heart of the city for students, writers, readers, and browsers who frequently stop in to read and rub shoulders with their own kind.

Over forty years ago George Whitman opened his doors to lovers of the English written word, selling mostly secondhand volumes from England and America. In name and in spirit the shop reflects an earlier bookstore run by American Sylvia Beach that became a gathering place for expatriate writers such as Hemingway and Fitzgerald. It was Sylvia Beach who dared to publish James Joyce's *Ulysses*.

Whitman's small shop across from Notre Dame has an appropriately homey air of comfortable con-

fusion and is a must-stop for anyone with a fascina-
tion for our expatriate writers, particularly if you
need a good read for the trip home. And who
knows? If you pen a good line he just may invite
you to stay on for a few days in his writer's room,
to carry on a grand tradition.

90. DIPTYQUE
Scented candles, room scents, soaps, and toilette waters

Candles in fifty-six natural scents, good prices, and
lovely packaging make this boutique a worthwhile
stop for gift givers or for those who want the familiar fragrances of France in their own homes.
　　Begin with *foin coupé* (fresh-cut hay) or
chevrefeuille (honeysuckle) before you take on heavier
scents such as lavenders and musks or the newest
scent, "Narcisse." The white-glassed candles (36€)
burn for sixty hours, slower in cold temperatures,
faster where it's warm. Buy more than one, because
once you become used to these scents at home, you
won't be able to live without them.

ADDRESS
34 Boulevard St-Germain, 5th
TELEPHONE
01.43.26.45.27
METRO
Maubert-Mutualité
OPEN
Mon–Sat, 10 a.m.– 7 p.m.
CREDIT CARDS
V, AE, MC
$$

91. LIBRAIRIE GIBERT JEUNE
Books and records

In the heart of the Latin quarter, just across from
the Sorbonne, you can mingle with students and
professors from around the world as they seek out
new and used books, notebooks, and CDs. Begin at
the racks set up outside the store and proceed to
the fourth floor for books in English.

ADDRESS
26, 30, 32, 34 Boulevard Saint
Michel, 6th
TELEPHONE
01.44.41.88.88
METRO
Odéon or Cluny
HOURS
Mon–Sat, 10 a.m.– 7:30 p.m.
CREDIT CARDS
V, AE, MC
$$

☕ BRASSERIE BALZAR
Brasserie-Restaurant

ADDRESS
49 Rue des Écoles, 5th
TELEPHONE
01.43.54.13.67
METRO
Cluny-La Sorbonne
OPEN
Daily, 8 a.m.–midnight
CREDIT CARDS
V, AE
$$

When a jaded Left Bank Parisian longs for the tummy-soothing experience of days past, he'll head for the Balzar, a thoroughly authentic example of the classic Parisian bistro that has defied modern trends without a tarnish to its well-shined mirrors and mahogany.

Order a roast chicken with sautéed spinach and fries and you'll understand the meaning of comfort food. Or consider the plates on their way to your neighbors' tables. For an amiable mix of food and company, you can't go wrong here. Reserve for dinner.

ADDRESS
35 Rue Daubenton, 5th
TELEPHONE
01.47.07.28.90
METRO
Censier-Daubenton
OPEN
Mon, 1–7 p.m.;
Tue–Sat, 10:30 a.m.– 7 p.m.
CREDIT CARDS
V, AE
$$

92. LA TUILE À LOUP
Pottery and handcrafted tableware from around France

Make only a slight detour from central Paris to discover these regional table arts of France, guaranteed to de-gentrify your dining. The Joblin-Depalle family travels throughout the French countryside to bring works from the finest traditional ceramic craftsmen, glass-blowers, and basket-weavers to this rustic urban outpost, a well-known source for nearly extinct crafts. In a recent year, the shop lost thirty-five suppliers who could no longer find enough market for their work.

Large wooden tables are stacked high with pottery plates and bowls of various shapes and shades, which to the learned eye represent the clays and glazes of rural France. Choose from the exceptional baskets and fill them with handblown glasses from a factory established in 1475, earthy egg cups, and an olivewood cheese tray. Or pick a large urn from Provence and a dozen settings of glazed earthen-

ware dinner plates from the Savoie, and let the
establishment do the shipping. You may want to
call ahead to make sure the owners, who speak
English, will be in. If you read French, take a look
at the selection of books on French regional history
and customs. The trip here is well worth it.

Along the Way

Some of my most sentimental purchases have been from the *bouquinistes* (booksellers)
along the quais on both banks of the Seine. From mid-morning until dusk these collectors of old books, maps, prints, and postcards open their stalls to lookers and buyers alike, who are free to poke through their treasures. Most have their specialties.

If you're in the market for a first-edition Colette, surrealist postcards, or a hand-
colored poster of Marie Antoinette, you have a good chance of finding them here.
Open Tue–Sat, or at the whim of the free-spirited vendor.

THE ISLANDS

The historical and geographical heart of Paris lies between the left and right banks of
the Seine on two small islands, the ÎLE DE LA CITÉ and the ÎLE ST-LOUIS, joined
by the bridge PONT ST-LOUIS. It was on the wild Île de la Cité that a tribe of fish-
ermen calling themselves Parisii came to settle in the third century BC.

Today these are two islands of relative serenity in the Seine captured in time
between the modern bustle of the left and right banks. The islands are a good spot to
catch your breath after a whirlwind shopping tour, or to spend a Sunday when most
of the rest of the city is closed down.

On a Sunday, head to the Île de la Cité to attend the 4:30 p.m. organ concert at
NOTRE DAME. Perhaps you'll also catch a candle-lit concert at SAINT CHAPELLE
(4 Boulevard du Palais), a gothic chapel with dazzling acoustics, stained glass, and
starlit ceiling.

The famous flower market (open Mon–Sat, 8 a.m. to 7 p.m.) at PLACE LOUIS
LEPINE becomes the famous bird market on Sundays (8 a.m. to 7 p.m.). On this
island, shopping is limited to the souvenir stands.

Cross over to the Ile St-Louis, which wakes up early Sunday afternoons to enjoy
its reputation as one of the only open shopping areas in Paris. If you're really hungry,
stop at the BRASSERIE DE L'ÎLE ST-LOUIS, N.55 Quai de Bourbon (open Fri–Tue,

noon to 1 a.m., and Thurs dinner) for *Alsatian choucroñte* (sausage-garnished sauer-kraut) and beer, shoulder-to-shoulder with the regulars, and be prepared to make new friends.

It is said that there are local residents who never leave the island. And why not? It is among the choicest addresses in the city, and its outstanding seventeenth-century *hôtels particuliers* (private residences) are inhabited by the Baron de Rothschild and the pretender to the throne of France, whose once-royal family still doesn't celebrate Bastille Day.

Pick up an ice cream or sorbet from BERTHILLON, the best in Paris and sold at nearly every café and tea salon on the island as well as the original store, N.31 Rue St-Louis-en-Ile, and you're on your way down the main street. Rue St-Louis-en-Ile is only a few short blocks, and given over to souvenir shops and galleries as well as necessities for local residents, so prepare to browse.

PYLONES, N.57 Rue St-Louis-en-Ile, carries its own brand of humorous sus-penders and neckties, made of latex and just the right thing to lighten up that tuxe-do. You'll congratulate yourself on your good taste when you see more of the same in the gift shop at the Pompidou Center. YAMINA, N.56 Rue St-Louis-en-Ile, special-izes in hand-painted scarves and women's clothing.

At LE GRAIN DE SABLE, N.79 Rue St-Louis-en-Ile, it's fun to coordinate your accessories for the season from among the large collection of hats with scarves, gloves, and purses.

Rive Droite

The Right Bank is where you'll find the crème de la crème. If you are most comfortable in a setting of grand hotels, luxurious boutiques, couture labels, and first-rate service, begin your shopping tour here. From the Ritz to Dior, from Christofle to Hermès, you'll recognize names that have set standards of taste for generations.

Even if you consider yourself more of a Left Bank type, don't miss this opportunity to explore the prestigious addresses of the Right Bank. For an education in classically French fashion, art, and home furnishings, make your way down the Avenue Montaigne and the Faubourg Saint-Honoré, the Rue Royale, and the Place Vendôme. The dazzling window displays along these boulevards will turn your head and capture your imagination, and you're bound to come away with something ineffably French.

For more intimate shopping and less intimidating price tags, visit the elegant Palais Royale and neighboring arcades. Join the French to discover the next trend in fashion at the Place des Victoires, and shop where they do in the renovated region of Les Halles, the former city market where cutting utensils still take their place next to the latest cuts in clothing.

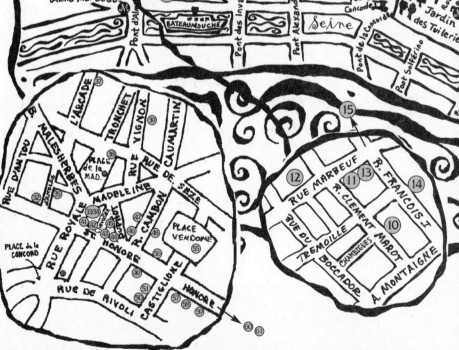

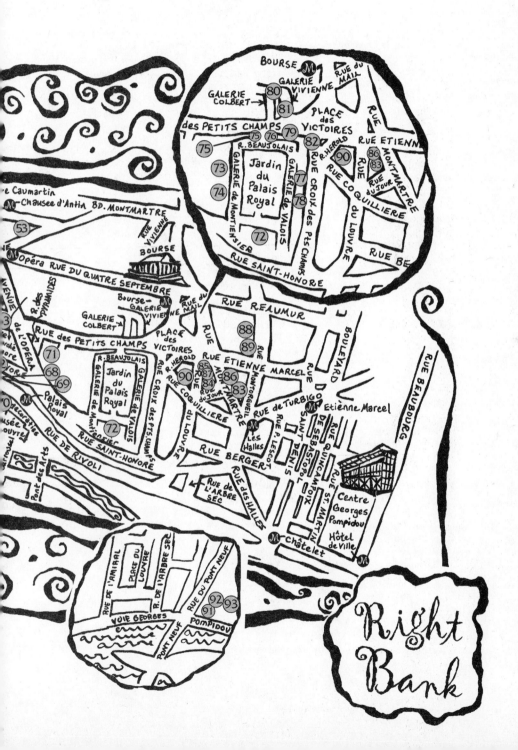

Map Key

1. Drouot Montaigne
2. Inès de la Fressange
3. D. Porthault
4. Christian Dior
5. Parfums Caron
6. Fouquet
7. Barbara Bui
8. Artcurial
9. Nina Ricci
10. Nouez-Moi
11. Boutiques Vignon
12. René Mancini
13. Alain Figaret
14. Courrèges
15. Morabito
16. Hermès-Motsch
17. Drugstore Publicis
18. Louis Vuitton
19. Sephora
20. Monoprix
21. Naf-naf
22. The Virgin Megastore
23. Pavillon Elysées Lenôtre
24. Christian Lacroix
25. Anna Lowe
26. Roger Vivier
27. Hermès
28. Casoar
29. Institut Carita
30. Façonnable
31. Jean de Bonnot
32. Renaud Pellegrino
33. Lalique
34. Pavillons Christofle
35. Rosemarie Schulz
36. Daniel Cremieux
37. Gien
38. Fauchon
39. Lafont et Fils
40. Kiosque Théâtre

41. Cassegrain
42. Au Nain Bleu
43. Longchamp
44. Hervé Chapelier
45. Le Jacquard Français
46. Victoire
47. Chanel
48. Fifi Chachnil
49. Cadolle
50. Jean Patou
51. Catherine Gift
52. Comptoir Sud Pacifique
53. Galeries Lafayette
54. Repetto
55. Charvet
56. Pierre Barboza
57. Alexandre de Paris
58. Goyard
59. Jean-Paul Hévin
60. Colette
61. Chantal Thomass
62. Cachemire Crème
63. Philippe Model
64. Brentano's
65. W.H. Smith
66. Denise Francelle
67. Maréchal
68. Galignani
69. Gault
70. 107 Rivoli
71. Paris Office de Tourisme
72. Le Louvre des Antiquaires
73. Les Drapeaux de France
74. Didier Ludot
75. La Boutique du Palais-Royal
76. Anna Joliet

77. Le Prince Jardinier
78. Delage
79. Small Is Beautiful
80. Jean-Paul Gaultier
81. Casa Lopez
82. Atelier Mercadal
83. Claudie Pierlot
84. Agnès B.
85. La Droguerie
86. Comptoir de la Gastronomie
87. Duthilleul & Minart
88. Stohrer
89. A. Simon
90. Dehillerin
91. Kenzo
92. Le Cèdre Rouge
93. Le Jardin de Victoria

107 Rivoli - 70
A. Simon - 89
Agnes B. - 84
Alain Figaret - 13
Alexandre de Paris - 57
Anna Joliet - 76
Anna Lowe - 25
Artcurial - 8
Atelier Mercadal - 82
Au Nain Bleu - 42
Barbara Bui - 7
Boutiques Vignon - 11
Brentano's - 64
Cachemire Crème - 62
Cadolle - 49
Casa Lopez - 81
Casoar - 28
Cassegrain - 41
Catherine Gift - 51
Chanel - 47
Chantal Thomass - 61
Charvet - 55
Christian Dior - 4
Christian Lacroix - 24
Claudie Pierlot - 83
Colette - 60
Comptoir de la
   Gastronomie - 86
Comptoir Sud
   ∫ Pacifique - 52
Courrèges - 14
D. Porthault - 3
Daniel Cremieux - 36
Dehillerin - 90
Delage - 78
Denise Francelle - 66
Didier Ludot - 74
Drouot Montaigne - 1
Drugstore Publicis - 17
Duthilleul & Minart - 87

Façonnable - 30
Fauchon - 38
Fifi Chachnil - 48
Fouquet - 6
Galeries Lafayette - 53
Galignani - 68
Gault - 69
Gien - 37
Goyard - 58
Hermès - 27
Hermès-Motsch - 16
Hervé Chapelier - 44
Inès de la Fressange - 2
Institut Carita - 29
Jean de Bonnot - 31
Jean Patou - 50
Jean-Paul Gaultier - 80
Jean-Paul Hévin - 59
Kenzo - 91
Kiosque Théâtre - 40
La Boutique du Palais-
   Royal - 75
La Droguerie - 85
Lafont et Fils - 39
Lalique - 33
Le Cèdre Rouge - 92
Le Jacquard Français - 45
Le Jardin de Victoria - 93
Le Louvre des
   Antiquaires - 72
Le Prince Jardinier - 77
Les Drapeaux de France - 73
Longchamp - 43
Louis Vuitton - 18
Maréchal - 67
Monoprix - 20
Morabito - 15
Naf-naf - 21
Nina Ricci - 9
Nouez-Moi - 10

Parfums Caron - 5
Paris Office de
   Tourisme - 71
Pavillon Elysées Lenôtre - 23
Pavillons Christofle - 34
Philippe Model - 63
Pierre Barboza - 56
Renaud Pellegrino -32
René Mancini - 12
Repetto - 54
Roger Vivier - 26
Rosemarie Schulz - 35
Sephora - 19
Small Is Beautiful - 79
Stohrer - 88
The Virgin Megastore - 22
Victoire - 46
W.H. Smith - 65

Where to Stay

The Right Bank is full of wonderful grand hotels, with the incomparable HÔTEL RITZ (www.ritz.com), an inspiration to all that follow. In that tradition are the GEORGE V (www.fourseasons.com/paris) and the BRISTOL (www.lebristolparis.com). But if money is a consideration, you'll find better values elsewhere. Included here are some more moderately priced deluxe hotels in the heart of the district.

HÔTEL PLAZA ATHÉNÉE

ADDRESS
25 Avenue Montaigne, 8th
TELEPHONE
01.53.67.66.67
METRO
Alma-Marçeau
Single rooms from 555€;
Doubles from 690€
Breakfast 35€
CREDIT CARDS
V, AE, MC, DC
INTERNET
www.plaza-athenee-paris.com

Not one of the moderately priced hotels mentioned above, the PLAZA ATHÉNÉE is a perfect choice for those who love luxury, beauty, and shopping the Avenue Montaigne. The elegant lobby maintains some of the most admired floral arrangements in Paris, a complement to a richly updated classic décor which runs throughout, with the exception of the top two floors done in art deco style. Even if you're not staying here, stop by for lunch at the chic RELAIS PLAZA bistro, or dinner at the ALAIN DUCASSE restaurant, tea in the GALERIE, or a late-night drink in the bar.

HÔTEL LANCASTER

ADDRESS
7 Rue de Berri, 8th
TELEPHONE
01.40.76.40.76
FAX
01.40.70.95.51
METRO
George V
Double rooms from 410€
Breakfast 30€
CREDIT CARDS
V, AE, MC, DC
INTERNET
www.hotel-lancaster.fr

This must certainly be one of the prettiest homes in Paris, and its guests are fortunate to be living here, if even for just a few days. The elegant nineteenth-century townhouse has been restored to perfection and filled with a mix of antique and modern pieces covered in period reproduction fabrics with a modern color sensibility. Don't miss breakfast in the Asian-inspired garden. The location, between the Champs-Elysées and Saint-Honoré, is slightly off-beat.

REGINA

An old-world hotel, the REGINA is loved for her enormous rooms filled with period pieces, some overlooking the Louvre and Tuileries gardens. In the stately lobby of this quiet hotel, beautiful old clocks keep time for the major European capitals.

ADDRESS
2 Place des Pyramides, 1st
TELEPHONE
01.42.60.31.10
FAX
01.40.15.95.16
METRO
Tuileries
Double rooms from 395€
Breakfast 20€
CREDIT CARDS
V, AE, MC
INTERNET
www.regina-hotel.com

HÔTEL COSTES

The hotel of the moment, HÔTEL COSTES shuns the minimalism of the past decade to flaunt its gorgeous interiors that teeter the fine line between Napoleonic luxe and Italian bordello. Yes, models and stars stay here, and are often visible as all dining areas and bars look onto the interior courtyard where meals are served in fine weather. American guests will further appreciate here that rarity in Paris, a fitness center and pool.

ADDRESS
239 Rue St-Honoré, 1st
TELEPHONE
01.42.44.50.50
FAX
01.42.44.50.01
METRO
Tuileries
Double rooms from 350€
Breakfast 30€
CREDIT CARDS
V, AE, MC, DC

CHAMBIGES ELYSÉES

Romantic and intimate, this small hotel simply oozes charm and is wonderfully located for shopping the golden triangle. You'll love coming back to your warmly decorated room with your armsful of shopping bags. Sink into an overstuffed chair, close your eyes, and imagine this is home.

ADDRESS
8 Rue Chambiges, 8th
TELEPHONE
01.44.31.83.83
FAX
01.40.70.95.51
METRO
Alma-Marçeau or Franklin D. Roosevelt
Double rooms from 250€
Breakfast complimentary
CREDIT CARDS
V, AE, MC
INTERNET
www.hotelchambiges.com

HÔTEL THÉRÈSE

ADDRESS
5–7 Rue Thérèse, 1st
TELEPHONE
01.42.96.10.01
FAX
01.42.96.15.22
METRO
Pyramides
Double rooms from 134€
Breakfast 12€
CREDIT CARDS
V, AE, MC
INTERNET
www.hoteltherese.com

This convenient location will appeal to those who want to be near the Louvre in the morning, shop Saint-Honoré in the afternoon, dine under the arcades of Palais Royal, and end the evening at the Opéra. A short walk back to the hotel and the sleepy traveler is in a quiet room of understated refinement and contemporary comfort. What more could one want?

Culture Along the Way

TUILERIES GARDENS

These former gardens of King Louis XIV run from his palace (now the Louvre Museum) to the Place de La Concorde. A stroll through its manicured hedges and bronze statues offers respite from the nearby crowds and a vantage point for a clear view through the Arc de Triomphe to the newer Arche de La Défense, and the Louvre Pyramid. Its *Jeu de Paume National Gallery*, once Paris's impressionist museum, now exhibits contemporary art. Open Thur, noon to 9:30 p.m.; Fri, noon to 9 p.m.; and Sat & Sun, 10 a.m. to 9 p.m. Closed Monday.

MUSÉE DES ARTS DECORATIFS

ADDRESS
107 Rue de Rivoli, 1st
METRO
Palais-Royal or Tuileries or Louvre
TELEPHONE
01.44.55.57.50
OPEN
Tue–Fri, 11 a.m.–6 p.m.; Sat & Sun, 10 a.m.–6 p.m.; Closed Monday

You'll learn more about historically correct and avant-garde style here than by thumbing the pages of a lifetime's worth of fashion and decorating magazines. The museum for the decorative arts shows French interiors from medieval times to present-day. The spectacular new GALERIE DES BIJOUX (the history of jewelry collection) is at this address, as well as the MUSÉE DE LA MODE (fashion museum) housing temporary exhibitions only, and the MUSÉE DE LA PUBLICITÉ (advertising museum), also with temporary exhibits.

MUSÉE NATIONAL DU LOUVRE

Europe's largest palace holds collections from ancient times to mid–nineteenth century. Need one say more?

ADDRESS
Enter through glass Pyramid off Cour Napoléon, 1st
METRO
Palais-Royal
TELEPHONE
01.40.20.53.17
OPEN
Mon, Thur, Sat, Sun, 9 a.m.–5:30 p.m.; Wed & Fri, 9 a.m.–9:30 p.m.
Closed Tuesday

MUSÉE NATIONAL D'ART MODERNE (POMPIDOU CENTER)

The most visted attraction in France not only contains the national collection of twentieth-century art in a controversial modern structure, but has a priceless view over the rooftops of Paris from the top floor.

ADDRESS
Place Beaubourg, 4th
METRO
Hôtel-de-Ville or Rambuteau
TELEPHONE
01.44.78.12.33
OPEN
Wed–Mon, 11 a.m.–9 p.m.;
Closed Tuesday

MUSÉE NISSIM DE CAMONDO

The aristocratic home of the Camondo family was left to France by Moise de Camondo in 1935, and its private apartments were opened to the public in 2003. It is filled with their outstanding collections of furniture, paintings, and art objects, most from the mid to late eighteenth century.

ADDRESS
63 Rue de Monçeau, 8th
METRO
Monçeau
TELEPHONE
01.53.89.06.40
OPEN
Daily, 10 a.m.–5 p.m.

Right Bank Shops

The neighborhood flanked by the Avenue Montaigne, the Rue François I, and the Avenue George V is known as the GOLDEN TRIANGLE, and as you stroll down the Avenue Montaigne in particular, you'll know why. The enormous chic is matched only by the price tags. Nobody treats fine merchandise quite as well as the French do, so whether you're buyer or browser, don't hesitate to step through those intimidating facades and explore a little.

If you buy here, you'll carry away with you a true Parisian luxury, wrapped so beautifully you may never want to open it. Rarely too crowded, particularly during the week, this is my favorite area for luxury goods, and there are always some very good buys.

Those pursuing a top-notch wardrobe less likely to be found at American stores may want to continue on to the following addresses: On the Rond Point des Champs Elysées, CARVEN (N.6) for men and women offers couture as well as ready-to-wear; on Avenue François I are HÉLÈNE ROCHAS (N.33), whose designs by Olivier Theyskens are highly esteemed for their quality and sophistication, and both FRANCESCO SMALTO (N.44) and GENTLEMEN GIVENCHY (N. 56) for men; on Avenue George V, BALENCIAGA (N.10) is where you'll find Nicholas Ghesquière's headturning couture collection and men's and women's ready-to-wear are in adjoining boutiques, and GIVENCHY (N.3 for women and N.8 for accessories only).

ADDRESS
15 Avenue Montaigne, 8th
TELEPHONE
01.48.00.20.80
METRO
Alma-Marçeau
OPEN
Mon–Fri, 9:30 a.m.–1 p.m. &
noon–6 p.m.;
check ahead for times of viewings and sales

HÔTEL DROUOT
ADDRESS
9 Rue Drouot, 9th
TELEPHONE
01.48.00.20.20
METRO
Richelieu-Drouot
OPEN
Mon–Sat, 11 a.m.–6 p.m.;
exhibitions 11 a.m.–6 p.m., day
before sale; 11 a.m.–noon, day
of sale; check ahead for auction
times

1. DROUOT MONTAIGNE
Auction house of fine art and antiques

DROUOT MONTAIGNE is considered "the best" branch of the renowned Paris auction house Drouot, which happens to be the oldest auction institution in the world. In keeping with the address, you'll find the most prestigious sales at this location. Not that the original Hôtel Drouot isn't brimming with treasures, and with professional dealers.

To browse or to buy, first pick up a copy of the weekly auction guide "La Gazette de L'Hôtel Drouot" at any newsstand, and an auction catalog that schedules and defines every lot at the front desk. Arrive early enough to visit each room before bidding so you can get your bearings and determine how active you plan to be. Registration isn't necessary. The bidding is fast and in French, so you should be equipped with a calculator and possibly a translator (available through the front desk).

Keep in mind the 10 to 18 percent commission you'll be paying the house above the bid price, and the cost of shipping. The house will suggest the transporter Jet Art Services (ph: 01.45.23.38.39) to be called before storage fees on your purchases accrue (after 24 hours).

It is best to pay cash for your merchandise, avoiding possible shipping delays waiting for a check to clear; the in-house bank can help you with currency exchange.

If you're feeling mystified, hold on to that vision of the chandelier from the Paris Opera above your dining table and go for it. The auction system here is highly professional and so are your bidding competitors, so keep your wits about you and remember, not only are these heirlooms the real thing, they're at wholesale prices.

Payment in cash in Euro dollars or French check only
$$-$$$$
INTERNET
www.drouot.fr
www.drouot.catalogues.com

2. INÈS DE LA FRESSANGE
Women's clothing, shoes, costume jewelry, linens, luggage

To this promenade of old-world taste and new world money came the fresh view of younger-minded aristocrat Inès de la Fressange. Formerly top model for Chanel, her personal style was inspiration to its superstar designer Karl Lagerfeld. When the French government honored her by

ADDRESS
14 Avenue Montaigne, 8th
TELEPHONE
01.47.23.08.94
METRO
Alma-Marçeau
OPEN
Mon–Sat, 10 a.m.– 7 p.m.
CREDIT CARDS
V, AE, MC
$$$

Inès de la Fressange

requesting to make her the official face of France, or "Marianne," as the French call this tradition, she accepted and was immediately dropped by Chanel. It didn't take long for her to launch herself into the store project, carrying out her own designs in her relaxed uniform of narrow black trousers, white shirt, blazer, and ballerina flats.

Though the line is now hers in name only, the lighthearted interior is still an antidote to this serious street, with its plank walls painted in pinks, greens, yellows, and blues that reflect Inès's preference for an upbeat, pared-down look that has been adopted by an entire generation of well-bred French women who want to be more casual than their mothers.

If you want an understated look that speaks with a husky French accent, get in line and let the sales staff help you put it together.

ADDRESS
18 Avenue Montaigne, 8th
TELEPHONE
01.47.20.75.25
METRO
Alma-Marçeau
OPEN
Mon, 9:30 a.m.–1 p.m. &
2–6:30 p.m.;
Tue–Fri, 9:30 a.m.–6:30 p.m.;
Sat, 10:30 a.m.–1 p.m. &
2–6:30 p.m.
CREDIT CARDS
V, AE, DC
$$$$

3. D. PORTHAULT
Bed, bath, and table linens, children's clothes

Even if you don't spend thousands of dollars on your bed sets, you must visit PORTHAULT simply to educate yourself in the crème de la crème of French linens. Like the Princess and the Pea, there are those who reportedly don't leave home without their Porthault, requesting that their beds in the finest hotel rooms be remade before they can properly rest.

Porthault is a prime example of a family business that won't compromise its high standards and original vision. It was the Porthaults who, inspired by the impressionists, introduced the first printed sheets to a society that knew only white embroideries and initials. Since their first designs in 1925, they have also created exclusive motifs for such discerning clients as Jacqueline Onassis, the Duchess of Windsor, and the Shah of Iran, in designs from florals to Greek key motifs. Even the *prêt-à-porter* collection of this house of couture linen is woven, dyed, and embroidered to specification.

If you're prepared to splurge, consider the thickest of terry robes and scalloped toweling, the exquisitely embroidered organdy table linens, and bed linens covered in pink hearts with matching breakfast dishes (the Porthault heart is copied everywhere, but never with the charm of the original). Or simply, a heart-covered showercap (30€); you can dress up your bed with a double-ruffled boudoir sham cut from the same fabric. Be sure to peek into the children's area in back to gaze upon exquisite crib and cradle linens for little sleeping beauties, and beautifully smocked children's clothing (newborn to age eight in dresses, to age two in boys clothes). If you're in town in January, don't miss the house sale!

4. CHRISTIAN DIOR
Women's, men's, and children's clothing, accessories, shoes; women's couture clothing and furs, lingerie, cosmetics, fragrances; household linens, accessories, and gifts

The HOUSE OF DIOR is a historic landmark in the world of fashion. M Dior opened his first small boutique here (the first couture house on the avenue) in 1947, bringing *la mode féminine* (feminine fashion) back to a dreary postwar society with his New Look. The original image of elegant chic, propelled by a visionary business sense, has not faltered, and today the House of Dior is clearly the grande dame of the Avenue Montaigne. Everything Dior, licensed or made in the couture workshops, is to be found here behind the pearl gray facade. The fabulous interior, completely redone in a neo–eighteenth-century style by architect Peter Marino for the fiftieth anniversary of the boutique, is a modern marriage of classicism and whimsy. The set-up, like

ADDRESS
30 Avenue Montaigne, 8th
11 bis Rue François I (Men's boutique)
TELEPHONE
01.40.73.54.44
METRO
Franklin D. Roosevelt

ADDRESS
46 Rue du Faubourg St-Honoré, 8th
TELEPHONE
01.44.51.55.51
METRO
Concorde

ADDRESS
25 Rue Royale, 8th
TELEPHONE
01.53.05.51.61
METRO
Concorde

ADDRESS
16 & 18 Rue de l'Abbaye, 5th
TELEPHONE
01.56.24.90.53
METRO
St-Germain-des-Prés

OPEN
Mon–Sat, 10 a.m.–7 p.m.
CREDIT CARDS
V, AE, DC
$$-$$$$

ADDRESS
34 Avenue Montaigne, 8th
TELEPHONE
01.47.23.40.82
FAX
01.47.23.67.01
METRO
Franklin D. Roosevelt
OPEN
Mon–Sat, 10 a.m.–6:30 p.m.

ADDRESS
90 Rue du Faubourg St-
Honoré, 8th
TELEPHONE
01.42.68.25.68
METRO
Champs-Elysées-Clémençeau
OPEN
Mon–Sat, 10 a.m.–7 p.m.
CREDIT CARDS
V, AE, MC, DC
$$-$$$$

a small department store, makes it easy to navigate.

With John Galliano as head couture designer there is always excitement in the House of Dior. His romantic genius is meant to attract the next generation of stylish clients, and these fitting rooms are among the busiest on the avenue. His collections can be most affordable if you're in town for the sales. Menswear, designed by Hedi Slimane, is back in a big way for those with a slim build. The Monsieur Dior signature is a silk vest with matching tie.

You may rely on the good taste of Dior for gifts in all price ranges, packaged to perfection. As a testimony to its classicism, I recognize gifts bought during my student days—the same mink-trimmed leather gloves I gave my mother and lavender sweater brought back for my brother, now available in cashmere. This is a must stop for presents that radiate Parisian refinement.

5. PARFUMS CARON
Perfumes

Little-publicized CARON is my favorite perfume house in Paris. Its allure is not only in its sumptuous interior—half a grand chandelier reflected in an antiqued mirror magnifies this small sanctum to magnificence in gilt, glass, and marble. I come here for the re-editions of their perfumes from a bygone era; for their exquisite selection of flacons both new and antique (from 60€ for something lovely, or 280€ to 2500€ for a limited-edition Baccarat); for their bath pearls filled with Nocturnes, lavender, or champagne perfumes (5€ for ten) and my choice of porcelain boxes to hold them; for the hypo-allergenic loose powder in a dozen shades, boxed (35€), and the fluffiest pink ostrich powder puffs (25€). These items are all musts. If you don't believe me, take your new bath pearls back to the deep tub in your room and have a good soak, perhaps inviting monsieur to share in the lavender?

Thank goodness you can reorder your favorites by fax with your credit card. A few of the scents are available in U.S. stores, but most of the thirty or so perfumes and toilet waters are exclusively here, stored in glass urns. The loyal, even lifelong, clientele can choose from eighteen reissued scents, or the famous classics such as Montaigne, or the romantic newcomer Aimez-Moi. For younger women I would recommend Lady Caron.

Parfums Caron

ADDRESS
22 Rue Francois 1, 8th
TELEPHONE
01.47.23.30.36
FAX
01.47.23.30.56
METRO
Alma-Marçeau or Franklin D. Roosevelt
OPEN
Mon–Sat, 10 a.m.–7:30 p.m.

ADDRESS
36 Rue Laffitte, 9th
TELEPHONE
01.47.70.85.00
METRO
Le Peletier
OPEN
Mon–Fri, 10 a.m.–6:30 p.m.
CREDIT CARDS
V, DC
$$-$$$$

6. FOUQUET

Candies, condiments, teas, and such

Just a step off the Avenue Montaigne is my favorite shop for edible gifts. It is here that the Fouquet family has been busy since 1852 conjuring up sweets and spices to comfort Parisian palates for four generations—though today's clientele is international. And, the shop is happy to ship.

Beyond the baskets, boxes, trays, and tins are shelves lined with all manner of bottles and brown-lidded glass jars filled with distinctively Fouquet jams, mustards, scented honeys, nuts and fruits, chocolates, and champagnes. Chances are, Fréderic and Catherine Fouquet will be in the back room conducting experiments for the sweet tooth that have produced such marvels as nuts, fruits, or caramels encased in sugar, or a new variety of hand-made chocolate. I dare you to make it home without sampling some of these beautifully displayed goodies.

Perhaps you're better advised to carry back some of the prepackaged gifts that the Fouquet family execute so famously. Ask them to fill one of their colorful house tins with the hard candies in fruit or caramel flavors (90€ a kilo), and don't overlook the more modest gifts—like an assortment of their own six mustards, touched with cognac, shallot, honey, or fine herbs (23€), a jar of delicately scented honey (5€), or a small jar filled with chocolate beads to delight the children.

Fouquet

7. BARBARA BUI

Women's clothing, shoes, and accessories

Barbara Bui, who has been among the ranks of
French designers since the 1980s, has definitely
made her way to the forefront with three floors
showcasing her creations to their most contemporary advantage in the cleanly designed Avenue
Montaigne store. To her trademark crisply cut
leather pieces, flowing silks, and knits, she has
added a finely tuned line of shoes and bags, all in
keeping with her elegantly modern look. Her fabric
choices are top quality and her colors are always up
to date. The top floor here is casual wear, with tee's
already vacuum-packed in plastic for your next
tropical vacation. The Etienne-Marcel location has
the BARBARA BUI CAFÉ next door and her husband William Halimi's three KABUKI men's and
womenswear shops down the block.

ADDRESS
50 Avenue Montaigne, 8th
TELEPHONE
01.42.25.05.25
METRO
Franklin D. Roosevelt
OPEN
Mon–Sat, 10 a.m.–7 p.m.

ADDRESS
23 Rue Etienne-Marcel, 1st
TELEPHONE
01.40.26.43.65
METRO
Etienne-Marcel
OPEN
Mon–Sat, 10:30 a.m.–7:30 p.m.

ADDRESS
67 Rue des Saints Pères, 6th
TELEPHONE
01.45.44.37.21
METRO
Sèvres-Babylone
OPEN
Mon–Sat, 10 a.m.–7 p.m.

ADDRESS
43 Rue des Francs-Bourgeois,
4th
TELEPHONE
01.53.01.88.05
METRO
Saint-Paul
OPEN
Tue–Sat, 11 a.m.–7 p.m.

ADDRESS
35 Rue de Grenelle, 7th (outlet
store)
TELEPHONE
01.45.44.85.14
METRO
Rue du Bac
OPEN
Mon–Sat, 10 a.m.–7 p.m.
CREDIT CARDS
V, AE, MC, DC
$$-$$$

ADDRESS
7 Rond Point des Champs-
Elysées, 8th
TELEPHONE
01.42.99.20.20 (auction
house)
01.42.99.16.16 (gallery)
01.42.99.16.19 (bookstore)
METRO
Franklin D. Roosevelt
OPEN
Auction house: Mon–Fri,
9 a.m.–7 p.m.
Bookstore and gallery:
Mon–Sat, 10:30 a.m.–7 p.m.
CREDIT CARDS
V, AE, DC
$$$-$$$$

8. ARTCURIAL

Auction house, art and jewelry, bookstore; specializing in twentieth-century art

Enter through the gates of the beautiful Hôtel Dassault, a haven for lovers of modern and contemporary art. In 2002 the space and concept were revised to incorporate the auction house alongside the gallery and bookstore. You'll find here the city's second-largest collection of books on the arts (over 8,000 volumes here; the art bookshop in the Louvre Museum claims to be the largest in the world). The gallery has editions of art, furniture, rugs, and jewelry designed for ARTCURIAL.

Artcurial

9. NINA RICCI
Women's ready-to-wear, lingerie, accessories, makeup
Menswear and accessories

If you are familiar with NINA RICCI only as maker of one of the world's best-selling perfumes, "L'Air du Temps," you'll be happily surprised when you walk through the portals of the impressive Avenue Montaigne store. An empire of luxe has grown discreetly from the Ricci couture name established in the 1930s. Under the stylist Lars Nilsson the women's collection is known for its glamorous femininity, no longer dressing exclusively the grande dame. Be sure to stop at costume jewelry, which is traditional and among the best of its kind. The shawls are lovely and varied, and the stylish footwear is just right for the Ball. The famous lingerie is, of course, exquisite. The newest perfume, "Love in Paris," makes an easy gift.

ADDRESS
39 Avenue Montaigne, 8th
TELEPHONE
01.40.88.64.96
METRO
Alma-Marçeau or Franklin D. Roosevelt
OPEN
Mon–Sat, 11 a.m.–7 p.m.
CREDIT CARDS:
V, AE, MC, DC
$$-$$$$

10. NOUEZ-MOI
Linens for bed, bath and table, baby linens, and gifts

A mere peek into this charming shop will have you restocking your linen closet with its distinctive yet practical frivolities for your bedroom, bath, and dining table. Parisian decorator Lillian Pons-Seguin, the owner and designer, makes your choices easy with embroideries in all colors for your made-to-order monogrammed, or otherwise ready-to-go, embellished linens. Boudoir pillows with funny sayings in French or in English (65€) , terry cloth guest towels, decorated and monogrammed, and toiletry bags (from 22€) fly out of here for good reason. They are oh so French in design and creation and at these prices offer an alternative to some of the more serious, longer established lines. You'll find lots of gift possibilities here. The shop in the Sixteenth is somewhat smaller.

ADDRESS
8 Rue Clément-Marot, 8th
TELEPHONE
01.47.20.60.26
FAX
01.47.20.53.50
METRO
Alma-Marçeau
OPEN
Mon, 2–7 p.m.; Tue–Sat, 10:30 a.m.–7 p.m.

ADDRESS
27 Rue des Sablons, 16th
TELEPHONE
01.47.27.69.88
FAX
01.47.04.89.05
METRO
Trocadéro
OPEN
Mon, 2–7 p.m.; Tue–Sat, 10 a.m.–7 p.m.
CREDIT CARDS
V, AE, MC
$$

ADDRESS
14 Rue Marbeuf, 8th
(Gastronomy de luxe)
TELEPHONE
01.47.20.24.26
OPEN
Mon–Fri, 8:45 a.m.–8 p.m.;
Sat, 9 a.m.–7:30 p.m.

ADDRESS
13 Rue Clément-Marot, 8th
(fruits & vegetables and baskets)
TELEPHONE
01.47.20.10.01
OPEN
Mon–Fri, 9 a.m.–7:45 p.m.

ADDRESS
25 Rue Jean Mermoz, 8th
(wines and table arts)
16 Rue Clément-Marot, 8th
TELEPHONE
01.47.20.16.18 and
01.42.56.07.49
OPEN
Mon–Sat, 9 a.m.–8 p.m.
METRO
Franklin D. Roosevelt
CREDIT CARDS
V, AE, MC
$$-$$$

11. BOUTIQUES VIGNON
Gourmet take-out

One of the prettiest of neighborhood take-outs, VIGNON is a good address for window-shopping or elegant picnic fare. Enter through the marble facade and choose something delicious to keep in your hotel minibar. Menu choices change daily, and M Vignon is particularly celebrated for his terrine of foie gras and game pâtés. Delivery within the 8th *arrondissement* is free.

 CHEZ ANDRÉ
Restaurant

ADDRESS
12 Rue Marbeuf, 8th
TELEPHONE
01.47.20.59.57
METRO
Franklin D. Roosevelt
OPEN
Noon to midnight, daily
CREDIT CARDS
V, AE, MC, DC
$$

When I'm staying in the area, I eat here every day. Somehow the faces always seem familiar, the waitresses seem to know you, and the food is everything you hope for in bourgeois French cuisine. Among the customers, I've noticed business people from nearby broadcasting and couture houses, groups of chic singles, families celebrating, older couples, even a gentleman with his lapdog. Make no mistake, this is a popular spot and has been so since 1937.

Chez André

12. RENÉ MANCINI
Women's shoes

It is remarkable to me that this small and highly
popular shop has so many beautiful and stylish
models on display, available in a variety of colors,
for sale only at this location and now their boutiques in Geneva and New York. Last time I bought
here, one of the satin evening slippers from my
shoebox was at the design workshop being copied
for another season. It is this high level of effort that
keeps the line in tow. René Mancini made the first
black-tipped shoe for Chanel, and now it is his
daughter Claire who oversees production of the
handmade styles designed for them and produced
in Italian factories. You can find lots of casual shoes
here, including Parisian tennies, sandals, many
models of loafers (called *escarpins* in French and a
classic day shoe for the relaxed Parisienne) in colored leathers, denim, and more, and certainly some
very sexy dress shoes.

ADDRESS
5 Rue Marbeuf, 8th
TELEPHONE
01.47.20.18.93
FAX
01.47.23.03.27
METRO
Alma-Marçeau
OPEN
Mon–Sat, 10:30 a.m.–7 p.m.
CREDIT CARDS
V, AE, MC
$$$-$$$$

Alain Figaret

ADDRESS
14 bis Rue Marbeuf, 8th
TELEPHONE
01.47.23.35.49
METRO
Franklin D. Roosevelt
OPEN
Mon–Sat, 10 a.m.–7 p.m.

ADDRESS
30 Avenue Franklin D.
Roosevelt, 8th
TELEPHONE
01.42.89.08.31
METRO
Miromesnil
OPEN
Mon–Sat, 10 a.m.–7 p.m.

ADDRESS
18/20 Place de la Madeleine,
8th
TELEPHONE
01.40.06.94.90
METRO
Madeleine
OPEN
Mon–Sat, 10 a.m.–7:30 p.m.

ADDRESS
21 Rue de la Paix, 2nd
TELEPHONE
01.42.65.04.99
METRO
Opéra
OPEN
Mon–Sat, 10 a.m.–7:30 p.m.

13. ALAIN FIGARET

Men's shirts, ties, and furnishings, women's blouses and accessories

You'll like shopping here because it's small, there's plenty of service, and the choice is so great you're sure to find what you want. Since 1968 the Figaret family has kept a watchful eye over every aspect of its production, available exclusively in its own shops, in order to maintain a classic styling paired with smart colors. ALAIN FIGARET is tops for quality ready-to-wear shirts, available in any of 600 double-twisted Egyptian cottons, with a choice of five traditional collars and simple or French cuffs (76€). The same fine cotton goes into their boxers, three to a pack (60€); and, my favorite, the classic pajama with drawstring waist (137€), also available in women's sizes, a perfect gift for matching bedmates. A hand monogram can be added. Also for women are a large assortment of blouses and stunning shawls in wool (from 69€) or reversible colored silk.

Alain Figaret

ADDRESS
24 Rue Saint-Sulpice, 6th
TELEPHONE
01.43.29.84.04
METRO
St-Sulpice
OPEN
Mon–Sat, 10 a.m.–7:30 p.m.

ADDRESS
16 Rue de Sèvres, 7th
TELEPHONE
01.42.22.03.40
METRO
St-Sulpice
OPEN
Mon–Sat, 10 a.m.–7:30 p.m.

ADDRESS
99 Rue de Longchamp, 16th
TELEPHONE
01.47.27.66.81
METRO
Pompe
OPEN
Mon, 1–7 p.m.; Tue–Sat, 10
a.m.–7 p.m.
CREDIT CARDS
V, AE, MC, DC
$$-$$$
INTERNET
www.alain-figaret.fr

14. COURRÈGES
Women's clothing

Remember the futuristic fashions of André
Courrèges in the late 1960s? They're back,
designed by Mme Courrèges in the style of her
husband, and they still look like the twenty-first
century. The new boutique coincides with a renew-
al in the popularity of COURRÈGES' distinctive
concepts: stark white accessories, A-line dresses in
candy colors, geometric shapes, and lots of shiny
plastics. The vinyl jacket (550€) and miniskirt
(250€) with Courrèges' short boots will look just
right on the woman of today.

Next door to the boutique is its CAFÉ BLANC
where the neighborhood stops for a bagel sandwich
lunch, only 10€ including wine or Coke, all served
in shiny white surroundings.

ADDRESS
40 Rue François I, 8th
TELEPHONE
01.53.67.30.73
METRO
Franklin D. Roosevelt
OPEN
Mon–Sat, 10 a.m.–7 p.m.
CREDIT CARDS
V, AE, MC
$$$

LA MAISON DU CHOCOLAT

Chocolates, tea salon

ADDRESS
52 Rue Francois I, 8th
TELEPHONE
01.47.23.38.25
METRO
Franklin D. Roosevelt
OPEN
Mon–Sat, 9:30 a.m.–7 p.m.

ADDRESS
225 Rue du Faubourg St-Honoré, 8th
TELEPHONE
01.42.27.39.44
METRO
Ternes

ADDRESS
8 Boulevard de la Madeleine, 9th
TELEPHONE
01.47.42.86.52
METRO
Opéra or Madeleine

ADDRESS
19 Rue de Sèvres, 6th
TELEPHONE
01.45.44.20.40
METRO
Sèvres-Babylone

ADDRESS
89 Avenue Raymond Poincarée, 16th
TELEPHONE
01.40.67.77.83
METRO
Victor-Hugo
$$-$$$

Owner Robert Linxe is the acknowledged master of chocolate in Paris and perfector of chocolate for the modern taste that is very rich, less sweet, even a little bitter. The chocolate brown interior and serving help literally enrobed in chocolate will leave you with little desire for anything else, so make your way to the tea salon at the rear of the shop where you can indulge your sweet tooth in any of five unctuous hot chocolates, flagrantly rich pastries, and iced summer specialties. What better pick-me-up for the pooped shopper?

15. MORABITO
Handbags, luggage, and leather goods

For a handbag that is expensive and truly looks it, come to MORABITO. The top of the line here would be a custom crocodile bag, handfinished in Paris and guaranteed for a lifetime (6,500€). Or, you can choose from a number of exotic skins and colors and Morabito will put it together for you in a week if you can't find it on the shelves. There is also a sportier line of textured calfskin bags made in Italy (from 530€) with the same elegant styling and touch of gold plating. The desk accessories and small leather goods are equally handsome, with prices beginning at 1,000€ for ostrich. Everything Morabito is of Hèrmes quality, but less expensive and easier to order.

ADDRESS
55 Rue François I, 8th
TELEPHONE
01.53.23.90.40
FAX
01.53.23.90.41
METRO
George V
OPEN
Mon, 2:30–6:30 p.m.; Tue–Sat, 10:30 a.m.–7 p.m.
CREDIT CARDS
V, AE, MC
$$$$

16. HERMÈS-MOTSCH
Men's and women's hats, clothing, and accessories

Probably the most notable men's hatter in Paris (designs for women are less plentiful here), MOTSCH had been a father-son establishment since 1887 until coming under the management of Mlle Christine Motsch, and was recently sold to HERMÈS, who now sells a selection of its luxury goods at the same address. Motsch continues to top off numerous heads in France with traditional designs ranging from their bestselling plain felt and Borsolino, to caps, berets, and Panamas, each made from excellent materials and old-world methods exclusively for Motsch. The huge stock, beautifully paneled interior, and expert fitters assure that this stop is worthwhile, though the sales staff here does not always make you feel welcome.

ADDRESS
42 Avenue George V, 8th
TELEPHONE
01.47.23.79.22
FAX
01.47.20.59.60
METRO
George V
OPEN
Mon, 10:15 a.m.–1 p.m. & 2:15–6:30 p.m.; Tue–Sat, 10:15–6:30 p.m.
CREDIT CARDS
V
$$$

Hermès-Motsch

Along the Way

The Champs-Elysées—no longer the Elysian Fields for which it was named, transforms from a crowded rush of humanity during the day to an open-air social club at night. Walk fast along this still-beautiful avenue to avoid close encounters and beware of the pickpockets. You'll always find a celebrity crowd at LE FOUQUET (N.99), the landmark café-restaurant. This is a good street for teen shopping, beginning with MORGAN (N.92), whose racks crammed with clothes from sleazy to chic beckon from the sidewalk from 10 a.m. until midnight, while preppy boys and girls of all ages may prefer the flagship LACOSTE (N.95), where everything is noticeably less than stateside, and the loungewear is as popular as the collared tennis shirt.

ADDRESS
133 Avenue des Champs-Elysées, 8th
TELEPHONE
01.47.20.39.25
METRO
Charles de Gaulle-Étoile
OPEN
Daily, 9–2 a.m.
CREDIT CARDS
V, AE, MC, DC
$$-$$$

17. DRUGSTORE PUBLICIS
Restaurant, pharmacy, books and magazines, food, gifts

When the first DRUGSTORE opened on the Champs-Elysées, curious Frenchmen and homesick Americans came in droves for the burgers, fries, and ice cream sundaes, and its boutiques offered a destination for night owls prowling the Champs. Now a Drugstore exists at both ends of the avenue, giving everyone so inclined an excuse to roam back and forth til the wee hours. Since then, the Champs address has been completely redone and is still worth a stop. While you're there have a peek at the photo exhibit in the Eisenhower Gallery of Agence Publicis, dedicated to the liberation by American soldiers at the end of WWII.

If you're stuck with last-minute gift needs or a late craving for a good read in English, come here to find anything from toys and cigars to travel bags.

ADDRESS
101 Avenue des Champs-Elysées, 8th
TELEPHONE
01.53.57.24.00
METRO
George V
OPEN
Mon–Sat, 10 a.m.–8 p.m.

ADDRESS
6 Place Saint-Germain-des-Prés, 6th

18. LOUIS VUITTON
Men's and women's clothing, shoes, leather goods, jewelry and watches, writing accessories

Vuitton is at the tip-top of brand names in France, and this Champs-Elysées flagship, the largest boutique in Europe at 4,000 square feet, is not to be missed! Opened in fall of '05, to coincide with the 150th anniversary of LOUIS VUITTON, it promises to be jam-packed and brilliantly merchandised. Vuitton has come a long way from simply produc-

ing stylish luggage, and for good reason. An extraordinary level of quality and design breathe long
life into everything carrying the name.

19. SEPHORA
Perfumes and cosmetics

Enter the twilight zone when you enter here.
SEPHORA.com's flagship store on the Champs-
Elysées is a cutting-edge makeover for the perfume
and cosmetics warehouse known for its universal
inventory and cut-rate prices. Everything about this
enormous space is futuristic, from the young sales-
girls in long black robes and gloves, to the word-
less, haunting music that never stops.

It's a virtual world unto itself where you'll find
virtually any brand you're seeking, many at a savings of about 20 percent. If you're working toward
the all-day face, don't miss the special room where
you can test your makeup under lighting conditions
from day to night. Manicures and make-ups are also
offered, and this may be the only address in Paris
for an off-hours or Sunday manicure.

If the world described above isn't for you, try
the more exclusive GUERLAIN (N.68) next door,
with its luxurious art deco interior. Guerlain fragrances are pure French sophistication and only
available at the Guerlain boutiques in France. Ask
to try those that are not available in the U.S. Also
at this address is a highly recommended Guerlain
skin treatment institute. Boutique open Mon–Sat,
10:30 a.m. to 8 p.m.; Sun, 3 to 7 p.m.; For institute
hours and appointments, telephone 01.45.62.11.21.

TELEPHONE
01.45.49.62.32
METRO
Saint-Germain-des-Prés
OPEN
Mon–Sat, 10 a.m.–7 p.m.

ADDRESS
22 Avenue Montaigne, 8th
TELEPHONE
01.45.62.47.00
METRO
Franklin D. Roosevelt
OPEN
Mon–Sat, 9:30 a.m.–7 p.m.
CREDIT CARDS
V, AE, MC, DC
$$$-$$$$

ADDRESS
70-72 Avenue des Champs-
Elysées, 8th
TELEPHONE
01.53.93.22.50
METRO
Franklin D. Roosevelt
OPEN
Sun–Thur, 10 a.m.–midnight;
Fri–Sat, 10 a.m.–1 a.m.

ADDRESS
50 Rue de Passy, 16th
TELEPHONE
01.53.92.28.20
METRO
Muette
OPEN
Mon–Sat, 9:30 a.m.–7:30 p.m.
CREDIT CARDS
V, AE, MC
$$
INTERNET
www.sephora.com

ADDRESS
52 Avenue des Champs-
Elysées, 8th
TELEPHONE
01.53.77.65.65
METRO
Franklin D. Roosevelt
OPEN
Mon–Sat, 9 a.m.–midnight

ADDRESS
21 Avenue de L'Opéra, 1st
TELEPHONE
01.42.61.78.08
METRO
Opéra or Pyramides

ADDRESS
18 Rue de Passy, 16th
TELEPHONE
01.45.20.17.52
METRO
La Muette

ADDRESS
25 Avenue des Ternes, 17th
TELEPHONE
01.43.80.43.76
METRO
Ternes
OPEN
Mon–Fri, 9 a.m.–10 p.m.; Sat,
9 a.m.–9 p.m.
CREDIT CARDS
V, AE, MC
$$

20. MONOPRIX

Household items, groceries, clothing for men, women, and children

MONOPRIX is a mini–department store with locations throughout the city. It is extremely well merchandised and well priced. Everyone shops at these stores—even Princess Stephanie has been seen at Monoprix rounding out her wardrobe. As a student I made wardrobe purchases here that continued to draw compliments ten years later. Parisiennes come here for the Bourjois cosmetics line, which is Chanel makeup under a different label at very low prices. It is a favorite family stop for stylish and inexpensive children's clothing.

For good gift buys during the less crowded off-hours, latch on to a shopping cart and grab some "typically French" items like kitchen gadgetry or Provençal pottery. Or head to the food halls, among the best-stocked in the city.

21. NAF-NAF
Children's, junior, adult clothes

The NAF-NAF line, named after the youngest of the Three Little Pigs, experienced instant success with its first design: a very wide, printed jumpsuit, now much-copied. Even though it calls itself the "big, bad look," the casual collection is identifiable by its gay colors and shapes, and is most popular with teenagers.

ADDRESS
52 Avenue des Champs-Elysées, 8th
TELEPHONE
01.45.62.03.08
METRO
Franklin D. Roosevelt

ADDRESS
33 Rue Etienne-Marcel, 1st
TELEPHONE
01.42.36.15.28
METRO
Etienne-Marcel

ADDRESS
168 Blvd. Saint-Germain, 6th
TELEPHONE
01.43.26.98.09
METRO
St-Germain-des-Prés
OPEN
Mon–Sat, 10 a.m.–7 p.m. (to 7:30 p.m. in 6th)
CREDIT CARDS
V, AE, MC
$$

22. THE VIRGIN MEGASTORE
Musical recordings, books, electronics

An English import (an offshoot of the Virgin Record label), this is the biggest record store in France, and a destination attraction on the Champs-Elysées. On a restless night it's a place to see and be seen.

Three floors and 35,000 square feet are a palais of high-tech design and technology, with headphones for sampling recordings from the international musical scene. Some top names in French rock 'n' roll are Ophélie Winter and M. C. Solaar. Not in the past noted for this particular genre of music, but never to be culturally outdone, the French have instituted the post of Minister of Pop Music, with a big budget for finding and promoting local talent. The law requires French radio to play 60 percent French music.

You'll find every kind of music here, on record, cassette, or CD, as well as an excellent selection of books. For a mid-browse pick-me-up, find a spot upstairs at the VIRGIN CAFÉ.

ADDRESS
52-60 Avenue des Champs-Elysées, 8th
TELEPHONE
01.49.53.50.00
METRO
Franklin D. Roosevelt
OPEN
Mon–Sat, 10 a.m.–midnight;
Sun, noon–midnight

ADDRESS
Galerie du Carrousel du Louvre, 99 Rue de Rivoli, 1st
TELEPHONE
01.44.50.03.17
METRO
Louvre
OPEN
Mon–Tue, 10 a.m.–8 p.m.;
Wed–Sat, 10 a.m.–11 p.m.
CREDIT CARDS
V, AE, DC
$$

Along the Way

The lovely AVENUE MATIGNON is a prime location for art and antiques galleries. A worthwhile stop here is GALERIE HOPKINS-CUSTOT (N.2), specializing in nineteenth- and early twentieth-century paintings along with contemporary painting and sculpture, and CHRISTIE'S FRANCE, the auction house, is at N.9. Poke around the stamp and old postcard collectors' market held on AVENUE MATIGNON and down the AVENUE GABRIEL on Thursdays, Saturdays, Sundays, and holidays from 10 a.m. to sunset.

Continue down to the CARRÉ MARIGNY (corner of Avenues Marigny and Gabriel) to the stamp market where licensed dealers buy, sell, and trade philatelia from booths set up on the sidewalks, keeping the same hours as above.

ADDRESS
Carré Marigny, 10 Avenue des Champs-Elysées, 8th
TELEPHONE
01.42.65.85.10
METRO
Franklin D. Roosevelt
OPEN
Mon–Sat, noon–11 p.m.;
Sun, noon–7 p.m.
CREDIT CARDS
V, AE, MC, DC
$$$

23. PAVILLON ELYSÉES LENÔTRE
Restaurant, gift shop, cooking courses

The marvelous presentations of the renowned pastry chef Gaston Lenotre have been brought into the twenty-first century with the Pavillon, bringing the concept of a gastronomical haven to this idyllic park setting between the Tuilleries Gardens and the Champs-Elysées. Outdoor dining overlooks the Grand Palais and indoor dining in the stylishly orange and chocolate brown setting only encourages one to think of the delicious chocolates sold here, lunching with friends, and of course, cooking, as the shop sells cookbooks and utensils and there is a full-fledged cooking school here with classes in nearly everything for children as well as adults. For more information on classes, telephone 01.42.65.85.10.

Couture Along the Way

The RUE DU FAUBOURG ST-HONORÉ is the best-known shopping street in Paris for good reason: it is lined with fine shops and many couture designers have prêt-à-porter boutiques here. Beginning across the street from the ELYSÉES PALACE (home of the French president) it's easy to spend a day going into every store down the Faubourg and its continuation, the Rue St-Honoré, or simply enjoying the window displays. English is spoken everywhere, and the *détaxe* and credit cards are no problem.

Among the many couture names to watch for on St-Honoré are LOUIS FÉRAUD (N.90), who designs alluring clothes that even a first lady can wear, as orders from the Palace across the street have proven; CHLOE (N.54–56) for Phoebe Philo's feminine, with-it designs ;YVES ST-LAURENT (N.38, women and N.32, men); LANVIN, where Alber Elbaz now brings his genius to a deceptively simple women's line (N.22), and the men's collection (N.15) offers outstanding tailoring.

24. CHRISTIAN LACROIX
Women's clothing, shoes, and accessories; men's collection

It's forever sunny chez LACROIX. No wonder he entered the world of couture in the lead. Fashions here are rich and colorful, inspired by the landscape of his native south of France. His interiors are worth a peek too, providing the backdrop for some of the most sought-after designs in Paris. Even the stewardesses on Air France are glorious in their Lacroix uniforms. Those who aren't quite prepared to step up to the price tags on his suits and gowns can dress up in costume jewelry that radiates his *joie de vivre*. For haute couture, shop at the boutique on St-Honoré.

ADDRESS
73 Rue du Faubourg Saint-Honoré, 8th
TELEPHONE
01.42.68.79.04
METRO
Miromesnil
OPEN
Mon–Sat, 10:30 a.m.–7 p.m.

ADDRESS
2–4 Place St-Sulpice, 6th
TELEPHONE
01.46.33.48.95
METRO
St-Sulpice
CREDIT CARDS
V, AE, DC
$$$$

25. ANNA LOWE
Discount women's clothing

ANNA'S is one of the better discount shops in Paris because here they are service-oriented even when offering the big names in couture at around 40 percent off. Many of the couture and haute couture models for day and evening come in right after the runway shows, so you can buy for the current season. During one visit I noticed a red Chanel suit in the window, offered for a third less than at the Chanel boutique down the street! Tags are marked with the original and discounted prices and you'll be helped in English with *détaxe* and alterations, of course.

ADDRESS
104 Rue du Faubourg Saint-Honoré, 8th
TELEPHONE
01.42.66.11.32
METRO
Franklin D. Roosevelt
OPEN
Mon–Sat, 10 a.m.–7 p.m.
CREDIT CARDS
V, AE, DC
$$-$$$

ADDRESS
29 Rue du Faubourg Saint-
Honoré, 8th
TELEPHONE
01.53.43.00.85
METRO
Concorde
OPEN
Mon–Sat, 10:30 a.m.–7 p.m.
CREDIT CARDS
V, AE, MC
$$$$

26. ROGER VIVIER
Women's shoes and bags

Contenders for "the most fabulous shoes in Paris,"
this is the rebirth of the extravagant styles created
in the '50s and '60s by Roger Vivier, inventor of the
high-high heel (he then engineered the steel rod
needed for inside support), the "virgule" or comma
heel, silk-satin knee boots, many of the above
adorned with jewels, and his most favored and simple pilgrim buckled pump. Now designed by Bruno
Frissonier, these styles have every bit the elegance
of the originals. Today's pilgrims (420€) with
matching suede bags (1,200€) are understated
standouts.

ADDRESS
24 Rue du Faubourg St-
Honoré, 8th
TELEPHONE
01.40.17.47.17
FAX
01.40.17.47.18
METRO
Concorde
OPEN
Mon–Sat, 10:30 a.m.–6:30 p.m.

ADDRESS
42 Avenue George V (Hermès-
Motsch)
TELEPHONE
01.47.20.59.60
METRO
George V
OPEN
Mon, 10:15 a.m.–1 p.m. &
2:15–6:30 p.m.; Tue–Sat, 10:15
a.m.–6:30 p.m.
CREDIT CARDS
V, AE, DC
$$$-$$$$

27. HERMÈS
Leather goods, men's and women's clothing, accessories,
jewelry, and tablewear

Everyone knows the name Hermès, but you don't
really know HERMÈS until you've visited this land-
mark store. Our present-day fascination with the
elegant country, horsey life has no better inter-
preter than the window and interior designers here,
and all of Paris knows it. Crowds come just to take
in the autumn scenes from the sidewalk, while
inside customers jam the aisles. At one time consid-
ered stodgy, the Hermès look has been revitalized
for a younger generation of trend setters. Once
again the scarf counter is mobbed with chic young
things who leave with their status-symbol silk twill
(over 200 different styles, averaging 227€) and the
little booklet that shows just how to tie it.

The incomparable leather clothing is classically
styled with the freshest of colors. And the Kelly
bag (carried by Princess Grace to Monaco for her
wedding) has been the best-selling handbag in the
world, with a customer waiting list of eighteen
months.

The success of Hermès, which began as a sad-
dlery in 1837, and its recent growth (the work-
shops just moved from this location to the outskirts
of Paris to make room for more selling space), are

thanks to the recognition of a new crop of customers appreciative of the first-rate craftsmanship in every Hermès product. Handbags, for example, are made by hand and guaranteed for life.

Those willing to pay Hermès prices will be thrilled not just with the image but with the perfect product. Leather connoisseurs note that Hermès skins always have a pleasant odor because the otherwise acceptable hide will be rejected if not up to the proper snuff. The useful small leather items are big sellers with relatively small price tags, and so are the distinctively Hermès men's neckties. If you just can't get enough of the look, ask to visit the upstairs museum.

The Hermès sales, held in mid-October and mid-March for a week, have customers lined up around the block and around the clock, just waiting their turn to enter the back rooms. Prices are about 40 percent off, and more.

At HERMÈS-MOTSCH, you'll find a small collection of Hermès basics alongside the Motsch hat collection.

ADDRESS
11 Rue du Faubourg St-Honoré, 8th
TELEPHONE
01.44.94.11.11
METRO
Concorde or Madeleine

October sale at Hermès

ADDRESS
15 Rue Boissy d'Anglas, 8th
TELEPHONE
01.47.42.69.51
FAX
01.40.07.04.17
METRO
Concorde
OPEN
Mon, 2:30–7 p.m.; Tue–Sat, 11 a.m.–1:30 p.m. & 2–7 p.m.

ADDRESS
29 Galerie Montpensier, 1st
TELEPHONE
01.42.96.39.54
METRO
Palais-Royal
CREDIT CARDS
V, AE
$$-$$$

28. CASOAR
Jewelry and decorative items in silver

When Mme Casoar first opened her shop, I would come here for her period designs in silverplate. Today her fantasies are realized in solid silver. The finely molded picture frames, jewelry, and perfume flasks are inspired by the styles of the art deco and Napoleonic periods and are made to last forever. But the store decor is always a surprise, as Madame redesigns the stylish interior monthly, carting the large furnishings back and forth from her country château. It is always a pleasure to enter here, particularly knowing you can pick up a sparkling beetle or firefly to pin to your scarf for 100€, or an enamel silver Empire frame from 108 to 1,080€. There is a second, teensy little Casoar on the Palais Royal.

Casoar

29. INSTITUT CARITA

Beauty salon offering hair, skin care, makeup, body treatments, skin products, and hair accessories

The Carita sisters, Rosy and Maria, were the first to offer treatments for skin, body and hair together, creating the concept of the beauty institute. The St-Honoré CARITA location is now the largest such temple of beauty in Paris, known for its premier quality treatments, ultra-stylish coifs, and celebrity clientele.

A beauty break in the luxury of this feminine salon is designed to tranquilize the nervous '90s. Make an appointment for your hair (91€ for an excellent cut), a classic facial, French manicure, makeup, massage, or come for a "Belle de Jour" package (249€ for facial, makeup, hair styling, manicure), and leave feeling completely pampered. Before you go, check the excellent selection of hair accessories. It's always busy here; the Parisienne visits her salon weekly.

ADDRESS
11 Rue du Faubourg St-Honoré, 8th
TELEPHONE
01.44.94.11.11
METRO
Concorde or Madeleine
OPEN
Tue–Sat, 10 a.m.–6:30 p.m. (salon) ;
Mon–Sat, 10 a.m.–6 p.m. (boutique and reservation line)

CARITA MONTAIGNE
ADDRESS
3 Rue du Boccador, 8th
TELEPHONE
01.47.23.76.79
OPEN
Tue–Sat, 9 a.m.–7 p.m.
CREDIT CARDS
V, AE, MC
$$$

30. FAÇONNABLE

Menswear and womenswear

A great place to find the American casual wear look with a European flair, FAÇONNABLE is otherwise described by an elegant American friend in Paris as "a French version of Ralph Lauren." Even if the rest of French sartorial style won't do for him, he'll surely be delighted with Façonnable.

Men's sportswear is designed with American comfort and French color consciousness in mind. French-cuffed corduroy shirts come in every hue from salmon to black and discreetly branded with the house logo (a bird holding a golf club). Visit upstairs for outerwear, including a few fashionable concessions to that rarity, the true sportsman.

While he's marveling at the hundreds of very wide ties and suspenders in every possible combination, surprise him with a pair of irresistible *caleçons* (boxer shorts) in mixed florals or patchwork checks.

In addition to the four floors of men's clothing, which includes suits, there is now a line of casual wear for women shown on the mezzanine.

ADDRESS
9 Rue du Faubourg St-Honoré, 8th
TELEPHONE
01.47.42.72.60
METRO
Concorde or Madeleine

ADDRESS
174 Boulevard St-Germain, 6th
TELEPHONE
01.40.49.02.47
METRO
St-Germain-des-Prés

ADDRESS
27 Rue Marbeuf, 8th
TELEPHONE
01.49.52.05.84
METRO
Franklin D. Roosevelt
OPEN
Mon–Sat, 10:30 a.m.–7 p.m.
CREDIT CARDS
V, AE, DC
$$-$$$

ADDRESS
7 Rue du Faubourg St-Honoré,
8th
TELEPHONE
01.42.65.44.71
FAX
01.47.42.28.02
METRO
Madeleine
OPEN
Mon–Fri, 9 a.m.–6:30 p.m.;
Sat, 9:30 a.m.–6:30 p.m.
CREDIT CARDS
V, AE, MC
$$$
INTERNET
www.jeandebonnot.fr

31. JEAN DE BONNOT
Rare books

The perfect gift for a serious bibliophile or student of French literature could be found here among the beautifully bound classics on the shelves at JEAN DE BONNOT. Each volume is bound in lambskin cut from a single piece and engraved by hand in 22-carat gold. If you don't find what you're looking for among their inventory they will seek it out for you, and have it bound and delivered. Single editions begin at about 40€.

ADDRESS
14 Rue du Faubourg St-
Honoré, 8th (in the courtyard)
TELEPHONE
01.42.65.35.52
METRO
Concorde or Madeleine
OPEN
Mon–Sat, 10 a.m.–7 p.m.
CREDIT CARDS
V, AE, MC
$$$-$$$$

32. RENAUD PELLEGRINO
Handbags

PELLEGRINO bags are like pieces of modern art, and among the most artful in Paris. For to M Pellegrino, a handbag is to be worn as jewelry, not as a mere tote. Thus his elegant designs come in compact, original shapes, often with whimsically molded handles, and in five sizes and many colors. The leather bags are quite costly, coming from the same skins as Hermès, including the lizard and ostrich; but the extraordinary satin evening bags,

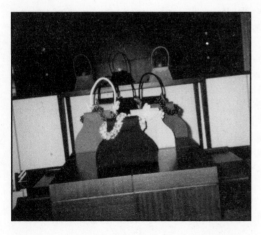

whether studded with semiprecious-looking stones or simply with a clear crystal necklace as a handle, are a real value (from 230€).

If you carry only a lipstick, keys, and phone money to your dressy soirées, why not indulge in something stunning? There are also a number of very pretty belts, leather goods, and silk scarves.

Renaud Pellegrino

Along the Way

The RUE ROYALE, leading up to the CHURCH OF LA MADELEINE, is where the rich and royal traditionally window shopped, perhaps on the way to the restaurant MAXIM'S (N.3), whose magnificent belle époque interior still draws a crowd, and so do its gift boutique and the art nouveau collection on view upstairs (open to tour at 2, 3:15, and 4:30 p.m., Wed–Fri); its more laid-back sidekick, MINIM'S (N.7), is a brasserie/restaurant/tea salon open from 8 a.m. (9 a.m. Sundays) to 10 p.m. daily. On this showcase street are some of the grandest names in French tableware. You'll pass BERNARDAUD LIMOGES (N.11), France's whitest and best-selling porcelain, whose lovely tea salon is tucked away in the pedestrian passage Galérie Royale (N.9); CRISTALLERIES DE ST-LOUIS (N.13), whose weighty hand-cut crystal dates back to royal tables of the 1700s; ODIOT (N.7 Place de la Madeleine), for collector's items for the table, where gorgeous pieces in gold, silver, and vermeil are cast in eighteenth- and nineteenth-century molds; BACCARAT (N.11 Place de la Madeleine) shows delicate crystal in a luxurious setting at prices up to 30 percent under U.S. retail, after shipping costs. At N.25 you'll find the entrance to the VILLAGE ROYALE, at first glance a well-preserved seventeenth-century village street, but actually a shopping mall redo of the royal barracks of that era.

33. LALIQUE
Crystal and table arts

Even if you've never longed for LALIQUE, you should take a peek at its crystal kingdom. From doorknob to chandelier, the Lalique touch glistens. Since René Lalique changed the face of glassware with his large deco-influenced sculptures at the turn of the century, Lalique has added facets to the range of the medium. Now working primarily in crystal and specializing in a marriage of clear and frosted glass, Marie-Claude Lalique is charged with assuring her family name is present in the gift bags of presidents and kings (Lalique is a typical gift from the French president to another head of state) as well as their countrymen.

ADDRESS
11 Rue Royale, 8th
TELEPHONE
01.53.05.12.12
METRO
Concorde
OPEN
Mon–Fri, 10 a.m.–6:30 p.m.;
Sat, 10 a.m.–7 p.m.
CREDIT CARDS
V, AE, MC, DC
$$$

For innovative wearable crystal, begin with the pendants, butterfly pins, and cabochon rings in fifteen different colors and ten finger sizes. If you are a fan of Lalique, the selection of figurines, vases, and tableware is at its best here, and prices are 30 percent less than in the U.S., with a further *détaxe* that's close to the price of shipping. Continue through the courtyard to their table arts boutique.

ADDRESS
9 Rue Royale, 8th
TELEPHONE
01.55.27.99.13
METRO
Madeleine
OPEN
Mon–Sat, 10:30 a.m.–7 p.m.
CREDIT CARDS
V, AE, DC
$$$

ADDRESS
112 Rue Amoise Croizat, Saint Denis (**Musée Bouilet-Christofle**)
TELEPHONE
01.49.22.40.40
METRO
Ligne 13, station St-Denis, Porte de Paris
OPEN
Mon–Fri, 9:30 a.m.–5:30 p.m.(closed on bank holidays)
Tickets 5€ less for students

34. PAVILLONS CHRISTOFLE
Silver and table arts

The dazzling CHRISTOFLE pavilion illustrates the fine French art of setting a beautiful table, and is one of the best addresses in the city for gifts. You'll find a wealth of beautiful, packable objects that simply ooze good taste, suited to a range of purposes (office, jewelry, entertaining) and prices.

A celebrated silversmith from the days when the haute bourgeoisie would dine with nothing less, Christofle has added an extensive selection of silverplated flatware as well as the real thing in designs from baroque to stark.

Go downstairs for tables set with an inspired mix of the major French table brands (Baccarat, Limoges, and others), including porcelain made for Christofle. Choose an adorable silver animal figurine (from 50€), a Louis XI bottle opener (38€), or a dozen silver dinner settings. A runaway hit for the couple who has everything is the silver straw touted for drinking champagne, packed as

Pavillons Christofle

two for 90€. Modernist André Putman has recently designed a distinctive line of solid silver jewelry with pieces from 75 to 450€. The shops are all set up for shipping treasures to America, so ask for a catalog for future orders.

The founding family, who has been running Christofle for six generations, maintains the Musée Bouilet-Christofle, a collection of over 2,000 of their silver pieces in an orginal Christofle workshop just outside Paris. A visit here is a simple excursion by metro and a fascinating trip through decorative arts styles since 1830.

Rosemarie Schulz

35. ROSEMARIE SCHULZ
Long-lasting floral and fruit arrangements

A rose is a rose with a magically long life chez Rosemarie Schulz, who has discovered a formula to keep her artful arrangements looking and smelling freshly picked for two years, at least. She works primarily with roses, preserving them with glycerin and organic colors and presenting them splendidly in silver bowls or simple leaf boxes. The preserved fruits, often oranges and limes geometrically designed, are also fragranced with their own scent. Delightful objects, like a life-size torso covered in rose petals (500€), or a wall mirror framed with flowers are available alongside roses in pots of all sizes (from 69€), topiaries, lifelike floral table sets, postcards, and scents.The shop packs well for shipping to a worldwide clientele.

ADDRESS
30 Rue Boissy d'Anglas (Galerie de la Madeleine), 8th
TELEPHONE
01.40.17.06.61
METRO
Madeleine
OPEN
Mon–Sat, 11 a.m.–7 p.m.
CREDIT CARDS
V, AE, MC, DC
$$

ADDRESS
6 Boulevard des Malesherbes,
8th
TELEPHONE
01.42.66.54.50
METRO
Saint-Augustin
OPEN
Mon–Sat, 10 a.m.–7:30 p.m.
CREDIT CARDS
V, AE, MC
$$$

36. DANIEL CREMIEUX
Sportswear

If you think you know this line from the U.S., for-get everything you've seen. This sporty shop houses a creative collection sold only here and in the south of France, where Daniel Cremieux launched his line with the golfer logo over thirty years ago. The colorful fabrics and refined finishes are contemporary French style for the seventeen- to fifty-five-year-old who takes his sportswear seriously. Between the regular line and the very casual weekend line you'll find suits (1,000€), shirts (150€), sport shirts, caps, jackets, underwear, everything you'll need, all of it distinctive. Made-to-measure is available.

Daniel Cremieux

37. GIEN
Faience tableware

At last, GIEN is on the rebound. This old favorite
has been known for the warm colors and lovely
shapes that have carried it through every trend in
table arts since the early nineteenth century. Taken
over recently by Louis and Fabienne Grandchamps,
an innovative couple who is wild about the arts of
the table and particularly the tradition of *faience*
(earthenware), the first Gien stores have opened in
Paris. The beautiful boutiques display many of traditional and contemporary patterns created for
them today, some inspired by the Gien past, others
as limited editions by known artists. Among them

ADDRESS
18 Rue de l'Arcade, 8th
TELEPHONE
01.42.66.52.32
METRO
Madeleine

ADDRESS
13 Rue Jacob, 6th
TELEPHONE
01.46.33.46.72
METRO
St-Germain-des-Prés
OPEN
Tue–Fri, 10:30 a.m.–7 p.m.;
Sat, 11 a.m.–6:30 p.m.
CREDIT CARDS
V, AE, MC
$$-$$$

Gien

are variations of flora, fauna, and nature and also a
series of Paris scenes, all available as table settings,
tea sets, cocktail sets, and serving pieces. Packaged
here, they make fine gifts. Many of the older patterns may still be ordered and, in original Gien tradition, they will hand-paint your coat of arms or
special occasion dates on their pieces. Tables are set
with their place settings and linens throughout, and
unique pieces are upstairs at Rue de l'Arcade.

ADDRESS
24-26-30 Place de la
Madeleine, 8th
TELEPHONE
01.70.39.38.00
01.70.39.38.78 (tea salon)
METRO
Madeleine
OPEN
Mon–Sat, 8 a.m.–9 p.m.; tea
salon Mon–Sat, 9 a.m.–8 p.m.
CREDIT CARDS
V, AE, DC
$$-$$$$
INTERNET
www.fauchon.com

 38. FAUCHON

Food hall, tea salon, wine cellar, and bar

No one who enjoys food will want to miss
FAUCHON, France's great homage to the glory of
grocery shopping. From a tiny greengrocer stand in
1866, Fauchon has gained landmark status for its
showstopping displays of over 20,000 food items in
its chic fuschia hued boutique.

From fresh exotic fruits and take-out mini-
Fauchon, make your way to the bustling pastry and
candy shop, and on to the tabletop and packaged
foods hall, where accommodating salespeople can
turn even the tiniest offering into a coveted treat
packaged à la Fauchon while you take your receipt
to the cashier.

Fauchon is the ultimate in quick-picks for food
items to send or carry home, if you can navigate the
crowds, because you'll find everything from wine
and pâté to Far-Eastern condiments, prepackaged to
carry or ship. Or, order from the online boutique.

Since its recent expansion you needn't content
yourself with drooling at the windows. The tea
salon offers Fauchon quality eats, and there's an epi-
curean restaurant upstairs that is open for dinner. I
highly recommend it.

Fauchon

39. LAFONT ET FILS
Eyewear

For three generations the *famille* Lafont has designed and sold eye-catching frames from this old-fashioned interior whose wares are always in tune with the times. Whether your look is strict or whacky, LAFONT has it, and can deliver it with your prescription (don't worry, these are international) within forty-eight hours.

This is Paris, and the establishment will custom style to your measure, color, and shape, upon request.

ADDRESS
11 Rue Vignon, 8th
TELEPHONE
01.47.42.25.93
METRO
Madeleine
OPEN
Mon–Sat, 10 a.m.–7:00 p.m.

ADDRESS
2 Rue Duphot, 8th
TELEPHONE
01.42.60.01.02
METRO
Madeleine
OPEN
Mon, 10 a.m.–1:30 p.m. & 2:30–7 p.m.; Tue–Sat, 10 a.m.–7:00 p.m.

ADDRESS
17 Boulevard Raspail, 7th
TELEPHONE
01.45.48.24.23
METRO
Rue du Bac
OPEN
Mon, 10 a.m.–1:30 p.m. & 2:30–7 p.m.; Tue–Sat, 10 a.m.–7:00 p.m.
CREDIT CARDS
V
$$-$$$

40. KIOSQUE THÉÂTRE
Discounted tickets to theaters and special events

Same-day ticket sales for some of the best (leftover) seats in the house. Theater, circuses, you name it. This last-minute commitment is an easy way for the harried traveler to partake of Parisian nightlife. And prices drop more than 50 percent off earlier ticket prices, before adding the 13 percent commission. As the Saturday lineup can be quite long, I recommend you arrive early that day.

ADDRESS
15 Place de la Madeleine, 8th
METRO
Madeleine
OPEN
Tue–Sat, 12:30–7:45 p.m.; Sun, 12:30–3:45 p.m.
NO CREDIT CARDS

LADURÉE
Tea salon, restaurant

ADDRESS
16 Rue Royale, 8th
TELEPHONE
01.42.60.21.79
METRO
Madeleine
OPEN
Mon–Sat, 8:30 a.m.–7 p.m.; Sun, 10 a.m.–7 p.m.

ADDRESS
21 Rue Bonaparte, 6th
TELEPHONE
01.44.07.64.87
METRO
St-Germain-des-Prés
OPEN
Mon–Sat, 8:30 a.m.–7 p.m.

ADDRESS
75 Avenue des Champs-Elysées, 8th
TELEPHONE
01.40.75.08.75
METRO
George V
OPEN
Daily, 7:30 a.m.–midnight
$$

The original LADURÉE on Rue Royale is my favorite tea salon, and I'm among its many ardent fans. Some love it for its morning café crème and flaky croissant; some claim it has the richest hot chocolate in the city; others rapture over the tea sandwich menu (eighteen varieties). But I come here for the cherub-frescoed ceiling and the chocolate macaroon, which is second to none.

At the more recently opened Champs-Elysées salon, interiors are inspired by the ironwork designs of Gustave Eiffel, and on Rue Bonaparte, at the former address of renowned decoratrice Madeleine Castaigne, the warm interior is neoclassic. The proprietors appropriately repeat the legendary menu.

Ladurée

41. CASSEGRAIN
Stationery and writing supplies

Since 1919, CASSEGRAIN has been a stationer of choice for those who appreciate the dying art of fine papers. An institution among the old guard, Cassegrain continues to hand-engrave in the manner of the last century, producing calling cards and personal stationery that stand apart.

If you wish to count yourself among its overseas customers, Cassegrain will ship. Allow three weeks for engraving. Don't fail to notice the luxurious desk accessories in bright colored leather, lizard or crocodile, with a lizard agenda at 375€. The best of name brand pens, writing gear that no child will want to put down, as well as a line of very stylish notebooks in all sizes make this a smart gift stop.

ADDRESS
422 Rue St-Honoré, 8th
METRO
Concorde or Madeleine
TELEPHONE
01.42.60.20.08
FAX
01.42.61.40.99
OPEN
Mon–Sat, 10 a.m.–6:30 p.m.
CREDIT CARDS
V, AE, DC
$$$-$$$$
INTERNET
www.cassegrain.fr

ADDRESS
406–410 Rue St-Honoré, 8th
TELEPHONE
01.42.60.39.01
METRO
Madeleine or Concorde
OPEN
Mon–Sat, 10:15 a.m.–6:30 p.m.
CREDIT CARDS
V, AE, MC
$-$$$$

42. AU NAIN BLEU
Toys

To a Parisian of a certain size, nothing can compare with the thrill of being offered a package wrapped in the distinctive paper of AU NAIN BLEU! One of the world's top toy stores, it has been run by the same family for five generations and attracts a celebrity clientele and children of all ages. Its original exquisite porcelain-faced dolls have grown into a large collection of beautifully dressed demoiselles, some in French folk costumes.

Today, a child can find the world's most popular toys here, but you'll probably want to look beyond the Beanie Babies and Barbies to more typically French items, like knight and Pierrot costumes, toy soldiers, marionettes, and lots of inventive, inexpensive gadgets that children find so appealing.

For the mademoiselle who has everything, the store has designed an elaborate nursery kit complete with cribs, strollers, changing tables, and babies with their nannies. There are tea sets with wine glasses, napkins, and plates patterned after Maman's, side by side with porcelain tea sets that would fit on a quarter for just a few euros.

Boys on their way to play in the Luxembourg

Au Nain Bleu

or Tuileries gardens will want a Nain Bleu carrying case of twenty-three metal vehicles for land, air, and sea or an inexpensive wooden sailboat, neither of which needs a translator. Happily, Au Nain Bleu ships internationally.

43. LONGCHAMP
Luggage, purses, small leather goods

With all the fashion-conscious handbags to choose from in Paris, I come to LONGCHAMP for my classic, functional day bags. The price-to-quality ratio is excellent in these detailed yet sturdy pieces in leather, nylon, or canvas, with every bag made to last like a piece of luggage (which is sold upstairs).

While young mothers might be drawn to a leather-cornered nylon zip bag that looks more structured than the luggage it's made to be and per-fectly designed for stuffing with leaky baby bottles (it's rubberized), camera, and diapers, you might go for the grainy leather hobo in a sleek color—a sophisticated, well-detailed bag that will look good and fetch compliments beyond one season. The briefcases are a smart buy, and there's a stylish selection of gloves and belts, as well as lots of small leather goods in brilliant colors.

ADDRESS
404 Rue St-Honoré, 1st
TELEPHONE
01.42.60.00.16
METRO
Madeleine

ADDRESS
21 Rue du Vieux-Colombier, 6th
TELEPHONE
01.42.22.74.75
METRO
St-Sulpice or Sèvres Babylone
OPEN
Mon–Sat, 10 a.m.–7 p.m.
CREDIT CARDS
V, AE, MC
$$-$$$

44. HERVÉ CHAPELIER
Nylon bags

This is where to come to buy gifts for college-bound girlfriends, and while you're here, pick up something for yourself. Handbags, travel bags, backpacks, and accessories, all nylon with zippers in luscious, trendy colors. This location is conve-niently close to LONGCHAMP, making it easy to go back and forth to compare colors and styles. The nylon purses are a craze here and abroad.

ADDRESS
390 Rue St-Honoré, 1st
TELEPHONE
01.42.96.38.04
METRO
Concorde
OPEN
Mon–Sat, 10:15 a.m.–7 p.m.

ADDRESS
1 bis Rue du Vieux Colombier, 6th
TELEPHONE
01.44.07.06.50
METRO
Saint-Sulpice
OPEN
Mon–Sat, 10:15 a.m.–7:00 p.m.

ADDRESS
13 Rue Gustave-Courbet, 16th
TELEPHONE
01.42.27.83.66
METRO
Victor-Hugo
OPEN
Mon, 2–7 p.m.; Tue–Sat, 10:15
a.m.–7 p.m.
CREDIT CARDS
V, AE, MC
$$

ADDRESS
12 Rue du Chevalier Saint-
Georges, 1st
TELEPHONE
01.42.97.40.49
METRO
Madeleine
OPEN
Mon–Sat, 10 a.m.–7 p.m.
CREDIT CARDS
V, AE, MC
$$-$$$

45. LE JACQUARD FRANÇAIS
Table and bath linens

This is the first boutique for these superb damasks,
produced in the Vosges region since 1871. The
abundance of rich color here came with the influ-
ential stylist Primrose Bordier, who was an original
advocate of the colorful table in France. Her legacy
is linens that are beautiful and *très à la mode*. There
are solids and patterns in cotton and linen, and,
yes, you can still find whites. Video screens against
the pale gray walls show the collections, which are
updated twice yearly. Placemats, napkins, and table
cloths as well as robes, towels, and baby linens are
here, each in its own space. The shop can make
special sizes for your table, and it's easy to walk
away with a set of solid placemats and napkins in
colors with tantalizing names like "curry," "tango,"
and "potimarron."

ADDRESS
4 Rue Duphot, 1st (Women
and men)
TELEPHONE
01.55.35.95.05
METRO
Bourse

ADDRESS
12 Place des Victoires, 2nd
(Women)
TELEPHONE

46. VICTOIRE
Women's and men's casual wear

The Rue Duphot boutique is our favorite VICTOIRE,
where elegant sport and a breezy personal style are
paired so cleverly by owner/manager Florence
Riboud. If you put yourself in her hands, she will
choose an outfit that's just right for you, with fin-
ishing touches of belt, bag, coat, and shoes. This is
also the only address with both men's and women's

styles, and very popular among upscale Parisiens who want a relaxed look. All the stores carry the Victoire line with additional labels, and while choices for men are quite casual (e.g., top-quality linen shirts in beautiful solids at 100€), the styles for women are also very feminine (e.g., a cotton shirt dress for 170€, topped with a scarf).

01.42.61.09.02
METRO
Bourse

ADDRESS
1 Rue Madame, 6th (Women)
TELEPHONE
01.45.44.28.14
METRO
Saint-Sulpice

ADDRESS
16 Rue de Passy, 16th (Women)
TELEPHONE
01.42.88.20.84
METRO
Passy
OPEN
Mon–Sat, 10:30 a.m.–7 p.m.
CREDIT CARDS
V, AE, MC
$$-$$$

Victoire

ADDRESS
31 Rue Cambon, 1st
TELEPHONE
01.42.86.26.00
METRO
Concorde or Madeleine

ADDRESS
42 Avenue Montaigne, 8th
TELEPHONE
01.47.23.74.12
METRO
Alma-Marçeau

ADDRESS
21 Rue du Faubourg Saint-
Honoré, 8th
TELEPHONE
01.53.05.98.95
METRO
Madeleine
OPEN
Mon–Sat, 10 a.m.–7 p.m.
CREDIT CARDS
V, AE, MC
$$$-$$$$

47. CHANEL
Women's clothes, accessories, makeup

I once read that a vast majority of French women polled said that if they won the lottery they would run out to buy a CHANEL suit. If you are so lucky, you'll find the best service at the Rue Cambon store, right underneath Coco Chanel's apartment, which two decades after her death is as intact as the Chanel couture name.

Designer Karl Lagerfeld continues to revitalize the Chanel line with witty takeoffs on Mlle Chanel's innovations like the little black dress, costume jewelry, pants, and short hair for ladies, easy-to-wear jerseys, Chanel N.5—in short, much of what we take for granted in fashion today.

All the shops are typically crowded, and the Rue Cambon store has moved its makeup and costume jewelry down the staircase in the rear of the store. Even if you haven't won the lottery, make your way toward a classic quilted bag (from 1,000€) or a lipstick, perfume, and a makeup demonstration.

If you do decide on a suit, you'll find it as comfortable as a second skin, it won't become outdated, and as they will tell you in the boutique, "After you have worn this one, Madame, you'll be back every year for another."

Chanel

48. FIFI CHACHNIL
Lingerie

If you ever want to be called "Fifi," you can dress for the part here. Fifi Chachnil (a stage name, of course) has had a thing for the lingerie of the '50s for many successful years now, and her designs in *mousseline* and *charmeuse* (silk and cotton) are for girlie girls who don't just dress to be seen; these are also garments to please the wearer, and are easily worn under a business suit or jeans. The baby doll boutiques are lots of fun, and any monsieur would enjoy them too. Even Madonna shops here. A pack of seven day-of-the-week lace undies is 180€.

ADDRESS
26 Rue Cambon, 1st
TELEPHONE
01.42.60.38.86
METRO
Concorde

ADDRESS
231 Rue Saint Honoré, 1st (in the courtyard)
TELEPHONE
01.42.61.21.83
METRO
Tuilleries

ADDRESS
68 Rue Jean-Jacques-Rousseau, 1st
TELEPHONE
01.42.24.19.93
METRO
Les Halles
OPEN
Mon–Sat, 11 a.m.–7 p.m.
CREDIT CARDS
V, AE, MC
$$$

49. CADOLLE
Made-to-measure lingerie; ready-to-wear lingerie

Ever since Herminie Cadolle invented the bra in 1889, the CADOLLE touch has been devoted to underpinnings that are to sigh for. Chanel and Mata Hari and the dancers of the Crazy Horse Revue have all been shaped here. Now the sixth-generation descendant, Poupie Cadolle, has opened a new appointment-only address for the made-to-measure clientele, a luxurious space where the most sensuous of fabrics are made to give form to the body, the old-fashioned way. Her corsets are coveted eveningwear among the glamorous international crowd, who also comes for lacy bras with just the right lift and panties of all cuts, as well as hand-sewn nighties. This is also a favorite of the hard-to-fit. At the boutique just down the street on Rue Cambon you'll find her ready-to-wear collection of similar pieces.

ADDRESS
255 Rue Saint-Honoré, 1st (made-to-measure)
TELEPHONE
01.42.60.94.94
METRO
Concorde or Tuilleries
OPEN
Mon–Fri, 10 a.m.–1 p.m. & 2–6:30 p.m., by appointment only

ADDRESS
4 Rue Cambon, 1st (Cadolle Boutique)
TELEPHONE
01.42.60.94.22
METRO
Concorde or Tuilleries
OPEN
Mon–Sat, 10 a.m.–6:30 p.m.
CREDIT CARDS
V
$$$-$$$$

ADDRESS
5 Rue de Castiglione, 1st
TELEPHONE
01.42.92.07.22
METRO
Tuileries
OPEN
Mon–Sat, 10 a.m.–7 p.m.
CREDIT CARDS
V, AE, MC
$$$

50. JEAN PATOU
Perfumes and custom scents

The fashions of designer Jean Patou have not been seen since 1982, but his perfumes continue at this new and distinguished address. The elegantly modern boutique is equipped with a perfume bar where uniquely designed testers allow you to experience "Joy" (his greatest success, Joy was introduced after the crash of 1929 to improve the mood of morose Americans), and the new fragrances (1000, Sublime, Enjoy) developed by in-house parfumeur Jean-Michel Duriez. A downstairs workshop is for developing scents for the private client. Whether you come for a made-to-measure perfume and are treated to a private salon, or simply seek a new visual and olfactory experience, you will be warmly welcomed. Products in these fragrances begin with shower gels for 30€.

Jean Patou

51. CATHERINE GIFT
Discount perfumes and cosmetics

From the outside you'd never guess that CATHERINE has among the largest stock in town of the perfumes and cosmetics that no tourist can leave without. The trick is in the revolving-shelf wall that the salesgirl will put into action when you give her your order. Most major scents are offered here (Guerlain, Goutal, and Caron are exceptions) as well as beauty products for 25 percent off French retail (before *détaxe*) and up to 45 percent for purchases of 185€.

Shopping is made easy for Americans here, and you can request to be on the mailing list to continue ordering at these low prices from home and pay in dollars.

ADDRESS
7 Rue de Castiglione, 1st
TELEPHONE
01.42.61.02.89
FAX
01.42.61.02.35
METRO
Tuileries
OPEN
Mon, 11 a.m.–7:30 p.m.;
Tue–Sat, 9:30 a.m.–7:30 p.m.
CREDIT CARDS
V, AE, MC
$$

Along the Way

On the Place Vendome is the HÔTEL RITZ, whose parking lot is built under the cobblestones originally laid for the carriages of Louis XIV. Surrounding this bastion of luxury is a glittering array of fine jewelry houses: REPOSSI, N.6; FRED, N.7; CHAUMET, N.12; MAUBOUSSIN, N.20; VAN CLEEF & ARPELS, N.22; ALEXANDRE REZA, N.23; CARTIER, N.23; BOUCHERON, N.26. A well-kept secret among less conventional Parisians is JARS, upstairs in N.7, where American Joel A. Rosenthal works magic with gold and stones. For the most magnificent fakes since 1927, head directly to BURMA BIJOUX, 16 Rue de la Paix, 2nd.

☕ HÔTEL RITZ
Hôtel Ritz Tea Salon
Ritz-Escoffier Cooking School

ADDRESS
15 Place Vendôme, 1st
TELEPHONE
01.42.60.38.30
01.43.16.30.50 (cooking school)
METRO
Concorde
CREDIT CARDS
V, AE, MC
INTERNET
www.ritzparis.com

This beautiful hotel is still considered to be foremost in the world for its fine service among those who are fortunate enough to stay here, and it is an experience within reach at teatime. The three-course English Tea in the VENDÔME BAR (32.1€) or a cocktail on the terrace provides a welcome respite for the stressed shopper. Gentlemen, a necktie is de rigueur.

You'll want to call to reserve for a cooking demonstration/tasting class by the chefs at the exceptional RITZ-ESCOFFIER COOKING SCHOOL. Entrance to the school is at 38 Rue Cambon. Be sure to pick up information about the full range of cooking programs available or check the école link on their website (ritzparis.com).

While you're here, don't miss the shopping gallery down the wing to the right of the main hotel entrance, where display cases present a sampling from many nearby boutiques.

ADDRESS
17 Rue de la Paix, 2nd
TELEPHONE
01.42.61.74.44
METRO
Opéra
OPEN
Mon–Sat, 10 a.m.–6:45 p.m.
CREDIT CARDS
V, AE, MC
$$-$$$

52. COMPTOIR SUD PACIFIQUE
Beach and sun wear for men and women

Oh, what a Parisian concept: to live like you're vacationing in sun and sea when you're stuck in town. COMPTOIR SUD calls itself an evasion tactic. Come here in the summer and you'll find linens and cottons, and in the winter, knits and heavier cottons. Everything is in terrific colors (at this moment, orange, turquoise, and fuschia) from swimsuits and trunks, to men's pants and shirts, to sundresses, purses and beach bags, along with the appropriate accessories and toiletries.

Comptoir Sud Pacifique

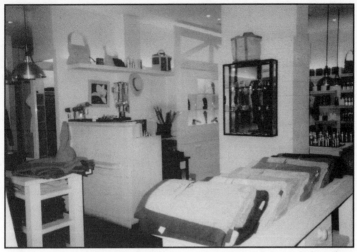

Comptoir Sud Pacifique

☕ CAFÉ DE LA PAIX
Cafe/Brasserie

ADDRESS
12 Boulevard des Capucines, 9th
TELEPHONE
01.40.07.36.36
METRO
Opéra
OPEN
Daily, noon–12:30 a.m.
CARDS
V, AE, MC, DC
$$-$$$

This elegant establishment was designed by Garnier, who also did the nearby opera house. Recently renovated, it is still a standout in *belle époque* style.

ADDRESS
40 Boulevard Haussemann, 9th
TELEPHONE
01.42.82.34.56
METRO
Chaussée d'Antin
OPEN
Mon–Wed & Fri–Sat, 9:30
a.m.–7:30 p.m.; Thur, 9:30
a.m.–9 p.m.
CREDIT CARDS
V, AE, MC
$$-$$$

53. GALERIES LAFAYETTE

Department store

Department store shopping in Paris has even less ambiance than in the States, and is a vivid contrast to the charm and service of Parisian boutiques. But it can offer the hurried traveler an overview of the major French labels and brands (helpful in deciding which boutiques to visit after leaving), as well as one-stop shopping, shipping, and a tax refund on the purchase total.

When I have dreams about shopping, I'm always in GALERIES LAFAYETTE. In no other Parisian department store is the merchandise as upscale as here, where 100,000 customers a day come to search out wardrobes, household goods, and gourmet foods.

Aimless wanderers can lose an entire day here. So come when the doors open and you're feeling fresh. It becomes so crowded by noon (all day on Saturdays) that you'll have trouble moving through the throngs and won't even notice the outstanding belle époque architecture.

If you plan to take advantage of the *détaxe* in addition to your 10 percent tourist discount be sure to spend over 175.01€ to qualify. Take your sales receipts and passport to the tourist tax refund (*détaxe*) office located on the mezzanine of the ground floor of the main store (Lafayette Coupole). Expect a wait of at least 20 minutes here. Select a method of reimbursement. You will then be issued a tax refund form (*bordereau de détaxe*) consisting of two sheets to be signed by the retailer and yourself. The person to whom the purchases are charged must be present when the tax refund form is issued. Purchases made at the store's Louis Vuitton boutique cannot be cumulated with other purchases from Galeries Lafayette.

The Galeries is really 110 departments in adjoining buildings. The store caters to Americans, and you can get help in English at the welcome desk, as well as a 10 percent discount card available only to tourists. If it's fashion you're after, you may attend weekly runway shows (telephone 01.48.74.02.30 to reserve a seat), or even put yourself in the highly capable hands of Mode Plus, a complimentary in-store service that will outfit you in keeping with your budget and personal style.

You're in the thick of French designers here, with a vast choice of both couture and avant-garde names on the first and second floors, many shown in their own mini-boutiques. If it's hot, you'll find it here, from the lower price ranges (their own stylish knockoff lines) to a main-floor Chanel boutique.

The main floor is a fertile hunting ground for presents (perfumes, leather goods, scarves, etc.). But don't miss children's wear, bed and table linens, housewares (you'll find Baccarat, etc., in the basement), and the very large gourmet food department with gold shopping carts and capped bellhops.

Menswear is in the neighboring Galfa Club building, and every *maman* in Paris knows about the high-styled children's clothes (and more) in the moderately priced MONOPRIX next door.

Galeries Lafayette's rival department store, PRINTEMPS, is located across the street at 64 Boulevard Hausseman. Similar in service and offerings, the store has been redone in an American look. Its new beauty department claims to be the largest venue for perfume-cosmetics and makeup in Paris, if not the world, and the luxury department is a venue for side-by-side comparisons of the top names in jewelry (Chanel, Bulgari, etc.), accessories, and bags. A LADURÉE restaurant is on the same floor.

54. REPETTO
Dancewear and ballet and street shoes

Ballerinas from all over Paris, from the prima ballerinas and *les petits rats* (youngest ballerinas) of the nearby Opéra Garnier to Angelina mouse-size preschoolers come to REPETTO for their toe shoes and tutus. And now that Repetto has begun making the same slippers with soles for streetwear, this line is all the rage for the rest of us, too.

Founded by the mother of famed choreographer Roland Petit fifty years ago, Repetto offers its own lines of everything for the dancer, beginning with ballet slippers and the pink Satin Opéra toe shoe (in sizes 6 to 24, medium width) considered to be the most supple, lightweight, and silent available. If you have a dedicated ballerina at home with a hard-to-fit foot, you may consider bringing an

ADDRESS
22 Rue de la Paix, 2nd
TELEPHONE
01.44.71.83.20
METRO
Opéra
HOURS
Mon–Sat, 10 a.m.–7 p.m.(store); Mon–Sat, 9 a.m.–6 p.m. (custom workshop)
CREDIT CARDS
V
$$

imprint to the custom workshop for a tailor-made toe shoe, available in ten days. For the smallest ballerina, what could be a greater inspiration than a hot pink four-skirted tutu?

Besides the scores of dance shoe styles, there are leotards, gymnastics attire, sweaters, and Repetto signature towels for the cooldown.

ADDRESS
28 Place Vendôme, 1st
TELEPHONE
01.42.60.30.70
FAX
01.42.96.27.07
METRO
Opéra or Tuileries
OPEN
Mon–Sat, 10 a.m.–6:45 p.m.
CREDIT CARDS
V, AE
$$$-$$$$

55. CHARVET
Men's shirts, neckwear, suits, women's shirts

The gentlemanly tradition is in good form at CHARVET, where meticulous souls as diverse as Proust, Chanel, and de Gaulle have been coming for tailored clothing since 1838. The philosophy here, to offer the greatest choice possible, may send you reeling if you don't enlist the counsel of the well-trained staff. The 1,000 *prêt-à-porter* models (from 210€) with fifty collars and fifteen cuff styles may be worn with your choice of hundreds of necktie designs, each available in twenty to sixty colorways (100 to 110€). The array is astounding and the standards are the highest.

Even the shirts are made one by one and are proudly touted to be as beautiful inside as out. If you opt for a custom shirt (no minimum) the

Charvet

tailors will have you choose from their 6,000 rolls of the finest shirting cottons and take no fewer than 25 measurements, requiring one fitting the following week (from 300€). Your particulars will be kept in copious client files (no computers here!) and in the future you may request fabric samples and place orders by mail.

For women, shirts come in three sizes, 60 colors, and many models (210€), including silks in styles Chanel herself wore.

For an elegant gift for a man, you can't go wrong with the trademark silk-knot cuff links (36€ for three pairs in a suede pouch, any colors) to versions in gold and silver. Charvet neckwear now rivals Hermès as a symbol of status at a lower price. There are suede slippers ready-to-travel in a bag; and the house blend of silk and cashmere is fashioned into scarves, polos, and robes.

56. PIERRE BARBOZA
Antique jewelry

The exterior is quite ordinary, but the antique jewels inside are of excellent quality and at reasonable prices, an unbeatable combination in the estimation of my French friends who have long relied on the honesty and good taste of the owners. You may tell M and Mme Gribe (the daughter of the original Barboza) in English what you want and depend on them to find it for you. The specialty here is nineteenth-century jewelry from 100€ to 5,000€, and the shop is also known for restyling tired looks like no one else.

ADDRESS
356 Rue St-Honoré, 1st
TELEPHONE
01.42.60.67.08
METRO
Tuileries
OPEN
Mon–Sat, 10 a.m.–1 p.m. &
2:30–6 p.m.
CREDIT CARDS
V, AE
$$-$$$

Pierre Barboza

ADDRESS
235 Rue St-Honoré, 1st
TELEPHONE
01.42.61.41.34
METRO
Tuileries or Concorde or Opéra
OPEN
Mon–Sat, 10:30 a.m.–7 p.m.
CREDIT CARDS
V, AE
$$$

57. ALEXANDRE DE PARIS
Hair ornaments

If you're looking for something to decorate your locks that's a bit more extraordinary than the department store offerings, you'll be overwhelmed with the three floors of bands, barrettes, bows, and combs at ALEXANDRE. These "jewels for the hair" as they're called here, are all handmade in France and Italy exclusively for Alexandre. The finest are embroidered by renowned Lesage, with the simplest velvet or raw silk bands from about 30€.

Take the spiral staircase in back to the third-floor bridal selection of bows, roses, and exquisitely veiled head pieces, all in white. If the choices at Alexandre don't fit your lifestyle, head for your corner *parfumerie* (perfume and cosmetics store) or for the large selection downstairs at GALERIES LAFAYETTES.

ADDRESS
233 Rue St-Honoré, 1st
TELEPHONE
01.42.60.57.04
METRO
Tuilleries or Concorde or
Opéra
OPEN
Mon–Sat, 10 a.m.–7 p.m.
CREDIT CARDS
V, AE, MC
$$$$

58. GOYARD
Leather goods and luggage

One of the city's oldest and most exclusive addresses for luggage, GOYARD is where to come when your own initials are enough. A family-run business since 1853, fifth-generation owner Isabelle Goyard continues to offer a luxurious collection of leather luggage, with the addition of a line in plastified canvas in their trademark design of gray and gold herringbone. The leather desk accessories, handbags, and toiletry bags are classics, and the dog collars are just the thing for the pooch who has everything.

59. JEAN-PAUL HÉVIN
Chocolates, tea room

Master chocolatier Jean-Paul Hévin (sounds like "heaven") has several chocolate/pastry shops around town, but this is the only one with a tea room. His contemporary interiors, warmly dark like his chocolates, are only the first evidence of his outstanding presentations. Not to be missed by the chocolate connoisseur.

ADDRESS
231 Rue St-Honoré, 1st
TELEPHONE
01.55.35.35.96
METRO
Tuileries or Concorde or Opéra
OPEN
Shop: Mon–Sat, 10 a.m.–7:30 p.m.; Closed 2nd week in Aug.; *Tea Room:* Mon–Sat, noon–7 p.m.; Closed Aug.
CREDIT CARDS
V, AE, MC, DC
$$$

60. COLETTE
Clothes, cosmetics, gadgets, books and magazines, water bar and restaurant

This is *the* boutique in Paris for trend spotters. There's always a crowd here, and the place is full of design, from fashion on the main floor to everything else downstairs. Though the goodies here come from all over the world, the merchandising is uniquely COLETTE, Paris.

ADDRESS
213 Rue St-Honoré, 1st
TELEPHONE
01.55.35.33.99
METRO
Tuileries
OPEN
Mon–Sat, 11 a.m.–7 p.m.
CREDIT CARDS
V, AE, MC
$$$

ADDRESS
211 Rue St-Honoré, 1st
TELEPHONE
01.42.60.40.56
METRO
Tuileries
OPEN
Mon–Sat, 11 a.m.–7 p.m.
CREDIT CARDS
V, AE, MC
$$-$$$

61. CHANTAL THOMASS
Lingerie

Chantal Thomass is at home in her new shades-of-pink boudoir. The ultra-feminine stylist has come into the twenty-first century with the ultimate marriage of frou-frou and contemporary in this boutique to show off her seductive indoors outfits. Downstairs you'll find quick pick-me-ups like heeled slippers, sexy stockings, swimsuits, and her pink-and-black umbrellas. Take the staircase up for the pleasure of seeing and trying the lacy black corsets (150€ to 1,300€) and little pink nothings for which she is so well known.

Chantal Thomass

62. CACHEMIRE CRÈME

Cashmere clothing for men, women, and children, and home accessories

For a fresh take on the old twin set, etc., see what they do here with British cashmere and French styling. The cuts are original and the colors just right. These are classics given a modern touch: from the oversized cashmere rose cum brooche (20€) to jackets (men's and women's), dresses, and keen little baby clothes as well as variations on the sweater idea for everyone.

ADDRESS
10 Rue du Marché St-Honoré, 1st
TELEPHONE
01.42.92.05.50
METRO
Pyramids
OPEN
Mon, 11 a.m.–7:30 p.m.;
Tue–Sat, 10:30 a.m.–7:30 p.m.
CREDIT CARDS
V, AE, MC
$$-$$$

Cachemire Crème

63. PHILIPPE MODEL

Women's hats and shoes

Creative designer boutiques have come and gone on the calm and fertile Place du Marché, but PHILIPPE MODEL has held his territory over time. Best known for his wildly imaginative headgear, his hats are always a sensation at the Prix de Diane horse races and are toned down only a little for more discreet ceremonial occasions. This is a chic address for custom orders (from 300€). You'll also find here shoes, belts, gloves, and purses.

ADDRESS
33 Place du Marché St-Honoré, 1st
TELEPHONE
01.40.20.96.12
METRO
Tuileries
OPEN
Mon–Sat, 10 a.m.–7 p.m.
CREDIT CARDS
V, AE, MC
$$$

ADDRESS
37 Avenue de L'Opéra, 2nd
TELEPHONE
01.42.61.52.50
FAX
01.42.61.07.61
METRO
Opéra or Pyramides
OPEN
Mon–Sat, 10 a.m.–7:30 p.m.
CREDIT CARDS
V, AE, MC
$$

64. BRENTANO'S
Books and magazines

BRENTANO'S bills itself as "The American Bookstore in Paris since 1895," and it is indeed an institution for Americans here. A favorite venue for American cultural activities that include frequent author readings, it is also an historic home for a huge number of volumes in both French and English. You'll find all the bestsellers from the U.S. and Britain here, a large selection of travel guides, magazines from around Europe and back home, and the usual bookstore departments. This lovely old building is a place to wander as well as shop. Discount cards are available for frequent purchases in English.

Brentano's

☕ CAFÉ RUC
Café/restaurant

ADDRESS
159 Rue St-Honoré, 1st
TELEPHONE
01.42.60.97.54
METRO
Louvre or Palais-Royal
OPEN
Daily, 8 a.m.–2 p.m.
CREDIT CARDS
V, AE, MC, DC
$$

This is a fine spot, both indoors and on the terrace, when you need a quick meal in that busy area between the Opéra, the Louvre, and Palais Royal. It's done by the Costes brothers, a restaurant duo who uphold a certain standard. Once you're settled, you may not want to get up from your red velvet chair.

Along the Way

The RUE DE RIVOLI is one of the most crowded, tourist-driven streets in Paris, but can hardly be avoided as it runs along the back side of the LOUVRE MUSEUM and TUILERIES GARDENS up to the PLACE DE LA CONCORDE. Its sheltering arcades can even be welcoming on a drizzly day, particularly if you're battling for a taxi. On a sunny day, don't miss the opportunity to detour through the gardens. Among the dozens of similar small shops announcing duty-free in their windows, you'll find a few worth a stop.

65. W. H. SMITH
Bookstore

ADDRESS
248 Rue de Rivoli, 1st
TELEPHONE
01.44.77.88.99
METRO
Concorde
OPEN
Mon–Sat, 9 a.m.–7:30 p.m.;
Sun, 1–7:30 p.m.
CREDIT CARDS
V, AE, MC
$$

The largest English-language bookstore in France, all the best British, French, and English magazines are to be found here, along with thousands of books in English. This British-based store is one of the oldest in Paris to serve the English-reading public. The former tearoom space on the second floor now displays coffee-table books. There is a children's book section, a large travel section, and even a room for the French to read about travel in the United States and Britain.

ADDRESS
244 Rue de Rivoli, 1st
TELEPHONE
01.42.60.76.15
METRO
Concorde
OPEN
Mon–Sat, 10 a.m.–7 p.m.
CREDIT CARDS
V, AE, MC
$$-$$$

66. DENISE FRANCELLE

Gloves for men and women, scarves, handkerchiefs, and hosiery

Mme Denise Francelle has been here since 1938, when this stretch of the arcades of the Rue de Rivoli housed many such *gantiers* (glovesellers). Among the competitive tourist trade that lines the street today, this establishment does business as it always has, taking care to size properly and search out just the right glove from the tremendous inventory kept beneath the shop.

You'll find gloves for every occasion here, from classic to fantasy designs, from driving gloves to handpearled elbow gloves, even mink cuffs. Because Mme Francelle has been buying for so long, you can find here many styles not available elsewhere, still at the original prices. And if it's not in her inventory, she will make to measure in any color. No wonder she has generations of repeat customers.

ADDRESS
232 Rue de Rivoli, 1st
TELEPHONE
01.42.60.71.83
FAX
01.42.60.33.76
METRO
Concorde or Tuileries
OPEN
Daily, 10:30 a.m.–6:30 p.m.
CREDIT CARDS
V, AE, MC
$-$$$
INTERNET
www.limogesmarechal.com

67. MARÉCHAL

Limoges boxes and souvenirs

Go directly downstairs for the hand-painted Limoges porcelain boxes that are so varied and collectible, and so well-priced here. This forty-year-old establishment claims to have the largest selection in France, including copies of traditional designs as well as new ones, beginning at 45€. The Limoges factory produces the gamut of theme box shapes in white ceramic, and sells them to only a handful of artists authorized to decorate to Limoges' standard. Each is an individual work of art. On weekdays here, there is an artist authorized to personalize your piece.

Be sure to be added to the mailing list for the bi-annual brochure, which pictures a new group with the pricing in dollars, including U.S. delivery—a bargain compared to what you would pay back home. There is also a fine range of tourist trinkets that make thoughtful but inexpensive gifts; perhaps the Eiffel Tower keychain at 4€. You can now order from the website.

Maréchal

 ANGELINA

Tea room

ADDRESS
226 Rue de Rivoli, 1st
TELEPHONE
01.42.60.82.00
METRO
Tuileries
OPEN
Daily, 9 a.m.–7 p.m.
CREDIT CARDS
V, AE, MC
$$

This beautiful and beloved tea room is long-favored by children from the turn of the century. The same, now-grown grandes dames, are seated amid the marble, murals, and mirrors, *en tête-à-tête* with friends or grandchildren. It is equally popular with fashion models who retreat here after couture shows nearby and with shoppers wishing to escape the modern hordes. The famous hot chocolate is so rich that it shouldn't be consumed before noon.

ADDRESS
224 Rue de Rivoli, 1st
TELEPHONE
01.42.60.76.07
METRO
Tuileries
OPEN
Mon–Sat, 10 a.m.–7 p.m.
CREDIT CARDS
V, AE, MC
$$$

68. GALIGNANI
Bookstore

A classic bookstore, GALIGNANI has been handed down from father to son since 1805. Though it is French, there is quite a selection of English and American books and an impressive collection of international art books. The beautiful interior naturally draws the book lover, and it is known as a very pleasant place to browse.

ADDRESS
206 Rue de Rivoli, 1st
TELEPHONE
01.42.60.51.17
FAX
01.42.61.63.82
METRO
Tuileries
OPEN
Mon–Sat, 10 a.m.–7 p.m.;
Sun, 11 a.m.–7 p.m.
CREDIT CARDS
V, AE, MC
$$-$$$

69. GAULT
Architectural miniatures

If you've always dreamed of a French period home built to old-world standards of craftsmanship, you'll find the practical answer here. The miniature ceramic homes and buildings entirely handmade by M Gault's southern French workshops follow the architectural detailing of various regions of France. Each is carved from raw clay, sculpted, fired, and painted individually, and like the real thing, promises to last centuries. Moreover, they are portable and affordable (dream homes from 38 to 380€). You may want a tiny French bakery, or to put together an entire Alsatian village or your favorite neighborhood in Paris. GAULT also does specific buildings to order. Any of these highly detailed recreations make terrific gifts. Fax for the catalog to order from home.

ADDRESS
105–107 Rue de Rivoli, 1st
TELEPHONE
01.42.60.64.94
METRO
Palais-Royal or Tuileries or
Pyramides
OPEN
Daily, 10 a.m.–7 p.m.

70. 107 RIVOLI
Boutique of the Decorative Arts Museum

This stop is a must for those who love fashion and the decorative arts, even if you're not staying to see the museum exhibits. The entrance to the new boutique (and museum) is indicated only by the street sign 107 RIVOLI. Inside the gift shop you'll find the best of the best in table arts, games and toys, stylish accessories, and the latest in jewelry, the finest books on the decorative arts, and exciting paper goods.

107 Rivoli

CREDIT CARDS
V, AE, MC
$$-$$$

☕ CAFÉ MARLY
Café and restaurant

ADDRESS
Cour Napoléon, 93 Rue de Rivoli, 1st
TELEPHONE
01.49.26.06.60
METRO
Palais-Royal
OPEN
Daily, 8 a.m.–2 a.m.
CREDIT CARDS
V, AE, MC, DC
$$

Located in the heart of Paris, overlooking the glass pyramid in the central courtyard of the Louvre, CAFÉ MARLY is a choice spot for a rendezvous. Even if you're not visiting the museum, you will want to linger over a drink on the terrace as all of Paris walks by, or take a light lunch in the sumptuous interior restaurant. Enter from the courtyard, Cour Napoléon.

ADDRESS
25 Rue des Pyramides, 1st
TELEPHONE
08.92.68.30.00 (special rate)
METRO
Pyramides
OPEN
Daily, 10 a.m.–7 p.m.
INTERNET
www.parisinfo.com

71. PARIS OFFICE DE TOURISME
Paris Office of Tourism

If you're still without a hotel room for the night or
need yet more tourist information, stop by the Office
of Tourism for the city of Paris. You can also access
them from home for help in planning your trip by
Internet, www.parisinfo.com. They give out free city
maps and sell guidebooks in English as well as gifts.

ADDRESS
2 Place du Palais-Royal, 1st
TELEPHONE
01.42.97.27.27
METRO
Palais-Royal or Louvre
OPEN
Tue–Sun, 11 a.m.–7 p.m.
CREDIT CARDS
V, AE, MC
$$$-$$$$
INTERNET
www.louvre-antiquaires.com

72. LE LOUVRE DES ANTIQUAIRES
Antiques

Probably the world's most-shopped antiques center,
this cooperative of 250 highly reputable dealers is
spread over three floors, providing civilized mall
shopping, complete with shipping agent and a
good restaurant (LE JARDIN DU LOUVRE). Amid
fine furniture and furnishings from every century
and continent you may get carried away, but you
won't get taken in, as these dealers represent the
most scrupulous and scrutinized in the trade. Each
piece is sold with a certificate of guarantee, and the
prices reflect it. On a rainy Sunday you'll hardly
find a better activity than to take a program and
wander the booths. Many of the dealers have Left
Bank shops with lower price tags. Pick up their
business cards if you're interested in their specialty.
You may also explore them on the Internet at
www.louvre-antiquaires.com.

Along the Way

Tranquil PALAIS-ROYAL was childhood home to Louis XIV, who nearly drowned in
the garden fountains, as every French student learns. Today, you may see children
playing hockey on roller skates in the palace courtyard. After centuries of ill repute,
the elegant quadrangle with the palace at one end, arcades along the three sides, and
gardens in the center is experiencing a renaissance with shops at ground level and
sought-after apartments above.

Colette wrote *Paris from My Window* from her own window overlooking the gardens, in the apartment now inhabited by decorator par excellence Jacques Grange. The Ministry of Culture offices are here, and resident Palais-Royalists feel they live at the most fortunate address in Paris.

73. LES DRAPEAUX DE FRANCE
Toy soldiers

Little boys press their noses to these windows to get a better view of the armies of thousands of soldiers on display in this phone-booth-size shop. Foot soldiers from most any Western war are 23€, with cavaliers at 39€.

Nearby is A. MARIE STUART (N.3, 4 & 5 Galerie Montpensier), a fourth-generation family shop selling civil and military decorations. Any *parvenu* can come here to purchase a *croix de guerre* for 1,817€. Just a few steps away are BACQUEVILLE (N.7 & 8) and RENÉ ANDRÉ (N.4) with like-minded inventories.

ADDRESS
13,14,15 Galerie Montpensier, 1st
TELEPHONE
01.42.97.55.40
METRO
Palais-Royal
OPEN
Mon–Sat, 10 a.m.–7 p.m.
CREDIT CARDS
AE
$$

74. DIDIER LUDOT
Vintage couture clothing, shoes, leather goods

This is where Parisians come to find their original Hermès "Kelly" bags, reworked crocodile luggage, stiletto heels that really are from the '50s, and their postwar-era Chanel suits. DIDIER LUDOT is the city's prime vendor of couture clothing and leather goods from the '20s through the '90s, and the racks are filled with labels like Dior, Grès, Balmain, and Jacques Fath at prices beginning under 150€.

If you've never done secondhand shopping, keep in mind that the evening gowns and daywear that may look a bit worn carry a great mystique and

ADDRESS
19–20 Galerie Montpensier, 1st (Couture)
23–24 Galerie Montpensier, 1st (Accessories and ready-to-wear)
125 Galerie de Valois (LA PETITE ROBE NOIRE)
TELEPHONE AND FAX
01.42.96.06.56
METRO
Palais-Royal
OPEN
Mon–Sat, 11 a.m.–7 p.m.
CREDIT CARDS
V, AE
$$-$$$

La Petite Robe Noire

simply cannot be had new. The hand-bags and luggage, also bearing grand labels and often from exotic materials, are reconditioned to endure.

His other venture, LA PETITE ROBE NOIRE, is devoted to that Parisian icon, the little black dress. A selection of vintage black dresses as well as a new collection by Ludot is available here, just across the gardens. Half-sizes may be ordered.

 MUSCADE
Tea salon, restaurant

ADDRESS
36 Rue de Montpensier, 1st
TELEPHONE
01.42.97.51.36
METRO
Palais-Royal
OPEN
Summer: Tue–Sat, 10 a.m.–10:30 p.m.;
Winter: Tue–Sat, 10 a.m.–8:30 p.m.
$$

This lovely spot overlooking the gardens is a pleasant place of respite for the busy shopper. The menu offers both Mediterranean and Breton specialties, and the delicious pastries are made on the premises.

75. LA BOUTIQUE DU PALAIS-ROYAL
Toys

Handcrafted toys, many of the sort meant to sit on your child's shelf forever, are here. The owner, Mme Baret, is influenced by the nearby Comédie Française (the French National Theater) to seek out those that add drama and originality to her shelves.

The marionettes by Jacques Picard in Provence are outstanding—especially the two-foot-tall Puss in Boots with a painted face, knitted collars, and velour hat (185€). Toy-happy adults will want to see the never-used pens from the '30s and '40s.

ADDRESS
9 Rue de Beaujolais, 1st
TELEPHONE
01.42.60.08.22
METRO
Palais-Royal
OPEN
Mon, 11 a.m.–7 p.m.;
Tue–Sat, 10 a.m.–7 p.m.
CREDIT CARDS
V, AE
$$-$$$

La Boutique du Palais-Royal

ADDRESS
9 Rue de Beaujolais, 1st
TELEPHONE
01.42.96.55.13
METRO
Palais-Royal
OPEN
Mon–Sat, 11 a.m.–7 p.m.
CREDIT CARDS
V, MC
$-$$$

76. ANNA JOLIET
Music boxes

You might miss this tiny shop if not for the magical sounds floating out its door. Inside is a huge variety of music boxes for all ages and pocketbooks, with origins from Switzerland to Japan. From the simplest transparent square playing Mozart to elaborate antique instruments with new interior workings, ANNA JOLIET offers them all, making this shop an attraction for the collector as well as a gift stop for the smallest child.

Along the Way

Continue on the GALERIE DE VALOIS for more notable boutiques. Be sure to step into the poetic decor at LES SALONS DU PALAIS ROYAL SHISEIDO (N.142), an exotic perfume house whose spicy oriental fragrances are made in France and sold exclusively at this address; and stop in at L'ÉCLAIREUR, where the space is as well designed as its top-notch creations of ready-to-wear and accessories for both sexes.

☕ RESTAURANT DU PALAIS ROYAL

ADDRESS
110 Galérie de Valois, 1st
TELEPHONE
01.40.20.00.27
METRO
Palais-Royal
OPEN
Mon–Sat, noon–2:30 p.m. & 7:30–10:30 p.m.;
Closed Sunday
$$

On most days, tables are set up in the Palais-Royal gardens, where you can spend a happy hour with a flute of champagne or over an open-air meal that can go courses beyond a typical picnic. This is a lovely spot to enjoy some sun and a cup of coffee. In wet weather everything moves indoors to a modern setting.

If you're in the mood for something more historical, head toward LE GRAND VEFOUR (N.17 Rue de Beaujolais), one of the city's finest and most beautiful restaurants, where famous names have feasted and conversed since the days when Napoleon dined here with Josephine. Call ahead for reservations, months ahead would be best (01.42.96.56.27).

77. LE PRINCE JARDINIER
Garden attire, decoration, and supplies

The Prince de Broglie opened a shop devoted to
his hobby, which has become the last word for
those who dress for and dress up their gardens.
Everything for the royal gardener is here: stylish
gardening clothing in heavy, beautifully colored
cotton solids and stripes that you'll even want to
wear in town; hats and gardening bags of all sizes
to match garden shoes; all of the above for men
and women with the discreet house logo; also pots,
garden tools, and picnic wear.

ADDRESS
117–121 Arcade Valois, 1st
TELEPHONE
01.42.60.37.13
METRO
Palais-Royal
OPEN
Mon–Sat, 10:30 a.m.–7 p.m.
CREDIT CARDS
V, MC
$$-$$$

Le Prince Jardinier

78. DELAGE
Shoes for men and women, gloves

These sumptuous shoes, handmade in Brittany, are
grand classics to begin with. When you execute
them in exotic leathers and vibrant colors, they
verge on the decadent. The family-run business is
willing to work with you and will make up any
color, in skins that range from calf to stingray, igua-
na, and ostrich. The fun comes with their ability to
mix skins and colors in one classic shoe. Off-the-
shelf prices begin at 300€. Or consider a conservative orange pump made from a single crocodile
hide for 2,000€. The golf shoe here, made with
mixed skins (1,200€), will certainly add some punch
to your swing. Superb gloves at 180€.

ADDRESS
159–161 Galerie de Valois
TELEPHONE
01.40.15.97.24
METRO
Palais-Royal
OPEN
Mon & Sat, 10:30 a.m.–1 p.m.
& 2–6:30 p.m.; Tue–Fri, 10:30
a.m.–6:00 p.m.
CREDIT CARDS
V, AE, MC
$$$-$$$$

Along the Way

Before leaving Palais-Royal you might stop by BEL GAZOU (N.5, Rue des Petits-Champs), an old-fashioned magazine shop given the nickname of Colette's daughter, to pick up photo-reproduction postcards of an older Paris and writing pens. The owners promise to procure for you any book in Paris within forty-eight hours of your order.

ADDRESS
5 Rue des Petits-Champs, 1st
TELEPHONE
01.42.86.00.88
METRO
Palais-Royal
OPEN
Mon–Sat, 10:30 a.m.–7 p.m.
CREDIT CARDS
V, AE
$$-$$$

79. SMALL IS BEAUTIFUL
Children's clothes

This adorable little boutique is almost as small as the clothing sold inside, made for boys and girls ages three through nine. But wait, there's something even more miniscule that the little girls will adore: with each dress comes a tiny mannequin wearing the same outfit, knitted. Even the life-size clothes are quite special, from the T-shirts (30€) to hand-pearled dresses (318€).

☕ WILLI'S WINE BAR

ADDRESS
13 Rue des Petits-Champs, 1st
TELEPHONE
01.42.61.05.09
METRO
Palais-Royal or Bourse or Pyramides
OPEN
Mon–Sat, noon–3 p.m. & 7–11 p.m. (bar open until midnight)
CREDIT CARDS
V, MC
$$

When the wine is as important as the company, a rendezvous over a carafe at the corner café just won't do. The Parisian who wants to pick and choose his vintage from small production wines to familiar favorites will go to a wine bar to taste and test. There he can order by the bottle or glass from quality house selections, often hand-picked by the bar owner at the vineyard and shipped in barrels directly to the bar.

At WILLI'S, among the most popular and elegant of these *bars à vins*, Englishman Mark Williamson will help you choose from 300 labels the bottle that is perfectly attuned to your entree or salad.

On the Rue Vivienne (N.4) is LE GRAND COLBERT, a classic brasserie beautifully restored and so typical it is a frequent movie set, open daily until 1 a.m. A bit farther at N.13 is a new concept truffle and wine bar, UN JOUR À PEYRASSOL, where you can order a truffle plate and glass of wine from this southern region of France (or the menu du jour, 15€), in a charming setting of stone and wood recalling their origins; open Mon–Fri, 10 a.m. to 7 p.m. A regional boutique is attached.

80. JEAN-PAUL GAULTIER
Women's and men's clothing

Certainly one of the most provocative Paris designers, at times the most outrageous, GAULTIER is
favored by Madonna, and both personify a modern
version of the baroque esthetic.

Whether or not you would be comfortable in
Gaultier, his past collections have pointed toward
the future of fashion and a peek into his boutique
promises to be a trip to another planet or a brilliant
vision of the future, depending on your sensibili-
ties; either way it's fun and well worth it. You'll be
surrounded by videos of his latest collection
(they're even set into the Pompeiian tile floor), and
metal manequins, reminding you that Gaultier is
out to create the future on the ruins of our past.
He's a designer who knows his history, being classically trained by Cardin and Patou, and has even
received the coveted French Fashion Oscar.

ADDRESS
6 Rue Vivienne, 2nd (enter
from the street)
TELEPHONE
01.42.86.05.05
METRO
Bourse
OPEN
Mon–Fri, 10 a.m.–7 p.m.;
Sat, 11 a.m.–7 p.m.

ADDRESS
44 Avenue Georges V, 8th
TELEPHONE
01.44.43.00.44
METRO
Georges V
OPEN
Mon–Sat, 10:30 a.m.–7 p.m.
CREDIT CARDS
V, AE, MC, DC
$$$-$$$$

Along the Way

The GALERIE VIVIENNE is a smartly renovated glass-vaulted shopping arcade,
where traditional proprietors are almost outnumbered by fashionable new boutiques.
Under the arched glass skylight at A PRIORI THE (N.35-37 Galerie Vivienne) is a
charming spot to sit with tea and brownie, a light lunch, or weekend brunch. Go
next door to EMILIO ROBBA (N.29) to see the best in fantasy or realistic artificial
flowers, some sold in uniquely designed vases. Just across at N.18 is WOLFF ET
DESCOURTIS where you can find extraordinary hand-detailed scarves and shawls of
silk, wool, velvet, or cashmere, many sumptuously embroidered or printed. Fabrics
are also sold by the meter. Farther down at N.68 is SI TU VEUX, a charming and
well-priced toy shop that any child would find irresistible. You would be sure to find
a young gift here. A super-stylish eyeglass frame shop, TRACTION, is at N.56.

Among the Galerie Vivienne's original tenants are DOMINIQUE ET FRANÇOIS
JOUSSEAUME (N.45-47), a warmly wooded book and prints shop with merchan-
dise that has been obtained anytime since 1826, and LEGRAND FILLE ET FILS
(N.1, but for the full effect of its nineteenth-century storefront go around to N.1 Rue
de la Banque), where the all-time bestseller is a little gingerbread pig sold as a good-
luck charm among bins of hard candy and shelves of wine bottles and preserves.

ADDRESS
39–41 Galerie Vivienne, 2nd
TELEPHONE
01.42.60.46.85
METRO
Bourse
OPEN
Mon–Sat, 11 a.m.–7 p.m.

ADDRESS
27 Boulevard Raspail, 6th
TELEPHONE
01.45.48.30.97
METRO
Rue du Bac
OPEN
Mon, 3–7 p.m.; Tue–Sat, 11
a.m.–2 p.m. & 3–7 p.m.

ADDRESS
58 Avenue Paul-Doumer, 16th
TELEPHONE
01.45.03.42.75
METRO
Muette
OPEN
Mon, 2–7 p.m.; Tue–Sat,
11 a.m.–7 p.m.
CREDIT CARDS
V, AE
$$

81. CASA LOPEZ
Rugs and needlepoint pillows

You will recognize the ravishing Casa Lopez petit point pillows at finely decorated addresses all around town since Mme Lopez brought them back into style. Her romantic raised designs of bows, florals, traditional Victorian and Greek patterns, and geometrics are woven by hand (except for certain carpeting) in her Portuguese workshop supplied with 90 shades of threads. The technique is ancient, dating from the Renaissance when the threads were embroidered onto fishnets.

Rugs are now the focus here in her ever-so-stylish designs, done in wool, quilted or woven, but also in jute, woven leather, and printed velours. All can be customized to decorating perfection with cute little rugs beginning at 60€. You can purchase a cushion cover, or needlepoint an identical one at home with a Casa Lopez kit (77€).

Along the Way

The PLACE DES VICTOIRES is prime real estate for fashion-forward boutiques whose designs have been termed avant-garde anytime from the recent past to the near future. Many of these designers are established, but certainly not passé. It's also a hunting ground for wardrobe shoppers eager for a bird's-eye view of the coming season.

ADDRESS
3 Place Des Victoires, 1st
TELEPHONE
01.42.33.86.22
METRO
Bourse or Louvre or Rivoli
OPEN
Mon–Sat, 10:45 a.m.–7 p.m.
CREDIT CARDS
V, AE, MC
$$-$$$

82. ATELIER MERCADAL
Men's and women's shoes, purses

Come here for shoes that are stylish and well-made but not terribly expensive. Most are between 165 and 200€. For men, they are of the narrow-toed European sort.

83. CLAUDIE PIERLOT
Women's clothes

A member of the fashion school of discretion, CLAUDIE PIERLOT offers a preppy look with charm. A few basic colors and sporty shapes make up the collection, which gives itself to easy mix-and-matching. You can find some dressier items here than at AGNÈS B., and prices are somewhat lower.

Claudie Pierlot

ADDRESS
1 Rue Montmartre, 1st
TELEPHONE
01.42.21.38.38
METRO
Les Halles

ADDRESS
23 Rue du Vieux-Colombier, 6th
TELEPHONE
01.45.48.11.96
METRO
St-Sulpice

ADDRESS
1 Rue du 29 Juillet, 1st
TELEPHONE
01.42.60.01.19
METRO
Tuilleries
OPEN
Mon–Fri, 10:30 a.m.–7 p.m.;
Sat, 10:30 a.m.–7:30 p.m.
CREDIT CARDS
V, AE
$$-$$$

84. AGNÈS B.
Men's, women's, and children's clothing

AGNÈS B. has won over Parisians with her deceptively simple styling and affordable price tags. Color and cut are outstanding and the look is casual, comfortable, and chic. Fabrics are natural and prices reasonable.

From her domain of five boutiques on the Rue du Jour, this knowing mother of five has brought her understated sophistication to entire families. A harried American mother can let her husband and

ADDRESS
6 Rue du Jour, 1st (Women)
TELEPHONE
01.45.08.56.56

ADDRESS
2 Rue du Jour, 1st (Children 3–6 years)
TELEPHONE
01.40.39.96.88

ADDRESS
3 Rue du Jour, 1st (Men)
TELEPHONE
01.42.33.04.13

ADDRESS
10 Rue du Jour, 1st (Men &
women)
TELEPHONE
01.45.08.49.89

ADDRESS
13 Rue du Jour, 1st (Layette to
3 years)
TELEPHONE
01.42.33.27.34
METRO
Les Halles

ADDRESS
13 Rue Michelet, 6th
(Women)
TELEPHONE
01.46.33.70.20
METRO
Luxembourg

ADDRESS
6 Rue du Vieux Colombier,
6th (Women)
TELEPHONE
01.44.39.02.60
METRO
St-Sulpice

ADDRESS
10–12 Rue du Vieux
Colombier, 6th (Men)
TELEPHONE
01.45.49.02.05
METRO
St-Sulpice

ADDRESS
17 Avenue Pierre I de Serbie,
16th (Men, women, children)
TELEPHONE
01.47.20.22.44
METRO
Alma-Marçeau or Iéna
OPEN
Mon–Sat, 10 a.m.–7 p.m.
CREDIT CARDS
V, AE
$$-$$$

children loose on the street, retreat into the shop at
N.6, allowing the salesgirl to outfit her from head
to toe (shoes and makeup are upstairs), and emerge
alluringly French. Agnès understands how to bring
the same discreet allure to a working woman or
preteen "Lolita."

If these quiet clothes don't speak to you from the
rack, slip on a colored cotton cardigan with pearl
snaps and you'll understand what they're saying.

Agnès B.

85. LA DROGUERIE

Dressmaker's trimmings

On Saturdays crowds line up at this bright and well-lit shop to find just the right touch for the outfits of their fantasies. Colorful yarns in cotton, wool, alpaca, tinsel, and chenille are sold by the 100 grams (3.5 oz. at 7–11€), along with very original knitting patterns. Embroidered ribbons from around Europe evoke the past or modernity in vinyl. There are buttons, beads, and jewelry-making items stocked in hundreds of little wooden drawers behind the sales counter. Fruits, flowers, and feathers are inviting adornments for the plain straw and felt hats.

Even if you enter feeling uninspired, there are plenty of imaginative examples of what you might knit, needlepoint, or string together on display. If you have an idea in mind, the salesladies will help you in your quest.

ADDRESS
9–11 Rue du Jour, 1st
TELEPHONE
01.45.08.93.27
METRO
Les Halles
OPEN
Mon, 2–6:45 p.m.; Tue–Sat, 10:30 a.m.–6:45 p.m.
NO CREDIT CARDS
$

La Droguerie

ADDRESS
34 Rue Montmartre, 1st
TELEPHONE
01.42.33.31.32
METRO
Les Halles
OPEN
Restaurant: Mon–Sat,
11 a.m.–11 p.m.;
Take-out: 6 a.m.–11 p.m.
CREDIT CARDS
V, AE, MC
$$
INTERNET
www.comptoir-
gastronomie.com

☕ 86. COMPTOIR DE LA GASTRONOMIE
Restaurant, takeout

This first-rate stop for French delicacies has been in the "belly of Paris" since 1894 and continues as a purveyor of gastronomic specialties both in the shop and over the Internet. Hundreds of products are here, from Burgundy snails to duck leg confit, foie gras, and champagnes. With the ambience of an older Paris and the freshest of ingredients, it is a wise choice for lunch in the neighborhood.

ADDRESS
14 Rue Turbigo, 1st
TELEPHONE
01.42.33.44.36
METRO
Étienne-Marcel
OPEN
Mon–Sat, 10 a.m.–7 p.m.
NO CREDIT CARDS
$$

87. DUTHILLEUL & MINART
Professional uniforms

If you're giving a formal dinner and the caterer doesn't show, you'll be able to dress the part after a trip to DUTHILLEUL & MINART, a shop with everything from the chef's *toque* (hat) and *waiter's tablier* (apron) to the *bleus de travail* (blue cotton work clothes) that are worn by more French than any couture label.

This place is all business, and while the dressing rooms are not elegant, a tailor is on staff to assure that even the corner butcher leaves with a perfect fit. There are also traditional craftsmen's uniforms and a large selection of restaurant-quality dish towels.

ADDRESS
51 Rue Montorgueil, 2nd
TELEPHONE
01.42.33.38.20
METRO
Les Halles
OPEN
Daily, 7:30 a.m.–8:30 p.m.
CREDIT CARDS
V, AE
$$

88. STOHRER
Pastries and prepared dishes

In 1725, when Princess Marie was sent from Poland to marry King Louis XV of France, she insisted that her pastry chef Stohrer follow her to Versailles. Five years later, M Stohrer opened this shop, which still serves many of his original recipes (his specialties were *babas* and *puits d'amour*). The history and beautiful interior, decorated by Paul Baudry in the

1800s and classified as an historic monument, make this a fascinating as well as delicious stop.

Stohrer

A. Simon

89. A. SIMON
Kitchen accessories

The light and calm atmosphere that prevails here and the very helpful sales staff make this an easy stop for cooks. Come for the lovely white porcelain dishes (plates from 3€), salt and pepper sets, decanters, mustard jars, and so forth, that are typically found in French cafés.

This is also a restaurant supply house and over 10,000 items are sold here. Fortunately, the establishment is happy to ship.

ADDRESS
48 & 52 Rue Montmartre, 2nd
TELEPHONE
01.42.33.71.65
METRO
Étienne-Marcel or Les Halles
OPEN
Mon, 1:30–6:30 p.m.; Tue–Sat, 9 a.m.–6:30 p.m.
CREDIT CARDS
V, MC
$$

ADDRESS
18–20 Rue Coquillière, 1st
TELEPHONE
01.42.36.53.13
FAX
01.42.36.54.80
METRO
Les Halles or Louvre
OPEN
Mon, 9 a.m.–12:30 p.m. & 2– 6
p.m.; Tue–Sat, 9 a.m.–6 p.m.
CREDIT CARDS
V, MC
$-$$$
INTERNET
www.dehillerin.com

90. DEHILLERIN

Kitchen utensils

A trip to this remarkable establishment, where the Dehillerin family has been in residence since 1820, is an unforgettable experience. Even if you think you already have every knickknack necessary for a well-equipped kitchen, a look around DEHILLERIN will show you the many ways you could stock your *batterie de cuisine*.

Shelves, floor, and ceiling are stocked with an exhaustively impressive supply of kitchenware from copper pots, properly lined with nickel and large enough to feed all the king's men, to tiny chocolate molds of infinite variety.

Restaurant chefs bump shoulders with housewives in an effort to locate just the right tool. Professional-size cookware is in the basement.

Though the store will ship, I never leave here without something in hand, be it a basic omelette pan to inspire small cooks at home or a pretty pastry shaper for a friend. Ask for the English catalog, covering a selection of knives, serving pieces,

Dehillerin

molds, and copper cookware so you can show the sales staff exactly what you want. Or fax for it from the States and send back a list of items that interest you, requesting prices and a shipping estimate. You may pay by mail with credit card, or over the web.

91. KENZO
Women's, men's, juniors, children's clothing

East and West have come to meet in the designs of Kenzo, the most successful and the most French of Japanese designers in Paris. A tourist who stayed on after top honors from his fashion school back home, Kenzo introduced wild mixes of colors, patterns, and aspects of Japanese tailoring that have permanently broadened French fashion and continue to be fresh and fun to wear.

The new flagship at Pont Neuf is where you'll find the most intense fusion clothes for everyone as well as a rooftop restaurant designed by Philippe Starck with an A-plus view, a beauty institute, and a sushi bar downstairs. The appealing Kenzo look is revitalized here.

Kenzo

ADDRESS
1 Rue du Pont-Neuf, 1st
(Women, men, juniors, children)
TELEPHONE
01.73.04.20.00
METRO
Pont-Neuf
OPEN
Mon–Sat, 10:30 a.m.–8 p.m.

ADDRESS
3 Place des Victoires, 1st
(Women, men, juniors)
TELEPHONE
01.40.39.72.03
METRO
Bourse or Louvre or Rivoli

ADDRESS
16 Boulevard Raspail, 6th
(Women, men, children)
TELEPHONE
01.42.22.09.38
METRO
Bac

ADDRESS
18 Avenue George V, 8th
(Women, men)
TELEPHONE
01.47.23.33.49
METRO
Alma-Marçeau

ADDRESS
60–62 Rue de Rennes, 6th
(Women)
TELEPHONE
01.45.44.27.88
METRO
St-Sulpice

ADDRESS
99 Rue de Passy, 16th
(Women)
TELEPHONE
01.42.24.92.92
METRO
Passy
OPEN
Mon–Fri, 10:30 a.m.–7:30 p.m.;
Sat, 10 a.m.–7:30 p.m.
CREDIT CARDS
V, AE, MC, DC
$$$

ADDRESS
22 Avenue Victoria, 1st
TELEPHONE
01.42.33.71.05
METRO
Châtelet
OPEN
Mon, 12:15–7 p.m.; Tue–Fri,
10:45 a.m.–7pm; Sat, 10:15
a.m.–7pm
CREDIT CARDS
V, AE
$$-$$$

92. LE CÈDRE ROUGE
Outdoor furniture and garden accessories

The garden pieces overflowing into the Place
Victoria are an invitation to enter this gardener's
Eden. As you do, be sure to pick up a house card at
the main desk for jotting down notes as you
explore the diverse collection of handsome patio
furniture that includes striking wrought-iron tables
with green-glazed ceramic tops, eighteenth-century
reproductions, and postmodern chaises. In the sec-
ond entrance are flowerpots and urns from regional
France and Italy, rustic basketry, citronella candles
to ward off garden bugs, and an irresistible supply
of small hostess gifts.

Though much of what you'll see won't fit into
your suitcase, the store will handle shipping when
pressed.

Le Cèdre Rouge

93. LE JARDIN DE VICTORIA
Garden tools, seeds, plants

After LE CÈDRE ROUGE, come next door to buy
authentically French seeds for your victory garden.
This gardener's supply house has been on the Place
Victoria since 1925, selling its own packaged seeds,
plants, and practical garden tools.

    You may want to bring home *sachets* (seed pack-
ets) of *haricots fins* (French green beans), herbs,
endive, or choose from among fifteen different
types of lettuce or hundreds of flower seeds. At 2€
for most packets, a tiny investment can nurture a
high-grossing yield.

    You may want to fax ahead for their catalog.

ADDRESS
24 Avenue Victoria, 1st
TELEPHONE
01.42.33.16.41
FAX
01.45.08.89.80
METRO
Châtelet
OPEN
Tue–Sat, 9:30 a.m.–6 p.m.
NO CREDIT CARDS
$

Along the Way

The PLACE DU LOUVRE is a lovely little square just in front of St-Germain
l'Auxerrois, where one can have a little rest on a fine day and listen to the church bells
and concerts. At one end of the bordering Rue de l'Amiral-Coligny is LE FUMOIR
(N.6), an airy modern café where you can sit from 11 a.m. to midnight reading the
American newspapers while having a bite. Opposite at N.2 is LE CADOR, a pretty
nineteenth-century tea salon facing the Louvre, and the perfect ambiance for an
omelette, salad, and *le petit Cador*, their own chocolate ganache with a butter cookie
infused with cassis.

Place du Louvre

The Marais

The maze of cobblestone streets that form the MARAIS (named for the "marsh" it was before it was drained and became the fashionable center of Paris in the 1400s) naturally deter traffic, but lure the adventuresome shopper who doesn't care to see crowds of fellow tourists. It's the French who flock here on weekends, anxious to explore a neighborhood where artisans live and trade next door to film stars, and fashionable boutiques thrive behind ancient facades.

A declared historic district of primarily medieval and Renaissance buildings, the Marais is wedged between those modern architectural statements, the BEAUBOURG and the BASTILLE OPERA, but has ably avoided the gentrification that often follows the crowds. This is a neighborhood in which to *flâner*, or wander and browse as the French do.

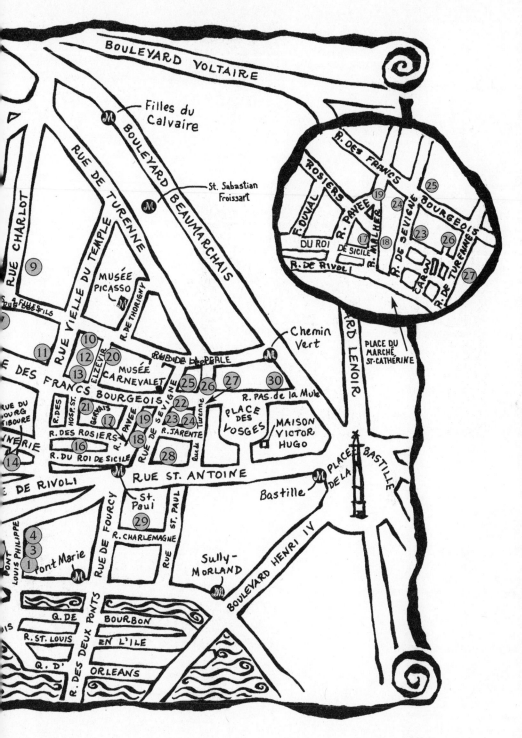

Map key on following page

Map Key

1. Calligrane
2. Galérie Agathe Gaillard
3. Orphée
4. Mélodies Graphiques
5. Papier Plus
6. Bazar de L'Hôtel de Ville
7. Jadis et Gourmande
8. Les Mille Feuilles
9. Agence Opale
10. Célis
11. Artis Flora
12. Art 75-Galérie Yves Di Maria
13. Zadig et Voltaire
14. France Ma Douce
15. Azzedine Alaia
16. Les Cadors
17. Jacqueline Darmigny
18. Suzanne
19. Paule Ka
20. Anne Becker
21. Boutique Paris-Musées

22. Meubles Peints
23. Formes
24. L'Agenda Moderne
25. Anne Fontaine
26. Manon Martin
27. Argenterie
28. La Vaissellerie
29. Village Saint-Paul
30. André Bissonnet

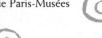

Where to Stay

5 RUE DE MOUSSY

ADDRESS
5 Rue de Moussy, 4th
TELEPHONE
01.44.78.92.00
FAX
01.42.76.08.48
METRO
Hôtel-de-Ville
CREDIT CARDS
V, AE, MC, DC
RATES
Two people, from 450€
Breakfast 25€

Not a hotel, this is the name and address of three suite-apartments done in style *moderne* by clothing designer Azzedine Alaia, in the central Marais complex housing his own living quarters, atelier, and boutique. Outfitted with his personal collection of 50s and 60s furnishings, this is for those who want calm, privacy and about 1,300 square feet of living space. It is unique luxury with concrete floors, wireless Internet, and a concierge.

PAVILLON DE LA REINE

ADDRESS
28 Place des Vosges, 3rd
TELEPHONE
01.40.29.19.19
FAX
01.40.29.19.20
METRO
Saint-Paul, Bastille
CREDIT CARDS
V, AE, MC, DC
RATES
Double rooms from 345€
Breakfast 20.25€
INTERNET
www.pavillon-de-la-reine.com

For those who prefer to stay in the picturesque Marais neighborhood, the Pavillon de la Reine is the luxury hotel of choice. A modern medieval lobby overlooks the square, and the duplexes facing the front have the same glorious view. Enter through the gates and flowered courtyards. Twenty-four-hour room service is only one of the amenities of a grand hotel in this fifty-five-room gem.

HÔTEL DU JEU DE PAUME

ADDRESS
54 Rue Saint-Louis-en-Ile, 4th
TELEPHONE
01.43.26.14.18
FAX
01.40.46.02.76
METRO
Pont Marie
CREDIT CARDS
V, AE, MC, DC
RATES
Double rooms from 240€
Breakfast 15€
INTERNET
www.jeudepaumehotel.com

The deluxe hotel on the island has a wood and stone interior, a glass elevator, and every pampering amenity. Ask for a room over the courtyard.

HÔTEL DU BOURG-TIBOURG

Guests here come home to a highly romantic stage set designed by master Jacques Garcia. Fringes and velvets in deep autumnal colors suggest the orientalism of the nineteenth century, with every convenience expected in a twenty-first-century hotel.

ADDRESS
19 Rue du Bourg-Tibourg, 4th
TELEPHONE
01.42.78.47.39
METRO
St-Paul
Doubles from 200€
Breakfast 12€
CREDIT CARDS
V, AE, MC, DC
INTERNET
www.hotelbourgtibourg.com

HÔTEL DES DEUX-ILES

Cozy and charming, this tiny hotel has rooms decorated in pretty Provençal prints with great views from the top, a lounging lobby below, and the allure of the island outside its doors.

ADDRESS
59 Rue St-Louis-en-Ile, 4th
TELEPHONE
01.43.26.13.35
FAX
01.43.29.60.25
METRO
Pont-Marie
Doubles from 164€;
Breakfast 11€
CREDIT CARDS
V, AE
INTERNET
www.2iles.com

HÔTEL CARON DE BEAUMARCHAIS

You're surrounded by the elegance of eighteenth-century Paris in any of the nineteen rooms in this lovely and comfortable hotel, personally run by the Bigeards, father and son. The Caron de Beaumarchais, a playwright and strong supporter of the American Revolution, once lived here, where he wrote *The Marriage of Figaro*. In rooms now equipped with wifi and satellite tv, the guests here can enjoy the best of both the eighteenth and twenty-first centuries.

ADDRESS
12 Rue Vieille-du-temple, 4th
TELEPHONE
01.42.72.34.12
FAX
01.42.72.34.63
METRO
Hôtel-de-Ville or Saint-Paul
Double rooms from 137€
Breakfast 9.80€
CREDIT CARDS
V, AE, MC, DC
INTERNET
www.carondebeaumarchais.com

ADDRESS
22 Rue Saint-Croix-de-la-
Bretonnerie, 4th
TELEPHONE
01.48.87.77.63
FAX
01.42.77.26.78
METRO
Hôtel-de-Ville
Doubles from 110€;
Breakfast 9.50€
CREDIT CARDS
V, MC
INTERNET
www.bretonnerie.com

HÔTEL DE LA BRETONNERIE

Set in a seventeenth-century townhouse on a quiet street, you can almost forget you're in the thick of an area that's lively night and day. This popular hotel has marble bathrooms and Louis XII decor.

Culture Along the Way

ADDRESS
23 Rue de Sévigné, 3rd
METRO
Saint-Paul
TELEPHONE
01.44.59.58.58
OPEN
Tue–Sun, 10 a.m.–6 p.m.;
Closed Monday

MUSÉE CARNAVALET

The graceful seventeenth-century townhouse and gardens that were home to the Marquise de Sévigné (who documented her own times in her famed letters) now house the venerable history of Paris in furniture, documents, and objects, including even the letter Robespierre was writing when the Revolutionaries found him in his tub.

ADDRESS
5 Rue Thorigny, 3rd
METRO
Saint-Paul
TELEPHONE
01.42.71.25.21
OPEN
Mon & Wed–Sun, 9:30 a.m.–
5:30 p.m.; Closed Tuesday

MUSÉE PICASSO

Picasso's favorite pieces were passed on to his heirs, whose donations to the state in lieu of inheritance taxes are now the world's definitive Picasso collection, on view in a sixteenth-century mansion. The outdoor restaurant serves a fine lunch.

Musée Picasso

MAISON VICTOR HUGO

In this former private home where Hugo lived from 1832 to 1848 are souvenirs and drawings left by the writer, and a great view of the Place des Vosges from his top window.

ADDRESS
6 Place des Vosges, 4th
METRO
Saint-Paul or Bastille
TELEPHONE
01.42.72.10.16
OPEN
Tue–Sun, 10 a.m.–6 p.m.;
Closed Monday

MAISON EUROPÉENE DE LA PHOTOGRAPHIE

Opened in a restored eighteenth-century home in 1990, this has become a major photography center, with a permanent collection of European and international works from 1950 on and rotating shows.

ADDRESS
5 Rue de Fourcy, 4th
METRO
Saint-Paul
TELEPHONE
01.44.78.75.00
OPEN
Wed–Sun, 11 a.m.–8 p.m.

ADDRESS
4 Rue du Pont-Louis-Philippe,
4th (Desk accessories)
TELEPHONE
01.48.04.31.89

ADDRESS
6 Rue du Pont-Louis-Philippe,
4th (Stationery)
TELEPHONE
01.40.27.00.74
FAX
01.40.27.84.08
METRO
Saint-Paul
OPEN
Tue–Sat, 11 a.m.–7 p.m.
CREDIT CARDS
V

$$-$$$

Marais Shops

1. CALLIGRANE
Stationery and desk accessories

For those who shift into mode *moderne* at work, CALLIGRANE will have the necessary function-abilia to dress your desk. Under ornately tiled ceilings are calculators to briefcases, staplers to agendas, in top Euro-designs that will captivate the contemporary critic. Black, red, and chrome reign in accessories, while the papers next door offer the rainbow.

Select a string-stitched sketch book from Austria with handmade papers and a red skin to capture Paris by pen, or letter paper that cleverly folds into an envelope. An unusual selection of paper sizes, shapes, colors, and materials lends itself to the particular client, and engraving is offered. Both stores are good gift stops, especially for an inscrutable male.

Calligrane

Calligrane

2. GALÉRIE AGATHE GAILLARD
Photography gallery

Mme Gaillard opened in 1975, encouraged by
Cartier-Bresson and Doisneau, among others, to
open a gallery showing both famous and new
names in photography. Still at her original address
she continues to show established and emerging
artists of quality in a gracious and well-lit space.
She is well known among collectors.

ADDRESS
3 Rue du Pont-Louis-Philippe,
4th
TELEPHONE
01.42.77.38.24
METRO
Saint-Paul
OPEN
Tue–Sat, 2–7 p.m.
CREDIT CARDS
V
$$-$$$

3. ORPHÉE
Antique musical instruments

A fascinating shop for both the musician and the
collector, ORPHÉE buys and sells musical instruments dating from the seventeenth century to the
mid-twentieth century. Virtually all types of
baroque, classical, and romantic strings and wood-
winds come through here. M Charbit will do his
utmost to locate and restore the instrument of your
desire.

ADDRESS
8 Rue du Pont-Louis-Philippe,
4th
TELEPHONE
01.42.72.68.42
METRO
Saint-Paul
OPEN
Mon–Sat, 2–7 p.m.
CREDIT CARDS
V, MC
$$-$$$

ADDRESS
10 Rue du Pont-Louis-Philippe,
4th
TELEPHONE
01.42.74.57.68
METRO
Saint-Paul
OPEN
Tue–Sat, 11 a.m.–7 p.m.;
Mon 2–7 p.m.
CREDIT CARDS
V, AE, MC
$$$

4. MÉLODIES GRAPHIQUES
Stationery and desk accessories

The fine Florentine papers found here are not for the modernist. These marbleized finishes are for the romantic writer—nearly every paper, pencil, and notebook is finished with a bath of dyes whose endless variations have fascinated since the process was created by the bookbinder to the court of Louis XIII.

Journals and stationery in vivid butterfly colorations lend themselves to literary prose, and the agendas and desk organizers are just the touch for a home library. A selection of lovely marbleized boxes in the shapes of hearts, butterflies, and crescent moons is easy to pack and carry home to delighted friends. And the richly colored, leather-bound book with blank pages (36 to 70€) would inspire anyone to write that long-contemplated novel.

Mélodies Graphiques

5. PAPIER PLUS
Stationery products, art supplies

Architects, artists, and fastidious laymen drop in from around the world to stock up on this exclusive supply of canvas-covered journals and portfolios meticulously executed by designer Laurent Tisné.

Formerly a publisher of art books, Tisné has brought his high standards and a strong graphic sense to the PAPIER PLUS line. The formula for his popular "little white book" has expanded to eight formats and fourteen solid colors in various dimensions and paper qualities from 19€, each volume beautiful and book-like enough to say "Keep me."

Come here for photo albums, address books, stationery, and more, neatly arranged by color on simple wooden shelves. The second entrance holds drawing papers and larger portfolios. Many of the items can be ordered from their website.

ADDRESS
9 Rue du Pont-Louis-Philippe, 4th
TELEPHONE
01.42.77.70.49
METRO
Saint-Paul
OPEN
Mon–Sat, noon–7 p.m.
CREDIT CARDS
V
$$
INTERNET
www.papierplus.com

Papier Plus

6. BAZAR DE L'HÔTEL DE VILLE (BHV)
Department store for home improvements

While it's not very touristique, the basement of the BHV is one of the most frequented retail spaces in Paris. A mecca of hardware and home improvement supplies, in styles designed to fit into the most historic or modern of domiciles, makes the trip down the central staircase a cultural experience.

Go to the fourth floor for latches and doorknobs in keeping with your Louis XVI furnishings or your contemporary castle, or for something

ADDRESS
52–56 Rue de Rivoli, 4th
TELEPHONE
01.42.74.90.00
METRO
Hôtel-de-Ville
OPEN
Mon–Tue & Thurs–Sat, 9:30 a.m.–7:30 p.m.;
Wed, 9:30 a.m.–8:30 p.m.
CREDIT CARDS
V, AE, MC
$-$$

hand-forged. You'll find beautiful bronze dinner bells (from 7€), voluptuous bathroom fixtures as well as old-fashioned and newfangled tools for the handyman in this basement bazaar. Don't ignore the broad variety of moderately priced upholstery fabrics, custom wood paneling, and window coverings such as the white lace and embroidered shades so hard to come by in the States. For fun, pick up the 100-page order guide. Purchases over 230€ will be delivered free of charge, in town.

Just outside the store on the Rue de Rivoli is a stand that sells common French signs. You might euphemise your guest bath with a plaque identifying the correct *toilette*, or provide a gentle reminder to your household to keep the door shut with the gift of a *fermez* sign to hang over the knob.

The CAFÉ BHV next door at 11 Rue des Archives is a fun stop for a snack, or flowers, books, and packaged foods in a well-designed space. Open Mon–Thurs, 9:30 a.m.–9 p.m.; Fri & Sat, 9:30 a.m.–11 p.m.; Sun, 11 a.m.–7 p.m.

ADDRESS
39 Rue des Archives, 4th
TELEPHONE
01.48.04.08.03
METRO
Hôtel-de-Ville
OPEN
Mon, 1–7:30 p.m.; Tue–Fri, 10 a.m.–7:30 p.m.; Sat, 10:30 a.m.–7:30 p.m.

ADDRESS
27 Rue Boissy d'Anglas, 8th
TELEPHONE
01.42.65.23.23
METRO
Concorde or Madeleine
OPEN
Mon, 1–7 p.m.; Tue–Sat, 10 a.m.–7 p.m.

ADDRESS
49 bis Avenue Franklin D. Roosevelt, 8th

7. JADIS ET GOURMANDE
Chocolates and candies

Come here to feel like a kid in a candy shop. This place is full of enticing presentations for all ages and chocolate concoctions for virtually any holiday and occasion, so just being here is a treat. You'll find chocolate bears for birthdays and "Bravo" tablets for great achievements among the many creative and delicious sweets here, including scrumptious hard candies. It's easy to find gifts, and special orders are taken for whatever you want to say in chocolate.

Jadis et Gourmande

TELEPHONE
01.42.25.06.04
METRO
Franklin D. Roosevelt
OPEN
Mon, 1–7 p.m.;
Tue–Sat, 9:30 a.m.–7 p.m.
CREDIT CARDS
V, MC
$$

8. LES MILLE FEUILLES/LES 2 MILLE FEUILLES

Flowers and decoration

These much-talked-about catty-corner boutiques are on the cutting edge of good taste, one for the old (LES MILLE FEUILLES), the other for the new (LES DEUX MILLE FEUILLES). Both are originals, and owners Pierre and Phillipe are experienced consultants for your home or entertaining events. The Rue Rambuteau boutique brings beautiful and unusual old objects into its florals, while the other has a clean and modern Provençal sensibility with linens and dishes.

ADDRESS
2 Rue Rambuteau, 3rd (Les Mille Feuilles)
59 Rue des Francs-Bourgeois, 4th (Les 2 Mille Feuilles)
TELEPHONE
01.42.78.32.93 (Les Mille Feuilles)
01.44.54.89.15 (Les 2 Mille Feuilles)
METRO
Rambuteau
OPEN
Tue–Sat, 11 a.m.–7:30 p.m.
CREDIT CARDS
V, AE
$$

ADDRESS
8 Rue Charlot, 3rd
TELEPHONE
01.40.29.93.33
METRO
Turbigo or Filles du Calvaire
OPEN
Mon–Fri, 9 a.m.–7 p.m.
CREDIT CARDS
None
$$-$$$

9. AGENCE OPALE
Photographs of writers

This is a real find for those literary souls who are inspired by the masters.

Founded in 1996, AGENCE OPALE is the first French photographic agency specializing in photographs of authors: Colette on the balcony of her Palais Royal apartment in 1942 (260€), Jean Cocteau at Milly–le-Foret, and other famous names such as Sartre, Hemingway, Faulkner, Malraux, and Marguerite Duras. Some portraits are by well-known photographers like Boubin, but most are from lesser-known photographers from whom Opale has bought the reproduction rights. Most are black and white; some are signed by the author; and all are sold framed.

Along the Way

The PASSAGE DE RETZ, 9 Rue Charlot, is a privileged destination. The privately owned seventeenth-century mansion has been renovated as gallery space for superb temporary shows in art and design from around the world. The owner's intent is that you look, then retreat to the Retz café to contemplate over a cold drink. Open Tue–Sun, 10 a.m.–7 p.m.

10. CÉLIS
Handmade knits

The proprietress here handknits everything you see in the workshop behind the boutique. One-of-a-kind pullovers and cardigans of alpaca, cotton, or wool for children and adults, hats and baby bonnets, finger puppets, children's mittens, everything with a playful motif. Adorable finger puppets for the Little Red Riding Hood characters are 7€ each, and a puppet theater (knitted, of course) is 18€. Wonderfully, it's all machine washable.

ADDRESS
72 Rue Vieille-du-Temple, 3rd
TELEPHONE
01.48.87.52.73
METRO
Hôtel-de-Ville or Saint-Paul
OPEN
Sun–Wed, 2–7 p.m.;
Thurs–Sat, 11:30 a.m.–7 p.m.
CREDIT CARDS
V, MC
$$

Célis

ADDRESS
75 Rue Vieille-du-Temple, 3rd
TELEPHONE
01.48.87.76.18
METRO
Saint-Paul
OPEN
Mon–Sat, 11 a.m.–7 p.m.
CREDIT CARDS
V, AE
$$-$$$

11. ARTIS FLORA
Tapestry reproductions

The tapestries hanging from the white walls and wood beams of what was a seventeenth-century home are meant to be lifted into the present. With great success, the ARTIS FLORA workshops outside Paris recreate famous medieval and renaissance tapestries found in the Cluny Museum and in the Louvre, working each piece individually and by hand. The process involves silkscreening onto a fabric woven of flax, cotton, and wool, capturing the color intensity of the original in its current condition and guaranteeing no fading.

Cushion covers decorated with forest animals, tapestries of hunting scenes and castle life can transform a living room into a "great hall," or add romance to a bedroom. The smallest cushions begin at 40€, and are easily packed as are small rolled-up tapestries. Tapestries can get quite large and Artis Flora is well versed in shipping. Be sure to ask for their beautiful, comprehensive order catalog.

Artis Flora

12. ART 75-GALÉRIE YVES DI MARIA
Vintage and modern photography and posters

A well-known dealer, Yves di Maria began by collecting old postcards, going on to build strong vintage and twentieth-century photograph and poster collections. He presents both in his spacious new gallery, including collector's items from the masters as well as interesting decorative prints. Prices begin at 100€ and attain levels the connoisseur will certainly understand. You may begin by perusing the collections online at www.photos-site.com.

ADDRESS
58 Rue Vielle-du-Temple, 3rd
TELEPHONE
01.42.71.70.26
METRO
Saint-Paul or Hôtel-de-Ville
OPEN
Tue & Fri–Sat, 10:30 a.m.–7 p.m.; Wed–Thur, 3–7 p.m.; or by appointment
CREDIT CARDS
V, AE, MC, DC
$$-$$$
INTERNET
www.photos-site.com

13. ZADIG ET VOLTAIRE
Women's clothing

This is a favorite among the young and hip who don't mind exposing a little skin to achieve a certain look, and then are willing to pay for it. The name is exploding here with boutiques all around town. This address is perhaps the busiest, while the most upscale, in the 8th, has an in-house spa. The outlet shop is nearby in the Marais.

ADDRESS
42 Rue des Francs-Bourgeois, 3rd
TELEPHONE
01.44.54.00.60
METRO
Saint-Paul
OPEN
Daily, 10:30 a.m.–7:30 p.m.

ADDRESS
18–20 Rue Francois I, 8th
TELEPHONE
01.40.70.97.89
METRO
Franklin D. Roosevelt
OPEN
Mon–Sat, 10:30 a.m.–7 p.m.

ADDRESS
22 Rue de Bourg-Tibourg, 4th (outlet)
TELEPHONE
01.44.59.69.62
METRO
Hôtel-de-Ville
OPEN
Tue–Sun, 1–7 p.m.
CREDIT CARDS
V, AE, MC
$$$, $$ (outlet)

Along the Way

On the Rue Vieille du Temple, in the heart of the Marais, is a suite of café/restaurants owned and designed by Xavier Denamur that attract crowds from 9 a.m. until 2 a.m., in keeping with the neighborhood. Each is unique, but each is typical of the Marais: LES PHILOSOPHES, at N.28; AU PETIT FER À CHEVAL, N.30; and L'ÉTOILE MANQUANTE, N.34.

ADDRESS
27 Rue du Bourg-Tibourg, 4th
TELEPHONE
01.44.59.38.03
METRO
Hôtel-de-Ville
OPEN
Tue–Sat, 11 a.m.–7 p.m.;
Sun, 2–7 p.m.
CREDIT CARDS
V, MC
$$

14. FRANCE MA DOUCE
Regional products

Full of charm, this old-fashioned shop sells traditional products at old-fashioned prices, and makes gift buying easy. Owners Elodie and Servane Guérin spent a year scouring the regions of France for their most authentic items, which they offer here. Among them are espadrilles from the Basque country, quimper dishes from Brittany, artisinal pastis from Provence, sailor shirts from St-Malo, violette candies from Toulouse, and much more. The Guérins have a large foreign clientele and are happy to gift wrap and box your choices for transport.

France Ma Douce

☕ MARIAGE FRÈRES
Tea salon and shop

ADDRESS
30–32 Rue du Bourg-Tibourg, 4th
TELEPHONE
01.42.72.28.11
METRO
Hôtel-de-Ville

ADDRESS
13 Rue des Grands-Augustins, 6th
METRO
St-Michel
TELEPHONE
01.40.51.82.50

ADDRESS
260 Rue du Faubourg St-Honoré
TELEPHONE
01.46.22.18.54
METRO
Ternes
OPEN
Tea Salon: Daily, noon–7 p.m.
Boutique: Daily, 10:30 a.m.–7:30 p.m.
CREDIT CARDS
V, AE, MC
INTERNET
www.mariagefreres.com

MARIAGE FRÈRES has been France's leading tea importer since 1854, and this salon-boutique has made a beautiful marriage of Eastern and Western traditions centered around the drinking of tea. In an exotic rattan and palm furnished salon you can sip your choice of over 400 teas to the strains of European arias.

Behind the scenes, master tea-makers still cut and stitch your tea bag by hand, while the dark counters up front are laden with varieties of loose teas, teapots either antique or authentically copied, and lovely tea services. A brunch that may be juice, eggs and salmon, pastry, tea, and toast is served from noon to 6; lunch is served noon to 3 p.m., and a formal tea takes place from 3 to 7 p.m. This is a must for tea lovers, but others take warning—coffee is not available! You may buy online at www.mariagefreres.com.

ADDRESS
7 Rue de Moussy, 4th
ADDRESS
18 Rue de la Verrerie, 4th
(outlet)
TELEPHONE
01.42.72.19.19
METRO
Hôtel-de-Ville
OPEN
Mon–Sat, 10 a.m.–7 p.m.
CREDIT CARDS
V, AE, DC
$$$$

15. AZZEDINE ALAIA
Women's clothes

This tiny Tunisian is in the forefront of creators with wild and slinky clothes that would change a doormouse into a femme fatale. Alaia's magic scissors are reputed to sculpt the body to the curves of the garment, a wile that fashion writers and artistic celebrities from Paloma Picasso to Tina Turner can't seem to deny themselves.

No less wild is the loft-like boutique designed with New York artist Julien Schnabel, where each sparse piece of furniture has a personality and forged-iron sculptures double as clothes racks. Buzz the building for admittance. Just around the corner, in a tamer space, is last season's collection at 30 to 50 percent off.

ADDRESS
12 Rue Ferdinand Duval, 4th
TELEPHONE
01.44.59.30.46
METRO
Saint-Paul

ADDRESS
11 Rue Princesse, 6th
TELEPHONE
01.43.29.90.17
METRO
Mabillon or Saint-Germain
OPEN
Mon–Sat, noon–7:30 p.m.
CREDIT CARDS
V, MC
$$$

16. LES CADORS
Dog and cat accoutrements

Here is a top chic boutique for the necessary little luxuries our dogs and cats deserve. The two owners, Stéphanie and Cécile, choose only what they would use for their own adorable pets, meaning the best in design and quality, with a touch of humor. How about a doggie bed fit for the *chien* of Louis XIV (290€), a Swarovski-studded collar (139€), their own hand-painted Limoges dishes, or faux fur coats? Everything for your Canine King and Aristocat.

☕ GOLDENBERG
Delicatessen

ADDRESS
7 Rue des Rosiers, 4th
TELEPHONE
01.48.87.20.16
METRO
Saint-Paul
OPEN
Daily, 9 a.m.–11 p.m.;
Closed Yom Kippur
CREDIT CARDS
V, MC
$$

This popular landmark delicatessen marks the heart of Paris's oldest Jewish quarter, where kosher butchers and bakers now trade alongside Moroccan fast fooderies and high-fashion outlets. If you're longing for a *plat du jour* (about 13€) of *boulettes grandmère* (chopped meatballs) or chou *farcie* (cabbage rolls) while you read the Jewish dailies, this is your place.

17. JACQUELINE DARMIGNY
Women's clothing

ADDRESS
3 Rue Malher, 4th
TELEPHONE
01.42.78.30.58
METRO
Saint-Paul
OPEN
Mon, 2–7 p.m.;
Tue–Sat, 11 a.m.–7 p.m.
CREDIT CARDS
V, AE, MC, DC
$$-$$$

In the spirit of the couture, stylist Jacqueline Darmigny designs for the elegant woman of approximately thirty to fifty-five. Her distinctive collection is both feminine and geometric, and has been drawing a faithful clientele to this address for eighteen years. A total look, from ensemble to co-ordinating hat, this is a good address for the woman who wants to make a statement without spending a fortune. Pantsuits run 500 to 650€ and dresses are from 200€. Silk, cashmere, and microfibre are star fabrics here.

ADDRESS
8 Rue Malher, 4th
TELEPHONE
801.44.61.04.67
METRO
Saint-Paul
OPEN
Mon–Sat, 11 a.m.–1:30 p.m. &
2:30–7:30 p.m.
CREDIT CARDS
V, MC
$$$

18. SUZANNE
Women's clothing

Amélie (from the film of that name) could come here for her wardrobe. Suzanne Grignard and her daughter Natalie run this charmingly original shop selling Suzanne's coquettish fashions. A costume designer for theater and film, she has dressed Vanessa Paradis and Isabelle Adjani early in the game and has worked with the greats: Dior, Givenchy, and Lagerfeld. While her resume is weighty, her designs are flirty and humorous, for the modern Parisienne of seventeen to sixty years of age. There are lots of corselets and bustiers to wear out (not under), and dresses begin at 500€. Made-to-measure is also available.

ADDRESS
20 Rue Malher, 4th
TELEPHONE
01.40.29.96.03
METRO
St-Paul
OPEN
Mon–Sat, 10:30 a.m.–1 p.m. &
2–7 p.m.

ADDRESS
45 Rue François I, 8th
TELEPHONE
01.47.20.76.10
METRO
George V

ADDRESS
192 Blvd. St-Germain, 7th
TELEPHONE
01.45.44.92.60
METRO
St-Germain-des-Prés
OPEN
Mon–Sat, 10:30 a.m.–7 p.m.
CREDIT CARDS
V, AE, MC
$$$

19. PAULE KA
Women's clothing, shoes, handbags, accessories

Even if you're from Paris, Texas, if you walk into PAULE KA for a new set of clothes you will walk out looking like the ultimate Parisienne. Designed by Serge Cafinger to dress the Parisian woman from head to toe, the collection accomplishes just that. The styles are simple, set off by a hint of sensual draping or a charming detail in that particular combination of sober and chic that says "Made in France." Each season is completely coordinated for mixing and matching, but if you have any doubts, or are in a hurry, let the sales staff put it together for you. Besides the street clothes there are lots of evening dresses and even wedding gowns. The shop in the Marais is the original, but the largest and newest is on François I.

20. ANNE BECKER
Bed, table, and bath linens

Simple yet extremely sophisticated, the linens of
Anne Becker could fit well in your mountain cabin
or your chateau. Duvet and pillow covers in burlap
or linen from the Pyranees are hand-embroidered
with fabulous monograms, trimmed in felt, and
thrown over sheets of cotton satin. Colors range
from the naturals to the likes of chestnut, eggplant,
saffron, and pinks, in
wonderful combina-
tions. American bed
sizes and custom table
linens of a similar
design can be ordered,
and bath linens co-ordi-
nate. Everything here is
magnifique.

ADDRESS
9 Rue Elzévir, 3rd
TELEPHONE
01.42.72.66.61
METRO
Saint-Paul
OPEN
Tue–Sat, 10 a.m.–12:30 p.m. &
2–7 p.m.
CREDIT CARDS
V
$$$

Anne Becker

Along the Way

The Rue des Francs-Bourgeois runs through the district and is a trendy shop-walk for
the fashionable up-and-coming, particularly on Sundays, when most boutiques here
remain open. At N.40, AMERICAN RETRO shows fabulous fifties vintage take-offs
for girls; DECALAGE at N.33 has lots of well-priced *fantaisie* jewelry and hippy-style
clothes; at N.22, JEAN-CLAUDE MONDERER sells his own casual shoe designs for
men and women, alongside other fun designers, all a good look and value; the
Bensimone collection at AUTOUR DU MONDE (N.12) is known for its take on
safari wear and tennis shoes for urban travels; and who could resist entering the
ABOU D'ABI BAZAR (N.10), for something slightly ethnic; SPRINT at N.8 is full of
tennis shoes for men/women that you may never find in the States; and CAMPER
(N.9) has those wonderfully hip walking shoes.

If you stop to take a break at N.24 Rue des Francs-Bourgeois, you'll have your
choice of two delightful restaurants: CAMILLE is a restaurant/tea salon on a corner
where the outdoor seating is a destination in fine weather; at CREPERIE SUZETTE
next door, you can sit at bar or table and enjoy delicious entrée and *desert crepes* or
salad. Both are open daily.

ADDRESS
29 bis Rue des Francs-
Bourgeois, 4th
TELEPHONE
01.42.74.13.02
METRO
Saint-Paul
OPEN
Mon, 2–7 p.m.; Tue–Fri, 11
a.m.–1 p.m. & 2–7 p.m.;
Sat, 11 a.m.–7 p.m.;
Sun, noon–7:30 p.m.
CREDIT CARDS
V, AE, MC, DC
$$

21. BOUTIQUE PARIS-MUSÉES
Museum gift shop selections

Smart selections from the boutiques of Museums of
the City of Paris include table accessories, jewelry
from emerging artists, and other treats.

ADDRESS
32 Rue Sévigné, 4th
TELEPHONE/FAX
01.42.77.54.60
METRO
Saint-Paul
OPEN
Tue–Sat, noon–6 p.m.
CREDIT CARDS
V, AE, MC
$$$
INTERNET
www.meublespeints.com

22. MEUBLES PEINTS
Painted wooden furniture

The popular painted armoires and chests that warm
this shop are transformed from tired and faceless
cast-offs of eighteenth- and nineteenth-century
households to splendid pieces of hand-painted
country furniture.

Jean-Pierre Besenval retrieves much from the
Alsacian countryside, working behind his storefront
to individually restore and color each piece with
egg-tempura motifs borrowed from the brightly
decorative traditions of eastern France, Swiss
baroque style, the Italian renaissance, and the Black
Forest. Whether you choose a blanket chest (from
1,832€) to cheer up a dreary corner or an armoire
(from 3,050€) to anchor an entire room, you'll
appreciate its individuality in a home setting. The
shop obligingly handles shipping for its many foreign customers. It also offers workshops teaching
the old techniques of painting on wood. Look up
their website at www.meublespeints.com.

ADDRESS
14 Rue de Sévigné, 4th
TELEPHONE
01.42.74.26.76
METRO
Saint-Paul

23. FORMES
Maternity clothing

For maternity wear that's really, really comfortable
and stylish enough to keep you feeling pretty,
witty, and gay for those nine months, come to
FORMES. The concept has been growing for twen-

ty years, producing wardrobes of creative, well-cut clothes for moms-to-be. The very feminine collection includes lovely lacy tops with a rose at the waist for the biggest of bellies. A portion of each season's collection may be ordered through their website at www.formes.com.

ADDRESS
22 Rue Cambon, 1st
TELEPHONE
01.49.26.00.66
METRO
Concorde or Madeleine

ADDRESS
10 Place des Victoires, 2nd
TELEPHONE
01.40.15.63.81
METRO
Bourse

ADDRESS
5 Rue du Vieux-Colombier, 6th
TELEPHONE
01.45.49.09.80
METRO
Saint-Sulpice

ADDRESS
41 Rue de Passy, 16th
TELEPHONE
01.46.47.50.05
METRO
La Muette
OPEN
Mon–Sat, 10:30 a.m.–7 p.m.
CREDIT CARDS
V, AE, MC
$$
INTERNET
www.formes.com

24. L'AGENDA MODERNE
Agenda books and small leather goods

Leather goods have been handmade here since 1829, and this elegant line is still created by artisans in the atelier behind the shop. They achieve perfection in ostrich, lizard, buffalo, crocodile, and calf, in a rich range of color and agenda styles to suit any need. Or, you may place a custom order.

ADDRESS
42 Rue de Sévigné, 3rd
TELEPHONE
01.44.54.59.20
METRO
Saint-Paul
OPEN
Mon–Fri, 10 a.m.–5:30 p.m.
CREDIT CARDS
V, MC
$$

ADDRESS
12 Rue des Francs-Bourgeois,
3rd
TELEPHONE
01.44.59.81.59
METRO
Saint-Paul
OPEN
Mon–Sat, 10 a.m.–7 p.m.;
Sun, 11:30 a.m.–7 p.m.

ADDRESS
50 Rue Etienne-Marcel, 2nd
TELEPHONE
01.40.41.08.32
METRO
Etienne-Marcel

ADDRESS
81 Rue des Saints-Pères, 7th
TELEPHONE
01.45.48.89.10
METRO
Sèvres-Babylone
OPEN
Mon–Sat, 10 a.m.–7 p.m.
CREDIT CARDS
V, MC, AE
$$

25. ANNE FONTAINE
Women's blouses and shirts

Brazilian-born Anne Fontaine brought a traditional love of pure white linen and its promise of good luck with her to France. Lucky Anne! French women are wild for her white blouses and shirts, and she continues to come up with a hundred or so new styles each season, almost exclusively in white, though there are always a few models in black. Fashioned in the traditional "whites" of cotton and linen, she includes a few modern textiles like stretch laces. Everything is elegant and comfortable, and feminine in its detail. You'll find simple, stylish tops galore for day or casual evenings. Prices average about 100€ for nearly anything.

Manon Martin

ADDRESS
19 Rue de Turenne
TELEPHONE/FAX
01.48.04.00.84
METRO
Saint-Paul
OPEN
Mon, 1:30–7:30 p.m.;
Tue–Sat, 11 a.m.– 7:30 p.m.
CREDIT CARDS
V, AE, MC
$$-$$$

26. MANON MARTIN
Hats and accessories for women and children

You'll find a perfect balance between the elegant and the whimsical in everything here. Marvelous headdresses for everyday or occasion or simply to hide under, rain or shine, are coordinated with bags, scarves, and jewelry, for a complete look. Once you start trying these on, you won't be able to stop, and it's easy to walk out with an adorable new *chapeau* for 130 to 290€.

27. ARGENTERIE
Antique silver and silverplate tableware

If you long to complete your dining service with
the family silver, but have none, you'll find history
altered here. Begin with baskets full of silverplated
flatware, worn but not weary, whose past life was
likely as a hotel service, selling for 61€/kilo (about
fifteen pieces).

Move on to the pure silver and choose from
among hundreds of forks, knives, and spoons,
engraved Christofle and the like, that earned their

rich patina at the tables of
fine French homes, sold
here at prices comparable
to new silverplate at
Christofle. Then turn to
coffee and tea services,
serving platters, and small
accessory items that make
wonderful wedding gifts.

The breadth of design
and origin of these pieces
allow you to set the palace
table or bistro kitchen.
Inventory here spans the
eighteenth, nineteenth,
and twentieth centuries. Let the
smiling and patient sales help
explain to you how to date
French silver by the markings on
the back side. Plan to pack or
mail your purchases as the shop
does not handle shipping.

ADDRESS
19 Rue de Turenne, 4th
TELEPHONE
01.42.72.04.00
FAX
01.42.72.08.24
METRO
Saint-Paul
OPEN
Tue–Sat, 10:30 a.m.–7 p.m.
CREDIT CARDS
V, MC
$$

Argenterie

Place du Marché-Sainte-Cathérine

Along the Way

On a lovely day you may want to turn off the Rue de Turenne at Rue de Jarente to sit at one of the casual cafés surrounding the charmingly hidden Place du Marché-Sainte-Cathérine. Among them LA BELLE HISTOIRE (N.6) offers Mediteranean cuisine daily on its terrasse and PITCHI POI (N.9) offers a Sunday brunch (24€). Next door at N.7 is SUZANNE ERMANN's collection of contemporary wedding gowns (open Tue–Sat, 11 a.m.–7 p.m.). Just outside the square at N.9 Rue de Jarente is the atelier-boutique of REINALDO ALVAREZ, couture designer of wedding gowns as well as mother-of-the bride and cocktail wear, open by appointment Tue–Sat (telephone, 01.42.77.66.51). At the next corner (N.14 Rue de Sévigné) you'll find FORMES for mothers-to-be, and just across the Rue de Sévigné at N.11 is CARABOSSE, adorable clothing for babies to boys age six and girls to age twelve (open Tue–Sat, 11 a.m.–7 p.m.; Sun, 3–7 p.m.).

Reinaldo Alvarez

28. LA VAISSELLERIE
Gifts and kitchenware

If you need some last-minute gifts or a memento of
Paris for your own kitchen, this is a terrific stop.
The many knickknacks, gadgets, and utensils here
are inexpensive, useful, and very French. You'll want
to bring home magnets in the image of Camembert
rounds and bottles of Bordeaux to hang on your
fridge or as a simple but stylish gift. Faïence dishes,
corkscrews, linens, oversized café-au-lait cups, and
cheese knives are just some of the offerings. Be sure
to request the store bags and stickers if you plan on
giving gifts.

ADDRESS
92 Rue St-Antoine, 4th
TELEPHONE
01.42.72.76.66
METRO
St-Paul

ADDRESS
85 Rue de Rennes, 6th
TELEPHONE
01.42.22.61.49
METRO
St-Sulpice

ADDRESS
332 Rue St-Honoré, 1st
TELEPHONE
01.42.60.64.50
METRO
Tuileries
OPEN
Mon–Sat, 10 a.m.–7 p.m.;
Sundays in December
CREDIT CARDS
V, MC, AE, DC
$-$$

ADDRESS
Enter at 14-15 Rue Saint-Paul, 4th
METRO
Saint-Paul
OPEN
Thur–Mon, 11 a.m.–7 p.m.
CREDIT CARDS
Accepted by some dealers
$-$$$

29. VILLAGE SAINT-PAUL
Antiques shops

This warren of antiques dealers and *brocanteurs* (sellers of bric-a-brac) tucked away in the courtyard between the Rue Saint-Paul and the Rue Charlemagne is perhaps the most charming antiques hunting ground in Paris, and a favorite among my Parisian friends.

The sixty-odd dealers trade in everything from fine antiques to *grandmère's* costume jewelry, with plenty of personality to liven up a serious search. Be sure not to miss AUX TROIS SINGES (N.23 Rue Saint-Paul). A perfect afternoon in the village should include a stop at THE RED WHEELBARROW BOOK-STORE (N.22 Rue Saint-Paul), a favored Anglophone bookshop, meeting place, and venue for literary readings run by Canadian Penelope Lemasson (open Mon–Sat, 10 a.m. to 7 p.m.; Sun, 2:30 to 6 p.m.).

Village Saint-Paul

Along the Way

The PLACE DES VOSGES is a beautifully symmetrical park surrounded by thirty-six slate-roofed, limestone townhouses. The oldest square in Paris (it was commissioned by Henry IV in the 1600s) has benefited from its restoration as centerpiece to the neighborhood.

Once again an aristocracy of intellectuals and artists compete to claim an address on the former PLACE ROYALE. A traditional spot to enjoy the architecture and activity is the café MA BOURGOGNE (N.19 Place des Vosges; open daily from 8 a.m. to 1:30 a.m.), where you can relax outdoors with a café au lait in the company of locals and well-known customers such as Inspector Maigret from the Simenon detective novels.

Take a peek at the beautiful Hôtel de Sully in the corner courtyard beyond N.5. Then stop at N.9 to see the contemporary art at GALERIE NIKKI DIANA MAR-QUARDT (hours vary with shows; telephone 01.42.78.21.00). Next door at the same address is one of my favorite romantic restaurants, L'AMBROISIE.

Stroll under the arcades to view the sophisticated black and white designs for the geometric body at POPY MORENI (N.13; open Mon, 11 a.m. to 7 p.m. and Tue–Sat, 10 a.m. to 7 p.m.) and the upstairs bridalwear. Peruse castoffs from the nineteenth century at LES DEUX ORPHELINES (N.21), perhaps even taking home some of its decor to create your own period room. A few steps away is the restaurant/tea room COTÉ PLACE (N.2 Rue des Francs-Bourgeois; open daily), a delightful stop for a hot or cold repast or refreshment.

Place des Vosges

ADDRESS
6 Rue Pas-de-la-Mule, 3rd
TELEPHONE/FAX
01.48.87.20.15
METRO
Bastille
OPEN
Mon–Sat, 2–7 p.m.;
Mornings by appointment;
Closed August
CREDIT CARDS
V, MC
$$$

30. ANDRÉ BISSONNET
Antique musical instruments

M Bissonnet began restoring antique musical instruments in the cold-storage room of his butcher's shop. When the instruments took over he packed away his cleavers, took off his apron, and hung a musician's sign over the butcher's plaque. Impassioned with the near-extinct instruments of the seventeenth, eighteenth, and nineteenth centuries, the engaging proprietor can explain them all, play many, and restore them to perfection. Even if you don't leave with a seventeenth-century harp, your visit here will be fascinating.

M Bissonnet

The Sixteenth

After you've chased the charm and history down each cobblestone street, seen the sights and bumped into too many tourists, it's time to retreat to the sedate Sixteenth for an afternoon of shopping that is reliably calm, comfortable, and conservative, in the neighborhood that the haute bourgeoisie discreetly calls home. The impeccable *fin-de-siècle* residences that line these streets shelter the BCBG (Bon Chic Bon Genre), the Parisian equivalent of the preppy, born and bred to carry on the values of that class. Leaving nothing to chance, the *Rallye* (coming out) of Mlle BCBG is a five-year process, and the young man she will eventually marry has likely attended one of the prestigious prep schools in the neighborhood.

In this primarily residential district you'll find an unhurried and uncrowded kind of shopping, with quiet neighborhood branches of many of the city's best boutiques, and resale shops of the highest caliber. Take a stroll down the elegant boulevard AVENUE VICTOR HUGO where many well-known fashion designers have shops offering their more conservative styles and attentive service to those who choose to shop in this neighborhood. Start with these names: APOSTROPHE, N.5, whose chic classics for the active Parisienne are not found in the U.S.; LOUIS FÉRAUD, N.17; GEORGES RECH, N.23; GIVENCHY, N.66, to name just a few, then on to footwear with ROBERT CLERGERIE, N.18; and STEPHANE KÉLIAN, N.20.

You'll find more fashion on the nearby RUE DE PASSY, as well as two worthwhile standbys: the newly renovated department store that tastefully clothes women of the neighborhood, FRANCK ET FILS (N.80), only crowded during its sensational sales in January and July; and SEPHORA (N.50), which offers hundreds of beauty products, perfumes, and cosmetics to the same *soignée* (well-groomed) crowd. Then there are the sidestreets, which shouldn't be ignored. All in all, the Sixteenth is among the most pleasant shopping areas in Paris, and if you are disposed toward the BCBG life, you'll love it here.

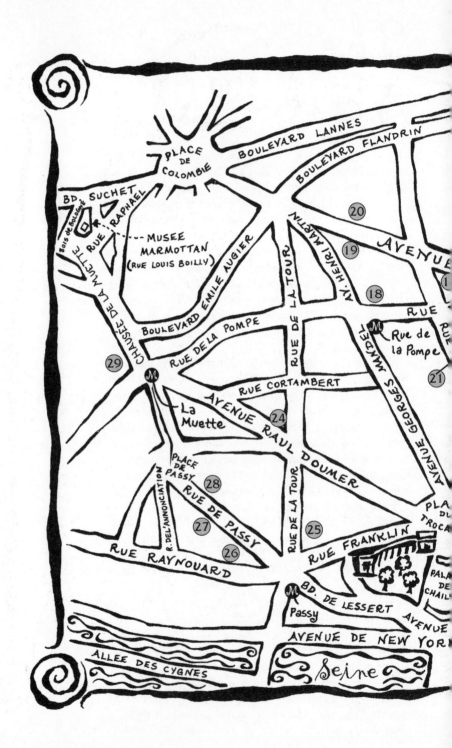

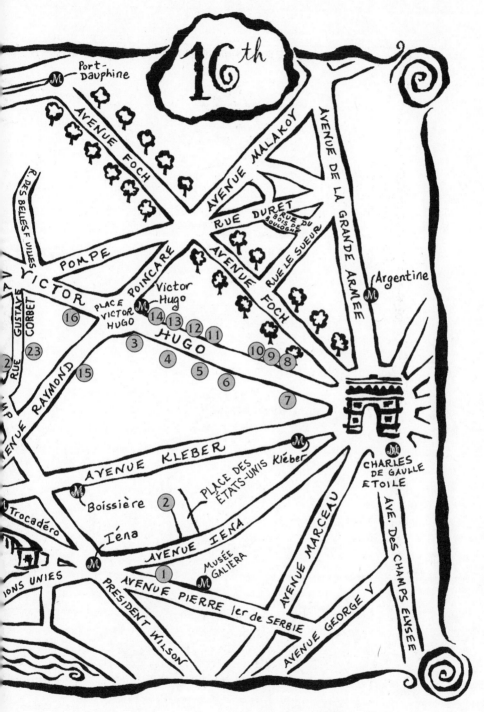

Map key on following page

Map Key

1. Noel
2. Baccarat
3. Marquise de Sévigné
4. Point à la Ligne
5. S.A. Maeght
6. O.J. Perrin
7. Céline
8. Boutique 22
9. Guibert
10. Armorial
11. Lolita Lempicka
12. Lenôtre
13. Ramosport
14. Petit Bateau
15. Parfums de Nicolai
16. J.M. Weston
17. Arthur and Fox
18. Réciproque
19. Aliette Massenet
20. La Châtelaine
21. Sap

22. Ligne 16
23. Axxon Marcus
24. Les Folies D'Élodie
25. Depôt-Vente de Passy
26. Regina Rubens
27. Mac Douglas
28. L'Entrepôt
29. Cyrillus

Where to Stay

SAINT JAMES CLUB

ADDRESS
43 Avenue de Bugeaud, 16th
TELEPHONE
01.44.05.81.81
FAX
01.44.05.81.82
METRO
Porte Dauphine
CREDIT CARDS
V, AE, MC, DC
RATES
Double rooms from 460€
Breakfast 20€
INTERNET
www.saint-james-paris.com

The only château-like hotel in Paris, the St-James Club is a unique opportunity for visitors wanting to experience *la vie au château* (chateau life). Once a home for visiting scholars, the magnificent library is now the setting for the piano bar in this altogether elegant establishment. Rooms are done in a luxurious '30s style, and there is a health club on the premises. The park-like grounds are open only to hotel guests and to members of the exclusive St-James Club.

TROCADÉRO DOKHAN'S

ADDRESS
117 Rue Lauriston, 16th
TELEPHONE
01.53.65.66.99
FAX
01.53.65.66.88
METRO
Trocadéro or Tour Eiffel
CREDIT CARDS
V, AE, MC, DC
RATES
Double rooms from 400€
Breakfast 27€

The interiors of this beautiful Haussemann-style mansion are newly redone by the talented Frédéric Méchiche, using Empire and Regency furniture, black and white stripes and marble countertops. The effect is strikingly comfortable and luxurious. Beyond the usual deluxe amenities, the hotel offers champagne tastings every Thursday night.

HÔTEL PERGOLESE

ADDRESS
3 Rue Pergolèse, 16th
TELEPHONE
01.53.64.04.04
FAX
01.53.64.04.40
METRO
Argentine
CREDIT CARDS
V, AE, MC, DC
RATES
Double rooms from 250€
Breakfast 12€
INTERNET
www.pergolese.com

A boutique hotel with first-rate service and amenities, this is a well-priced choice for those who appreciate elegant modern decor. Pale, uncluttered spaces defined by glass block and wall panels and filled with light ash and leather furnishings were designed by Phillipe Starck, with prints by Hilton McConnico.

Culture Along the Way

MUSÉE MARMOTTAN

This quiet and intimate gem tucked away from the crowds contains the premier collection of Monet's work, including his *Waterlilies*. Also enjoy other impressionists and medieval illuminated manuscripts.

ADDRESS
2 Rue Louis-Boilly, 16th
METRO
La Muette
TELEPHONE
01.44.96.50.33
OPEN
Tue–Sun, 10 a.m.–5:30 p.m.

MUSÉE GALLIERA

In the nineteenth-century palace of the Duchess of Galliera, the history of fashion is brought to life in a series of temporary exhibitions from the museum's 90,000-article collection.

ADDRESS
10 Avenue Pierre 1st de Serbie, 16th
METRO
Iéna or Alma-Marçeau
TELEPHONE
01.56.52.86.20
OPEN
Tue–Sun, during temporary exhibitions only, 10 a.m.–6 p.m.

BOIS DE BOLOGNE

The BOIS is the top destination for nature-loving Parisians. Rent a bike here and explore over 2,000 acres of lakes, gardens, restaurants, and the delightful JARDIN D'ACCLIMATATION (children's amusement park/zoo). The tulips, roses, and water lilies in the PARC DE BAGATELLE are not to be missed.

METRO
Porte Dauphine or Porte D'Auteil
OPEN
Summer, 9 a.m.–10 p.m.;
Winter, 9 a.m.–5:30 p.m.

The Sixteenth Shops

ADDRESS
1 Avenue Pierre de Serbie, 16th
TELEPHONE
01.40.70.14.63
METRO
Iéna
OPEN
Mon–Sat, 10:30 a.m.–7 p.m.
CREDIT CARDS
V, AE, MC
$$$-$$$$

1. NOEL

Embroidered household linens, sleepwear and loungewear, new-born gifts

This centenarian house carries on the tradition of delicate and sumptuous linens, maintaining its reputation as seamstress of some of the world's most beautiful table services of the organdy hand-embroidered sort finished to your table size.

Though the number of households in need of such refinement may seem to be dwindling, NOEL has 13,000 embroidery designs in its archives, sustained by an international customer list with a strong following in the States, and has added some machine embroideries to its repertoire. In the same tradition are embroidered table sets (48€), and toweling (a stitched guest towel makes a gift possible at 36€). Go downstairs for bed linens and sleepwear in cotton, silk, and cashmere. Like everything else here, the sleepwear can be made-to-measure.

Noel

For those who live in the modern world, Noel has taken a step in time and now offers T-shirts with truly wonderful embroideries of flowers, butterflies, fruit branches, and the like at a reasonable 92€. You can see and even order these lovely creations at the Noel website: www.noel.fr.

2. BACCARAT
Crystal museum, boutique and restaurant

The spectacular crystal palace created by BACCARAT with the help of designer Philippe Starck brings this prestigious brand into the twenty-first century. The unusual and beautiful in mirrors and glass mark your entrance into the former home of the Contesse de Nouilles, who held infamous society parties here pre-WWII. Chandeliers are everywhere, from contemporary styles with color to a magnificently ornate black showpiece. The tablewear and jewelry boutiques are just up the stairs with the museum and Cristal Room restaurant above. This is a must-see address in Paris, and the Cristal Room is a favorite table. Call to reserve.

ADDRESS
11 Place des États-Unis, 16th
TELEPHONE
01.40.22.11.00 (museum and boutique)
01.40.22.11.10 (restaurant)
METRO
Boissière
OPEN
Boutique and museum: Mon–Fri, 10 a.m.–9 p.m.; Sat, 10 a.m.–7 p.m.
Cristal Room restaurant: Mon–Sat, 8:30 a.m.–10:30 p.m.
CREDIT CARDS
V, AE, MC
$$$-$$$$

3. MARQUISE DE SÉVIGNÉ
Chocolates

These excellent chocolates carrying the name of the famous writer of letters, who suggested her daughter should eat a chocolate every day, were first produced in 1898. Beautifully boxed, the spe-

ADDRESS
1 Place Victor Hugo, 16th
TELEPHONE
01.45.00.89.68
METRO
Victor-Hugo

ADDRESS
32 Place de la Madeleine, 8th
TELEPHONE
01.42.65.19.47
METRO
Madeleine

ADDRESS
62 Rue de Seine, 6th
TELEPHONE
01.40.46.02.01
METRO
Mabillon
OPEN
Mon–Sat, 10 a.m.–7 p.m.
CREDIT CARDS
V, AE, DC
$$$

cialty is in pralines and ganaches, created in the
Burrus's family factory in eastern France. If you
should visit there, be sure to make a trip to their
outstanding chocolate museum.

Marquise de Sévigné

ADDRESS
67 Avenue Victor Hugo, 16th
TELEPHONE
01.45.00.87.01
METRO
Victor-Hugo or Kléber
OPEN
Mon–Sat, 10:30 a.m.–7 p.m.
CREDIT CARDS
V, AE, DC
$$

4. POINT À LA LIGNE
Decorative candles

An extraordinary collection of *trompe l'oeil* centerpiece candles lights up any style table and perfumes
the air. From a potted cactus or mushroom to a life-
size purple hyacinth growing out of a bulb, to a fra-
grant and abundant bouquet (30€), these still lifes
in wax are designed to tease and please the sensibil-
ities of your guests.

Depending upon the occasion, choose between
a formal row of miniature orange trees or the giant
pumpkin. Coordinating paper plates, cloths, and
napkins are also available.

5. S.A. MAEGHT
Old and new jewelry and silver

It's always an adventure to come here because you never know what treasure you might find. This shop has been buying and selling jewelry in this prosperous neighborhood for two generations and always has interesting pieces. Recently I spotted a Cartier necklace in the window. They also create, repair, and restyle.

ADDRESS
37 Avenue Victor Hugo, 16th
TELEPHONE
01.45.01.67.88
METRO
Kléber or Victor-Hugo
OPEN
Tue–Sat, 10:30 a.m.–6:30 p.m.
CREDIT CARDS
V, AE, MC, DC
$$

S.A. Maeght

ADDRESS
33 Avenue Victor Hugo, 16th
TELEPHONE
01.45.1.88.88
METRO
Victor-Hugo
OPEN
Tue–Sat, 10:30 a.m.–1 p.m. &
2–6:30 p.m.
CREDIT CARDS
V, DC
$$$-$$$$

6. O.J. PERRIN
Jewelry

The minimalist creations of this Parisian jeweler have captured the hearts of Parisiennes. Among his symbolic designs that have become all the rage are the heart pendant and the upside-down fleur-de-lis that can be seen in the simplest white gold dangling from the wrists of teens or in pavé diamonds on the chests of matrons. A handsome line of watches complements the modern jewelry designs.

O.J. Perrin

ADDRESS
3 Avenue Victor Hugo, 16th
TELEPHONE
01.45.01.80.01
METRO
Charles de Gaulle-Étoile or
Victor-Hugo or Kléber

7. CÉLINE
Women's clothing and leather goods

For that BCBG look that can be nothing other than Parisian, CÉLINE is it. You'll find the finest quality leather goods (shoes, belts, and handbags) in the classic, gold-trimmed tradition of Chanel and Hermès, without quite the same price tags. The collections of day and evening wear exhibit the same stylish good taste.

This should be your first stop for the leather skirt, silk blouse, and tweedy jacket that look so appropriate while shopping the Sixteenth.

ADDRESS
36 Avenue Montaigne, 8th
TELEPHONE
01.56.89.07.92
METRO
Alma-Marçeau

ADDRESS
58 Rue de Rennes, 6th
TELEPHONE
01.45.48.58.55
METRO
Saint Germain-des-Prés
OPEN
Mon–Sat, 10 a.m.–7 p.m.
CREDIT CARDS
V, AE, MC
$$$-$$$$

8. BOUTIQUE 22
Cigars

If you love cigars, you'll adore BOUTIQUE 22. This shop is at the top of the game, with a great classic cellar where you can also find the cherished rarity. The neophyte can receive a true education here, and even the connoisseur may learn something. Everything regarding cigars, except the actual tobacco products, may be ordered online at www.boutique22.fr.

ADDRESS
22 Avenue Victor Hugo, 16th
TELEPHONE
01.45.01.81.41
METRO
Charles de Gaulle-Étoile
OPEN
Mon–Sat, 10 am.– 7 p.m.
CREDIT CARDS
V, AE, MC, DC
$$$
INTERNET
www.boutique22.fr

9. GUIBERT
Equestrian gear

All you need for serious dressage is here on two luxurious wood-paneled floors—the chicest of regulation riding wear and hunting coats, divinely smooth saddles and sweet-smelling riding boots. There is even an exclusive line of silver jewelry, inspired by the horse bit (gamma collar necklace, 240€). You can make some purchases online at www.guibert.fr.

ADDRESS
22 Avenue Victor Hugo, 16th
TELEPHONE
01.53.64.74.74
METRO
Charles de Gaulle-Étoile
OPEN
Mon–Sat, 10:30 a.m.–7 p.m.
CREDIT CARDS
V, AE, MC
$$$
INTERNET
www.guibert.fr

ADDRESS
26 Avenue Victor Hugo, 16th
TELEPHONE
01.45.01.69.01
METRO
Kléber or Victor-Hugo
OPEN
Mon–Sat, 10 a.m.–7 p.m.
CREDIT CARDS
V, AE, MC, DC
$$$-$$$$

10. ARMORIAL

Stationery and desk accessories

This dignified establishment is best known for its engraved invitations, announcements, and visiting cards, which it executes regularly for the embassies, grand hotels, and private individuals that that make up its clientele. But you may also want to come here to choose from among the many elegant brief-cases and agendas, pens, and interesting desk décor. If you're looking for a gift, you're sure to find something very impressive here.

ADDRESS
46 Avenue Victor Hugo, 16th
TELEPHONE
01.45.02.14.46
METRO
Victor-Hugo
OPEN
Mon–Sat, 10:30 a.m.–7 p.m.
CREDIT CARDS
V, AE, MC, DC
$$$-$$$$

11. LOLITA LEMPICKA

Women's clothing

Don't imagine for a moment that in LEMPICKA's clothes you'll be dressed for market day in Krakow. This popular designer dresses the romantic wisp who loves to don ruffles and lace for her soirées. And her daytime clothes are just as appealing. The newly introduced second line, Lolita Lempicka Première, is less expensive without sacrificing any of the dreamy charm.

Lolita Lempicka

12. LENÔTRE
Pastries, candies, breads, prepared dishes

For inspiration at home, I keep a glossy fold-out of
LENÔTRE's *Merveilles de Patisseries* (Pastry Marvels)
on my fridge. Gaston Lenotre is known worldwide
for such luscious and lyrical cakes as Mozart
(gooseberries, Grand Marnier, and meringue) and
Opera (almond cake, coffee mousse, and chocolate
truffle) as well as for his candies, ice creams, decorated bread loaves, salads, and entrées.

There are seven branches in Paris alone, and
each lives up to his reputation, though those listed
may be most convenient. At lunchtime, stop in for
a delicious carry-out sandwich. The Victor-Hugo
shop is larger, and if you peek at the window displays, you won't be able to pass by without stop-
ping in for at least a bag of candies.

ADDRESS
48 Avenue Victor Hugo, 16th
TELEPHONE
01.45.02.21.21
METRO
Victor-Hugo
OPEN
Mon–Tue. 9:30 a.m.–9 p.m.;
Wed–Sun, 9 a.m.–9 p.m.

ADDRESS
121 Avenue de Wagram, 17th
TELEPHONE
01.47.63.70.30
METRO
Wagram

ADDRESS
40 Rue Cler, 7th
TELEPHONE
01.44.11.72.80
METRO
École-Militaire
OPEN
Mon–Sat, 9 a.m.–8 p.m.;
Sun, 9 a.m.–1 p.m.
CREDIT CARDS
V, MC
$$

13. RAMOSPORT
Women's raincoats

Yes, the trench is French. Stop in here during a
shower and walk out in the colors of the moment
worn with a French twist. Bye-bye, Burberry. The
founding family is said to have provided weather-
proof vests for the tsar's army before establishing
themselves in Paris in the 1920s, producing light-
weight, feminine rainwear for chic city life. Coats,
jackets, parkas, ponchos, hats, everything concern-
ing rainy weather is sold here by this generation's
mother-daughter team. Outerwear begins at 300€.

ADDRESS
50 Avenue Victor Hugo, 16th
TELEPHONE
01.45.00.12.62
METRO
Victor Hugo
OPEN
Mon–Sat, 10:30 a.m.–7 p.m.

ADDRESS
188 Boulevard St-Germain, 7th
TELEPHONE
01.42.22.70.80
METRO
St-Germain-des-Prés
OPEN
Mon, 2–7 p.m.;
Tue–Sat, 10 a.m.–7 p.m.
CREDIT CARDS
V, AE, MC
$$-$$$

ADDRESS
64 Avenue Victor Hugo, 16th
TELEPHONE
01.45.00.13.95
METRO
Victor-Hugo or Kléber
OPEN
Mon–Sat, 10 a.m.–7 p.m.

ADDRESS
116 Avenue des Champs-
Elysées, 8th
TELEPHONE
01.40.74.02.03
METRO
George V
OPEN
Mon–Sat, 10 a.m.–7:30 p.m.
CREDIT CARDS
V, AE, MC
$$

ADDRESS
69 Avenue Raymond Poincaré,
16th
TELEPHONE
01.47.55.90.92
METRO
Victor-Hugo
OPEN
Mon–Sat, 10 a.m.–7 p.m.

ADDRESS
28 Rue de Richelieu, 2nd
TELEPHONE
01.44.55.02.00
METRO
Palais-Royal
OPEN
Mon–Sat, 10 a.m.–7 p.m.

ADDRESS
80 Rue de Grenelle, 7th
TELEPHONE
01.45.44.59.59
METRO
Rue du Bac
OPEN
Tue–Sat, 10:30 a.m.–6:30 p.m.
CREDIT CARDS
V, AE, MC
$$$

14. PETIT BATEAU
Women's and children's clothes

Years ago we expected to outgrow this label one day, but it has kept up with its original customers in the most delightful way! They still make the basic cotton knit T-shirt, now in women's sizes, too. Also for grown-ups are oh-so-comfy sleepwear and loungewear of the same knit. The range here is much broader and prices much lower than what you might find in the States. PETIT BATEAU boutiques are all around town, but this address is possibly the least crowded. The Champs-Elysées address is fun—and a madhouse.

15. PARFUMS DE NICOLAI
Perfumes

Patricia de Nicolai, a descendant of Pierre Guerlain, has inherited the family nose for creating finely tuned scents from essential oils. After years of assiduous training, she is one of only a few women in the world of perfume, and an emerging star. She and her businessman husband founded the company in 1989 to develop, distribute, and sell her creations, which are not yet available in the U.S. Since, she has won an international title of Best Perfume Creator for her top-selling scent Number One. Her reputation has also won private clients like Pol Roger, who has commissioned a scented candle to go with their champagne. This line of excellence includes masculine and feminine fragrances (Sacré Bleu is the newest), a scent for children (Petit Ange), and ambient scents for the home.

16. J.M. WESTON
Men's and women's shoes

When a certain class of Frenchman sizes you up, he looks first at your shoes, and if they happen to be Westons he'll rest assured you are well-heeled. The WESTON shoe is a status symbol among the executive set, and to affluent teens, who save up for a conservative Weston as an American would for Air Jordans. The heavy leather shoes, classically styled, are pure quality. The famous Weston moccasin runs 370€, and the golf shoe is considered the best in the world (from 455€). There is even an additional strip of leather where the sole meets the top of the shoe to prevent leaks. At those prices, you should hope they will never wear out!

ADDRESS
97 Avenue Victor Hugo, 16th
TELEPHONE
01.47.04.23.75
METRO
Victor-Hugo
OPEN
Mon–Sat, 10 a.m.–7 p.m.

ADDRESS
114 Avenue des Champs-
Elysées, 8th
TELEPHONE
01.45.62.26.47
METRO
George V
OPEN
Mon–Sat, 10 a.m.–8 p.m.

ADDRESS
3 Boulevard de la Madeleine,
1st
TELEPHONE
01.42.61.11.87
METRO
Madeleine
OPEN
Mon–Sat, 10 a.m.–7:30 p.m.
CREDIT CARDS
V, AE, MC
$$$-$$$$

Along the Way

Mamans may want to stop in at any of these reasonably priced clothing shops for children and *bébés* along the Avenue Victor Hugo: DU PAREIL AU MEME (N.97); TILL (N.101); and TOUT COMPTE FAIT (N.115).

Among the shops for grown-ups who appreciate fine quality at a moderate price are: PHIST (N.130 Rue de la Pompe), for men's and women's classic attire, where a well-tailored men's suit is 299 to 359€, and a women's jacket 220€. Open Mon–Sat, 10 a.m. to 7 p.m.; VOTRE NOM (N.128 Rue de la Pompe), where women twenty to sixty stop in every season for easy but elegant, up-to-date sportswear. Open Mon–Fri, 10:30 a.m.–7 p.m., and Sat, 10 a.m.–7:30 p.m.; ERIC BOMBARD (N.17 Rue Gustave-Courbet), the king of cashmere that's very stylish and still well priced. Open Mon, 2–7 p.m., and Tue–Sat, 10:30 a.m.–7 p.m.; and for teens and twenty-something women is KOOKAI (N.2 Rue Gustave-Courbet), looking a lot less kookie than it once did. Open Mon–Sat, 10:30 a.m. to 7:30 p.m.

The animated restaurant/brasserie LE STELLA (N.133 Avenue Victor Hugo) is an institution in the *quartier*, serving fresh seafood and regional specialties daily until 1 a.m.

ADDRESS
133 Rue de la Pompe, 16th
TELEPHONE
01.45.53.05.15
METRO
Victor-Hugo

ADDRESS
13 Rue Marbeuf, 8th
TELEPHONE
01.47.20.65.59
METRO
Franklin D. Roosevelt
OPEN
Mon–Sat, 10:30 a.m.–7 p.m.
CREDIT CARDS
V, AE, MC
$$

17. ARTHUR AND FOX
Men's and women's tailored clothing

The name sounds British, but Arthur and Fox is a French company whose tailoring savvy leans toward the English tradition. Particularly at the end of the workday, these shops are bustling with smartly dressed customers who stop off to replenish their office wardrobes with classically cut suits in seasonable tweeds, linens, and silks, and fine cotton shirts (from 80€), which the excellent sales staff will help you put together with a savoir-faire that is distinctly French. Shirts and suits are also made-to-measure. Men's suits start at 710€ and women's pants at 200€.

But what may interest you even more than the reasonable prices and solid styling is that these stores welcome an order-by-mail clientele.

Arthur and Fox

18. RÉCIPROQUE
Resale designer clothing and gifts

Don't mistake this establishment for a mere neighborhood resale shop, though it most certainly reflects the bon ton that is the Sixteenth. In a city where some simply cannot be seen in the same couture threads twice, RÉCIPROQUE has brought respectability, high standards, and high style to the secondhand clothing trade.

On any business day you'll find the row of boutiques brisk with customers cruising the racks for this year's Ungaro gown, a Hermès scarf, a Cartier bag. The 30,000 or so fashionable items here are in immaculate condition and at least 50 percent less than when brand new. You'll notice that those who come to consign their clothing (perhaps a diplomat, a banker's wife, a student) leave with their bags as full as when they came in.

ADDRESS
88 Rue de la Pompe, 16th
(Housewares and gifts)

ADDRESS
89 Rue de la Pompe, 16th
(Women's accessories)

ADDRESS
92–93 & 95 Rue de la Pompe, 16th (Women's and children's clothing)

ADDRESS
101 Rue de la Pompe, 16th
(Menswear)

ADDRESS
123 Rue de la Pompe, 16th
(Women's outerwear)
TELEPHONE
01.42.04.30.28
METRO
Pompe
OPEN
Tue–Fri, 11 a.m.–7 p.m.;
Sat, 10:30 a.m.–7 p.m.
CREDIT CARDS
V, AE, MC
$-$$

19. ALIETTE MASSENET
Antiques, decoration, and gifts

Three generations of women from the Massenet family (relations of the nineteenth-century composer of that name) run this charming boutique specializing in anything and everything to decorate the home, with an inclination toward English design. Come here for a beautiful armchair or an interesting packable gift. All price levels are represented.

ADDRESS
169 Avenue Victor Hugo, 16th
TELEPHONE
01.47.27.24.05
METRO
Victor-Hugo
OPEN
Mon–Sat, 10 a.m.–6:30 p.m.
CREDIT CARDS
V, AE, MC, DC
$$-$$$

ADDRESS
170 Avenue Victor Hugo, 16th
TELEPHONE
01.47.27.44.07
METRO
Pompe
OPEN
Mon–Sat, 10 a.m.–7 p.m.
CREDIT CARDS
V, MC
$$$-$$$$

20. LA CHÂTELAINE

Children's clothing, household linens

Every indulgent *grandmère* in Paris knows that LA CHÂTELAINE will have the appropriate dresses, shawls, baptismal gowns, and gifts for their newest family member, and will outfit him/her in Bon Chic Bon Genre style to age ten.

European royalty come here for the hand-sewn collection exclusive to this shop, and the house seamstresses will fit a garment for your prince or princess at no extra charge. The lace pillowcases, embroidered bath towels, and organdy table sets are also fit for a princess, but accessible to regular customers during the store's very favorable sales.

La Châtelaine

ADDRESS
106 Rue de Longchamps, 16th
(children)
104 Rue de Longchamps
(juniors)
TELEPHONE
01.45.53.56.11 (children)
01.45.53.61.59 (juniors)
METRO
Trocadéro or Pompe
OPEN
Mon–Sat, 10 a.m.–7 p.m.
CREDIT CARDS
V, MC
$$-$$$

21. SAP

Children's and juniors clothing

Here is where many of the children of the Sixteenth come from babyhood on up to shop for the well-bred look their families like them to sport for casual and dress occasions. Suits for boys ages ten to sixteen are 183€, and a blazer alone is 122€. The shoe selection and junior wear create the most excitement among the younger clients.

22. LIGNE 16

Party dresses

The first time a girl comes here she's accompanied by her mother. She comes back whenever she's looking for something very special, for perhaps a first official date or a coming out party, or a cousin's wedding. Gowns and "cocktail" dresses are in silk, raw silk, mousseline, taffeta, and polyester. Some never stop shopping here. The helpful saleswomen give honest advice, and if all else fails you can take home a short skirt for 69€.

ADDRESS
100 Rue de Longchamps, 16th
TELEPHONE
01.47.27.63.05
METRO
Pompe
OPEN
Mon, noon–7 p.m.;
Tue–Sat, 10 a.m.–7 p.m.
CREDIT CARDS
V, AE, MC
$$

Ligne 16

ADDRESS
10 Rue Gustave-Courbet, 16th
TELEPHONE
01.47.27.00.49
METRO
Pompe
OPEN
Mon, 2–7 p.m.; Tue–Sat, 10:30 a.m.–7 p.m.
CREDIT CARDS
V, AE, MC
$$

23. AXXON MARCUS

Women's and men's pants, made-to-order

Have you ever wondered why French women look so good in their pants? They can't all be shopping at AXXON MARCUS, but this is known to be the boutique for the best cut in slacks. The specialty here is made-to-measure pants, delivered in three weeks. You may choose from English, French, and Italian bolts of fabric. Best of all, they ship, and you can continue to order from home.

Axxon Marcus

☕ Along the Way

You may want to stop at COFFEE PARISIEN (N.7 Rue Gustave-Courbet), a restaurant/café that is especially popular with the younger crowd. Open daily, noon to midnight.

CARETTE

Tea salon, ice creams

ADDRESS
4 Place du Trocadéro, 16th
TELEPHONE
01.47.27.88.56
METRO
Trocadéro
OPEN
Daily, 7 a.m.–midnight;
Closed August
Hot meals served until 4 p.m.
NO CREDIT CARDS
$$

A terrace table at this spacious tea salon is just the place to make a thorough study of the look and habits of the BCBG. Plant yourself here for a mid-morning chocolate and pastry and watch the world go by or stay for the lively lunch hours.

24. LES FOLIES D'ÉLODIE

Women's lingerie and evening wear

Since she opened, the exclusive Élodie label has caused a sensation. Simple but sexy dinner suits and evening gowns as well as some of Paris's most luxurious lingerie and sleepwear are seen in this shop, run by sisters.

Lingerie is done in silk satins, Calais lace, and microfibers, all sewn exclusively for them, in a look so alluring that many of the customers buying lingerie here are men buying for women. The Élodie workshop allows clients to choose from a wide range of fabrics and color, any standard style to be made up at no extra cost, ready for pickup or shipping in ten days. Or, you may purchase from the website, www.netfolies.com.

ADDRESS
56 Avenue Paul-Doumer, 16th
TELEPHONE
01.45.04.93.57
METRO
La Muette or Trocadéro
OPEN
Mon, 2:30–6:45 p.m.;
Tue–Sat, 10:15 a.m.–6:45 p.m.
CREDIT CARDS
V, AE, MC
$$$-$$$$
INTERNET
www.netfolies.com

25. DÉPÔT-VENTE DE PASSY

Designer resale and overstock clothing

Catherine Baril's resale shop of the stars and accompanying designer overstock handles only those items from the top designers (yes, you can also find accessories from Hermès, Chanel, and YSL) in top condition, and at prices any budget could bear.

ADDRESS
14 Rue de la Tour, 16th
TELEPHONE
01.45.20.95.21
METRO
Passy
OPEN
Mon, 2–7 p.m.; Tue–Sat, 10:30 a.m.–7 p.m.
CREDIT CARDS
V, MC, AE, DC
$$

Along the Way

On the Rue de la Tour, you'll find a group of antiques dealers. Three that stand out are: PATRICIA AND GUY MINOT ANTIQUITÉS (N.9); BENEDICTE DE LAFAURIE (N.3); and OPPOSITE (N.8). It's a fun browse, and the prices here may be discussed.

ADDRESS
15 Rue de Passy, 16th
TELEPHONE
01.45.20.56.56
METRO
La Muette
OPEN
Mon–Sat, 10 a.m.–7 p.m.
CREDIT CARDS
V, AE, MC
$$$

26. REGINA RUBENS
Women's clothing

It's easy to walk out of this boutique with an entire wardrobe. Each collection is designed to coordinate and be worn easily, and the pieces exude a feminine chic that take you through the day and out at night. Anything here can be made-to-measure upon request.

ADDRESS
27 Rue de Passy, 16th
TELEPHONE
01.42.88.96.02
METRO
Passy
OPEN
Mon, noon–7 p.m.;
Tue–Sat, 10 a.m.– 7 p.m.

ADDRESS
155 Rue du Faubourg Saint-Honoré, 8th
TELEPHONE
01.45.61.19.71
METRO
St-Philippe-du-Roule
OPEN
Mon–Sat, 10:30 a.m.– 7 p.m.

ADDRESS
9 Rue de Sèvres
TELEPHONE
01.45.48.14.09
METRO
Sèvres-Babylone
OPEN
Mon–Sat, 10 a.m.– 7 p.m.

27. MAC DOUGLAS
Leather clothing for women and men

MAC DOUGLAS has earned a reputation as a classic leather house that offers top quality at a good price. This is the place for jackets, coats, skirts, pants, and perhaps a matching bag in French-styled leather and seasonal colors. Maybe you'll fall for the pumpkin trench in ultra-soft lambskin (1,435€), or in pale pink calfskin (1,095€). A warm leather jacket is yours for 276€. Once you've entered these boutiques, it's hard to resist.

ADDRESS
20 Rue Pierre Lescot, 1st
TELEPHONE
01.42.36.15.48
METRO
Etienne-Marcel
OPEN
Mon, 12:30–7 p.m.; Tue–Fri,
10:30 a.m.– 7 p.m.; Sat, 10
a.m.– 7 p.m.
CREDIT CARDS
V, AE, MC
$$-$$$

28. L'ENTREPÔT
Home furnishings and accessories

No, it's not a French version of Home Depot, but it
is an institution. This one-of-a-kind shop sells every
style of French home décor. The loyal (and international) clientele come for gifts, accessories, mirrors,
armoires and armchairs, gloves, shirts, jewelry,
cards, et al. In each of the four departments (cozy
charm, office, ethnic, accessories) you'll find an
aproned salesperson waiting to be helpful.

ADDRESS
50 Rue de Passy, 16th
TELEPHONE
01.45.25.64.17
METRO
Passy
OPEN
Mon–Sat, 10:30 a.m.– 7 p.m.
CREDIT CARDS
V, MC
$$

L'Entrepôt

ADDRESS
1 Chausée de la Muette, 16th
TELEPHONE
01.42.15.50.82
METRO
La Muette

ADDRESS
16 Rue du Sèvres, 7th
TELEPHONE
01.42.22.16.26
METRO
Sèvres-Babylone
OPEN
Mon–Sat, 10 a.m.– 7 p.m.
CREDIT CARDS
V, AE, MC
$$

29. CYRILLUS

Clothes for men, women, and children

The CYRILLUS idea, which is to dress the whole family in classic, well-priced clothes, has become a phenomenon in France, with eight boutiques in Paris alone and order catalogs. The BCBG style here is particularly perfect for the families of the Sixteenth. At left are two convenient addresses.

Paris on a Budget

The shops of Paris are a feast for the eyes, but untempered indulgence can mean famine for the pocketbook. While the French themselves always appear so stylish and seem to consider window-shopping an appropriate national pastime, the tourist may well wonder how it's possible for the average wage-earner to play the part without going broke.

The typical Parisienne is a smart and seasoned shopper on a budget. She is used to window-shopping for ideas, then going to buy where she knows she'll get the best price.

Keep in mind that virtually every store has a major sale during the first three weeks of January and for six weeks beginning the last week in June. Two notable exceptions are the week-long October sale at HERMÈS, and the March and October sales at the department stores GALERIES LAFAYETTE and PRINTEMPS. For the tourist, shopping at these *grands magasins* offers the maximum variety in merchandise to achieve the *détaxe* minimum of purchases totaling more than 175€, and simplifies the reimbursement process. Before you shop here, go to the Welcome Desk for an additional 10 percent discount card available to tourists upon presentation of passport.

Keep your eyes open for the words *Soldes* (a sale is taking place), *Fin de Séries* (end of the collection), *Dégriffés* (labels cut out), *Stock* (overstock), or *Dépôt Vente* (resale establishment) for good values year-round.

Many style-conscious yet budget-minded haunts have already been mentioned in this book. Here's where else the smart shopper goes:

Discount Clothing Areas

If you're an experienced bargain-basement shopper, you won't be put off by the crowds or lack of service in some of these shops (Rue d'Alésia is more civilized than Saint-Placide). The ambiance is virtually nil, changing rooms in short supply, but discounts hover around 40 to 50 percent of original. prices.

METRO
Alésia
CREDIT CARDS
Accepted by some shops

RUE D'ALÉSIA, 14TH

Rue d'Alésia boutiques offer last season's designer fashions at great prices but in an inconvenient location. While you're here, you should stop at SR (N.64 and N.110-112) for Sonia Rykiel's timeless knits and velours of past seasons, open Tue, 11 a.m. to 7 p.m.; Wed–Sat, 10:30 a.m. to 7 p.m.; CACHAREL STOCK (N.114) for truly wearable Parisian style, open Mon–Fri, 10 a.m. to 7 p.m.; Sat, 10 a.m. to 7:30 p.m.; and JACADI (N.116) for children, open Mon, 11 a.m. to 7 p.m.; Tue–Sat, 10 a.m. to 7 p.m.

METRO
Saint-Placide
CREDIT CARDS
Accepted by some shops

RUE SAINT-PLACIDE, 6TH

Anything but placid, this short discount drag begins just outside the doors of the department store BON MARCHÉ, and if you're persistent, insistent, and under thirty-five, you're bound to find something quite up-to-the-minute. There are few designer labels here.

ADDRESS
3 Cours de Garonne
77706 Serris
TELEPHONE
01.60.42.35.00
CREDIT CARDS
Yes
OPEN
Mon–Sat, 10 a.m.–7 p.m.
Sun, 11 a.m.– 7 p.m.
Closed Christmas and New Year's days
INTERNET
www.lavalleevillage.com

LA VALLÉE VILLAGE

The die-hard bargain shopper won't want to miss this village-style outlet shopping center just 40 minutes outside Paris. You'll find 70 brand-name boutiques from AGNÈS B. to ZADIG and VOLTAIRE with merchandise discounted by a minimum of 33 percent. Let your concierge help with transportation options.

Fabrics

MARCHÉ SAINT-PIERRE
Upholstery and dressmaking fabrics, linens

At this fabric bazaar in the heart of the garment district, you can visit five floors of yard goods at all prices and all qualities. Be it Siamese silk or synthetic chinchilla, you'll find it at this well-frequented address. For the most luxurious, head for Tissus Reine on the first floor up.

ADDRESS
2 Rue Charles Nodier, 18th
TELEPHONE
01.46.06.92.25
METRO
Anvers
OPEN
Mon, 1:30–6:30 p.m.;
Tue–Sat, 10 a.m.–6:30 p.m.
NO CREDIT CARDS

Table Arts

RUE DE PARADIS, 10TH

A true paradise for those who love to create a beautiful table, the RUE DE PARADIS is lined with divine shops and showrooms paying homage to France's finest china, silver, and crystal. If you spend a few hours shopping this street, you will be able to put together the table of your dreams at prices more competitive than in the center of town, often with an additional discount for a quantity purchase. These shops can help you in English, usually accept credit cards, are reliable shippers, and will fill future orders sent via fax or Internet.

Be sure not to miss: MADRONET (N.34) for the top names in porcelain, crystal, and silver, open Mon–Sat, 10:30 a.m. to 6 p.m., www.limogesunic-madronet.com;

LUMICRISTAL (N.22 bis), open Mon–Fri, 9:30 a.m. to 6:30 p.m., and PARADIS13 (N.12), open Tue–Sat, 10 a.m. to 6 p.m., for their luxury lines and wedding registries;

MAISON DE LA PORCELAINE (N.21) for simple white or decorated porcelain and serving pieces that can be personalized with your initials or special design, open Mon–Sat, 10 a.m. to 6:30 p.m.

METRO
Château d'Eau
OPEN
Mon–Sat, 10 a.m.–6:30 p.m.
(most shops)
CREDIT CARDS
Accepted by most shops

ADDRESS
68 bis Avenue Denfert-
Rochereau, 14th
TELEPHONE
01.43.35.15.76
METRO
Denfert-Rochereau or Port
Royal
OPEN
Mon–Fri, 12–6:30 p.m.;
Sat, 2–7 p.m.
CREDIT CARDS
V, MC

Handcrafts

ARTISINAT MONASTIQUE
Embroidered linens, children's clothes, porcelains, gifts

In the vaults of a medieval convent you'll find handcrafts produced by monks and nuns living in cloisters throughout France. At prices that are quite reasonable you can take home beautiful hand- or machine-embroidered bed and table linens, or custom order monograms or special patterns, stationery printed to specification, and you'll be enchanted by little dresses embellished by loving hands, handmade books, painted porcelains, and gift items from this very special provenance.

ADDRESS
9–129 Avenue Daumesnil, 12th
TELEPHONE
01.44.75.80.66
METRO
Ledru-Rollin
OPEN
Mon–Fri, 9 a.m.–1 p.m. & 2–5
p.m. (a few shops open longer
hours and weekends)
CREDIT CARDS
Accepted by most shops
INTERNET
www.viaduct-des-arts.com

VIADUCT DES ARTS

Here in the Faubourg St-Antoine, hub of the fine furniture industry since the seventeenth century, city planners have revitalized an abandoned train viaduct by creating workshops and display for master craftspeople underneath a mile-long stretch of brick arches, and a planted promenade for strollers on top. The array of talents here is dazzling, showcasing the most skilled artisans representing a balance of the crafts.

A few that should not be missed are the silk flowers handmade at GUILLET (N.1, bis), in business for over 100 years; MAISON FEY (N.15), making cordoban and embossed and topstitched leather for their furniture pieces, desk accessories, and trompe l'oeil book libraries purchased by the meter, www.maisonfey.com; the magical LA BON-HEUR DES DAMES (N.17), for pieces in tapestry, stitching, and quilting, as well as at-home kits; GALERIE V.I.A. (N.29–35), showing the best of the modern movement under one roof: furniture, lighting, and accessories by the country's most innovative designers; at BAGUES (N.73), the 156-year-old firm who has remade chandeliers for Versailles, you can purchase a sconce fit for a queen for about 230€. For a convenient lunch stop at VIADUCT

CAFÉ (N.41). If you keep exploring, you'll find centuries' worth of home improvements under the viaduct's sixty arches. You can begin your adventure at home at www.viaduc-des-arts.com.

Flea Markets

A trip to the *marché aux puces* (flea market), that very French shopping experience, can be a welcome contrast to the luxury and prices of the city boutiques. Be sure to arrive early, because there is lots of competition for the better items.

Put on your most comfortable walking shoes and your drabbest attire if you intend to go far. Looking too glamourous can put a damper on the discount you may be able to secure—up to 30 percent off if you're really expert. Keep in mind that you have no protection against purchasing reproductions or fraudulent pieces, other than your own probing questions. The seller who responds that he doesn't know the answer is probably hiding something.

For a piece over 100 years old be sure to get a certificate of authenticity to avoid customs duty. Most dealers will help arrange shipping, which may seem high, so be sure to factor in your estimated savings by purchasing directly in France.

MARCHÉ AUX PUCES DE SAINT-OUEN (CLIGNANCOURT FLEA MARKET)
Antiques and secondhand furnishings and clothing

Welcome to LES PUCES, where you can rummage through centuries of discards from farmhouse attics and châteaux, along with Parisian housewives, tourists, and discerning dealers from around the world. A trip here is always fun and you're certain to find a treasure to take home, though a true find is rare.

If you have professional credentials, you will be allowed in on Friday mornings (dealers' day) when the bargains are bought up and the most important

ADDRESS
Porte de Clignancourt/Saint-Ouen, 18th
METRO
Porte de Clignancourt
OPEN
Sat, Sun, & Mon, 7 a.m.–6 p.m.; dealers only on Friday mornings
CREDIT CARDS
Accepted by some dealers; bring traveler's checks or cash. There are ATMs on the outskirts of the market.
$-$$$$

pieces change hands. Typically, prices at Les Puces run about 20 percent lower than in Paris. By Tuesday you can be sure that the best merchandise will be marked up for resale in a fancy antiques shop on the Left Bank or St-Honoré.

Located just outside the city limits of Paris, in the town of St-Ouen, this is the largest antiques/flea market in the world and much too big to cover in a day. Once the business address of a handful of ragpickers anxious to avoid city taxes on their sales, Clignancourt now has 3,000 savvy dealers working from permanent stands and portable tables.

The market center, where the better stalls are located, is a several-block walk from the Metro station, heading north on the Avenue Clignancourt (under the Périphérique), and turning left on the Rue des Rosiers. As you continue up this street you'll find separate markets on either side, each with a distinct personality and packed with individually owned stalls. Guides to the stalls and their specialties are sold at the information booths at the markets Biron, Paul-Bert, and Vernaison.

The following are your best bets:

The large and eclectic MARCHÉ VERNAISON (N.99 Rue des Rosiers and 136 Rue Michelet) sells small collectibles, linens, porcelains, and art deco knickknacks. Keep your eyes open for landscapes, still lifes, and ancestral portraits, which can go for a song when the artist is an unknown.

MARCHÉ BIRON and its annex MARCHÉ CAMBO (N.85 and N.75 Rue des Rosiers) deal in genuine antiques priced to impress, from rare furniture and Napoleonic objects to beautiful old dolls (Stand 50, Biron), early posters (Stand 137, Biron), perfect nineteenth-century table services (Stand 142, Biron), and antique lace (Stand 153, Biron).

MARCHÉ SERPETTE (N.110 Rue des Rosiers) is *très à la mode* with its specialty in pieces from 1900 to 1960. A favorite stop here is VOYAGES (Stand 15, allée 3) for luggage from Goyard, bags and accessories from Hermès, and trunks from Vuitton, dating to the days when up to fifty pieces per person were allowed on a transatlantic crossing (www.voyages.fr.com). A popular restaurant here is LA PETITE SALLE À MANGER (N.100).

MARCHÉ PAUL BERT (N.104 Rue des Rosiers and N.18 Rue Paul Bert) is the favorite of American buyers, full of affordable and stylish items in a charming setting. After you've chosen your gilt mirror and bathroom chandelier, mix with the young dealers over lunch at CAFÉ LE PAUL BERT (N.20 Rue Paul Bert), or in the belle époque decor of CHEZ LOUISETTE (N.130 Avenue Michelet). Whether or not you cook at home, don't miss BACHELIER ANTIQUITÉS (Allé 1, Stand 17), where Bachelier mother and son preside over gadgets for the kitchen, each an eye-catching bit of nostalgia guaranteed to be in working order.

MARCHÉ JULES-VALLES (N.17 Rue Jules-Valles) offers the least serious and least expensive shopping experience at Clignancourt. Here you can enjoy a good dicker over the price of countless curios with a dying breed of *brocanteurs* (secondhand dealers).

MARCHÉ MALIK (N.60 Rue Jules-Valles) is famous for its fripes (vintage clothing) and its pickpockets. Keep your euros well guarded throughout this excursion.

MARCHÉE AUX PUCES DE VANVES
Collectibles and small antiques

Small and convenient, VANVES offers a good alternative to Clignancourt. It can be fully inspected in two hours and is located just a few minutes from central Paris. Early Saturday mornings (better pickings than Sunday), is the best time to make the easy trip to this newly fashionable flea market.

You can uncover a choice pair of silver candlesticks, a bolt of ornate antique fabric, antique toys, nineteenth-century prints, and unusual furniture pieces at good prices.

This is the stuff of the *brocanteur*, somewhere between unusual antiques and collectible junk. The best dealers pull up shop at lunchtime and a group of true junk dealers moves in.

ADDRESS
Avenues Georges-Lafenestre et Marc Sangnier, 14th
METRO
Porte de Vanves
OPEN
Sat & Sun, 7 a.m.–7:30 p.m.
NO CREDIT CARDS
$$

When you've had enough, go next door to the old books market in the PARK GEORGES BRASSENS. Every Sunday morning from March to October the SQUARE GEORGE-LAFENESTRE becomes an open-air gallery, where you can buy paintings and sculpture directly from the artists.

Shop Talk

The following are translations of many French words and phrases used in this book. Although not exhaustive, this glossary should come in handy for you and your shopping companions:

arrondissement. An administrative zone. Paris is divided into 20 arrondissements.

atelier. Workshop.

bar à vins. Wine bar.

batterie de cuisine. Kitchen equipment.

belle époque. Turn of the century.

bleus de travail. Blue cotton worker's uniform.

Bon Chic Bon Genre. Preppy younger generation.

bon ton. Good taste.

bonne affaire. Good deal.

boulettes grandmère. Chopped meatballs.

brocanteur. Secondhand dealer.

caleçons. Boxer shorts.

carnet. Small book of tickets or forms.

Carte Bleue. Visa card.

chevrefeuille. Honeysuckle.

chez. At the house of.

chinoiserie. In the Chinese style.

choucroûte. Sauerkraut and sausage dish.

choux farcies. Stuffed cabbage rolls.

de rigueur. Required.

dégriffés. Labels taken out.

dégustation. Tasting.

dépôt vente. Resale establishment.

détaxe. Export discount.

doyenne. Eldest female of the group.

droite. Right.

duvet. Down comforter.

en vacances. On vacation.

Eurocarte. MasterCard.

faïence. Hand-painted earthenware.

fermé. Closed.

fermez. Please close.

fin de séries. End of the collection.

fin de siècle. End of the century.

flacon. Bottle, as for perfume.

flâner. Wander and browse.

foin coupé. Fresh cut hay.

folie. Something foolish.

fromage. Cheese.

galette. Pancake or flat cake.

gauche. Left.

givrette. Sugar-coated candy.

grand dame. Great lady.

grand magasin. Department store.

grandmère. Grandmother.

grêlon. Hailstone.

haricots fins. French green beans.

haute bourgeoisie. Upper middle class.

hôtel particulier. Private home.

joie de vivre. Love of life.

jardin. Garden.

jour de beauté. Day of beauty.

luxe. Luxury.

marché. Market.

marché aux puces. Flea market.

métis. Fabric blend of linen and cotton.

mode feminine. Women's fashions.

mode moderne. Modern style.

montgolfiers. Hot air balloons.

ouvert. Open.

pain. Bread.

pain aux noix. Nut bread.

palais. Palace.

parfumerie. Perfume store.

petit rat. Young member of the ballet.

plat du jour. Plate of the day.

premier étage. First floor above the ground floor (2nd floor in U.S.)

prés. Fields.

quartier. Neighborhood.

Rallye. "Coming out" for young women.

rez-de-chausée. The ground floor (1st floor in U.S.)

Rive Droite. Right Bank.

Rive Gauche. Left Bank.

sachet. Packet.

santons. Traditional figurines representing the people of southern France.

savoir faire. Know-how.

soldes. Sale.

stock. Overstock.

tablier. Apron.

tapénade. Olive and anchovy spread.

tapisserie. Tapestry.

tarte tatin. Apple tart.

toque. Chef's hat.

tout. All.

trompe l'oeil. Deceptively real-looking.

Fashion Shop Talk

The following French words are all related to fashion:

à la mode. In style.

bas. Stockings.

bottine. Boot.

ceinture. Belt.

chaussures. Shoes.

couture. The clothing business.

cravate. Tie.

demi-couture. Made-to-measure clothing.

écharpe. Scarf.

fripes. Secondhand clothes.

gant. Glove.

haute couture. Custom sewn clothing from a fashion house that meets rigorous industry standards.

jupe. Skirt.

manteau. Coat.

pantalons. Pants.

peignoir. Nightgown.

prêt-à-porter. Ready-to-wear.

pullover. Sweater.

retouche(s). Alterations.

robe. Dress.

sac. Purse.

taille. Size.

Shop Talk Phrases

When you enter a small shop, engratiate yourself with a *"Bonjour, Madame."* You will find the following phrases useful when you are shopping:

Do you accept credit cards or traveler's checks?
Acceptez-vous des cartes de crédit ou des chèques de voyages?

How much does this cost?
Ca coûte combien?

I would like the Export Sales Invoice for sales tax reimbursement.
Je voudrais l'imprimée pour la détaxe, s'il vous plaît.

Do you ship to the States?
Est-ce-que vous envoyez aux Étas-Unis?

I would like the package gift-wrapped, please.
Je voudrais un paquet cadeau, s'il vous plaît.

The Paris Shopping Companion will be updated for the next edition. If you find changes before I do or if you discover a shop you would like to see considered, please send me a note with your comments and any relevant information you may have. I welcome your feedback. Please send your comments to Susan Swire Winkler, c/o Cumberland House Publishing, 431 Harding Industrial Drive, Nashville, TN 37211.

Index

About the Authors

SUSAN SWIRE WINKLER was first fascinated by Paris as a young girl when she saw the movie *Gigi*. Her experiences in Paris as a college student, graduate student, fashion journalist, and importer of French linens for her own shop allow her to view the city in a personal, authoritative way. A former writer for *Women's Wear Daily*, she lives in Portland, Oregon, when she's not in Paris.

CAROLINE LESIEUR is a VIP personal guide and native Parisian. She may be reached at carolesieur@hotmail.com.

Notes

Notes

Notes

Notes